JAMES
A Commentary in the Wesleyan Tradition

*New Beacon Bible Commentary

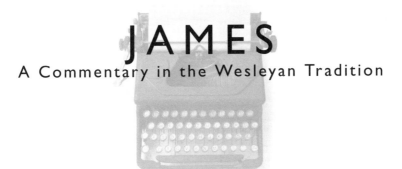

JAMES
A Commentary in the Wesleyan Tradition

C. Jeanne Orjala Serrão

BEACON HILL PRESS
OF KANSAS CITY

Library of Congress Cataloging-in-Publication Data

Serrão, C. Jeanne Orjala.
    James / C. Jeanne Orjala Serrão.
        p. cm. — (New Beacon Bible commentary)
    Includes bibliographical references and index.
    ISBN 978-0-8341-2405-9 (pbk. : alk. paper)
    1. Bible. N.T. James—Commentaries. I. Title.
    BS2785.53.S47 2011
    227'.91077—dc22

                                                                                    2010048279

10 9 8 7 6 5 4 3 2 1

DEDICATION

To my parents, Paul and Mary Orjala,
who encouraged my education both verbally and in
providing resources; and whose lives reflect a devotion
to the scholarly study of the Bible as well as
living out their faith in daily action.

COMMENTARY EDITORS

General Editors

Alex Varughese
   Ph.D., Drew University
   Professor of Biblical Literature
   Mount Vernon Nazarene University
   Mount Vernon, Ohio

Roger Hahn
   Ph.D., Duke University
   Dean of the Faculty
   Professor of New Testament
   Nazarene Theological Seminary
   Kansas City, Missouri

George Lyons
   Ph.D., Emory University
   Professor of New Testament
   Northwest Nazarene University
   Nampa, Idaho

Section Editors

Joseph Coleson
   Ph.D., Brandeis University
   Professor of Old Testament
   Nazarene Theological Seminary
   Kansas City, Missouri

Robert Branson
   Ph.D., Boston University
   Professor of Biblical Literature
      Emeritus
   Olivet Nazarene University
   Bourbonnais, Illinois

Alex Varughese
   Ph.D., Drew University
   Professor of Biblical Literature
   Mount Vernon Nazarene University
   Mount Vernon, Ohio

Jim Edlin
   Ph.D., Southern Baptist Theological
      Seminary
   Professor of Biblical Literature and
      Languages
   Chair, Division of Religion and
      Philosophy
   MidAmerica Nazarene University
   Olathe, Kansas

Kent Brower
   Ph.D., The University of Manchester
   Vice Principal
   Senior Lecturer in Biblical Studies
   Nazarene Theological College
   Manchester, England

George Lyons
   Ph.D., Emory University
   Professor of New Testament
   Northwest Nazarene University
   Nampa, Idaho

Frank G. Carver
   Ph.D., New College, University of
      Edinburgh
   Professor Emeritus of Religion
   Point Loma Nazarene University
   San Diego, California

CONTENTS

GENERAL EDITORS' PREFACE

The purpose of the New Beacon Bible Commentary is to make available to pastors and students in the twenty-first century a biblical commentary that reflects the best scholarship in the Wesleyan theological tradition. The commentary project aims to make this scholarship accessible to a wider audience to assist them in their understanding and proclamation of Scripture as God's Word.

Writers of the volumes in this series not only are scholars within the Wesleyan theological tradition and experts in their field but also have special interest in the books assigned to them. Their task is to communicate clearly the critical consensus and the full range of other credible voices who have commented on the Scriptures. Though scholarship and scholarly contribution to the understanding of the Scriptures are key concerns of this series, it is not intended as an academic dialogue within the scholarly community. Commentators of this series constantly aim to demonstrate in their work the significance of the Bible as the church's book and the contemporary relevance and application of the biblical message. The project's overall goal is to make available to the church and for her service the fruits of the labors of scholars who are committed to their Christian faith.

The *New International Version* (NIV) is the reference version of the Bible used in this series; however, the focus of exegetical study and comments is the biblical text in its original language. When the commentary uses the NIV, it is printed in bold. The text printed in bold italics is the translation of the author. Commentators also refer to other translations where the text may be difficult or ambiguous.

The structure and organization of the commentaries in this series seeks to facilitate the study of the biblical text in a systematic and methodical way. Study of each biblical book begins with an **Introduction** section that gives an overview of authorship, date, provenance, audience, occasion, purpose, sociological/cultural issues, textual history, literary features, hermeneutical issues, and theological themes necessary to understand the book. This section also includes a brief outline of the book and a list of general works and standard commentaries.

The commentary section for each biblical book follows the outline of the book presented in the introduction. In some volumes, readers will find section *overviews* of large portions of scripture with general comments on their overall literary structure and other literary features. A consistent feature of the commentary is the paragraph-by-paragraph study of biblical texts. This section has three parts: **Behind the Text**, **In the Text**, and **From the Text**.

The goal of the **Behind the Text** section is to provide the reader with all the relevant information necessary to understand the text. This includes specific historical situations reflected in the text, the literary context of the text, sociological and cultural issues, and literary features of the text.

In the Text explores what the text says, following its verse-by-verse structure. This section includes a discussion of grammatical details, word studies, and the connectedness of the text to other biblical books/passages or other parts of the book being studied (the canonical relationship). This section provides transliterations of key words in Hebrew and Greek and their literal meanings. The goal here is to explain what the author would have meant and/or what the audience would have understood as the meaning of the text. This is the largest section of the commentary.

The **From the Text** section examines the text in relation to the following areas: theological significance, intertextuality, the history of interpretation, use of the Old Testament scriptures in the New Testament, interpretation in later church history, actualization, and application.

The commentary provides **sidebars** on topics of interest that are important but not necessarily part of an explanation of the biblical text. These topics are informational items and may cover archaeological, historical, literary, cultural, and theological matters that have relevance to the biblical text. Occasionally, longer detailed discussions of special topics are included as **excurses.**

We offer this series with our hope and prayer that readers will find it a valuable resource for their understanding of God's Word and an indispensable tool for their critical engagement with the biblical texts.

Roger Hahn, Centennial Initiative General Editor
Alex Varughese, General Editor (Old Testament)
George Lyons, General Editor (New Testament)

ACKNOWLEDGMENTS

It is a privilege to be asked to write a commentary in this series. My gratitude goes to Beacon Hill Press for the vision to create this new series and to Bonnie Perry, director of Beacon Hill Press, for her encouragement and direction for this project.

My doctoral dissertation at the Claremont Graduate University applied sociological and anthropological methodologies to Paul's community letters. I attempted to illustrate how Paul adjusted his arguments and language to meet the needs of his audiences. My mentors—Karen Jo Torjesen, Vince Wimbush, James Robinson, and Burton Mack—profoundly influenced the scholar in me. Special appreciation goes to my dissertation chair, Karen Jo Torjesen, dean of CGU School of Religion and Margo L. Goldsmith Professor of Women's Studies, for her encouragement and continued interest in my work.

Many thanks to my professors at MidAmerica Nazarene University, European Nazarene College, and Nazarene Theological Seminary. Each contributed important aspects and methods to my understanding of the Bible. My father taught me my first year of Koine Greek and opened the world of the first-century Christians to me. Ralph Earle nurtured that love for the NT in its original language and encouraged me to pursue my study with grace and integrity.

This project took me into the Jewish-Christian world of James. Some of the cultural dynamics are similar to Paul's communities, but others, specific to Jewish Christians, were fascinating to discover. Wesley Hiram Wachob's 2000 study, *The Voice of Jesus in the Social Rhetoric of James*, was an excellent resource for me in the academic study of James.

I am also indebted to Mount Vernon Nazarene University for granting me a sabbatical leave during the spring of 2007 to work on this volume. Without their wholehearted support, this project would not have been possible. Special thanks to Alex Varughese, my mentor, both administratively and academically.

Thanks to my Greek students who gave editing and feedback comments, some of which have worked themselves into this book: Peter Blankenship, Evan Bunker, Stephanie Heayn, Craig Lamos, Julianne Meinecke, Shannon Pavlovic, Jannai Shields, Neil Taylor II, Christina Bush Bohn.

I am especially grateful to my family. My parents, Paul and Mary Orjala, always expected the best from me academically, spiritually, and ethically. Their modeling, along with their verbal and economic encouragement, gave me a firm foundation and made the writing of this commentary possible. My father's incurable curiosity for all things infected me and was an important part of why I wanted to investigate the world of James and not just remain in the comfortable world of the apostle Paul!

My mother, Mary; my sister Lorie; my brother Jon; and their families have put up with the priority of James over family visits and the timing of family get-togethers. My husband has encouraged me, giving me time and space to complete this project, including the James project taking over the dining room for months at a time!

Throughout this writing, I have sensed the help and blessing of God on this project. James has often been maligned. Even as I began this project, I received a homemade book on why no one should pay attention to James! But God has shown me that James is as relevant today as it was for James' community. We live in a world that is tired of the hypocrisy of so-called Christianity and is looking for those who will live out the message of Jesus in their everyday lives. My prayer is that this book will encourage each of its readers to "love their neighbor as themselves" and discover what that looks like in their own particular world of influence.

—C. Jeanne Orjala Serrão

ABBREVIATIONS

With a few exceptions, these abbreviations follow those in *The SBL Handbook of Style* (Alexander 1999).

General

A.D.	anno Domini (precedes date) (equivalent to C.E.)
B.C.	before Christ (follows date) (equivalent to B.C.E.)
ch	chapter
chs	chapters
ed(s).	editor(s), edited by
e.g.	*exempli gratia*, for example
esp.	especially
etc.	*et cetera*, and the rest
i.e.	*id est*, that is
ktl.	etc. (in Greek transliteration)
lit.	literally
LXX	Septuagint (Greek translation of the OT)
n.	note
n.d.	no date
MT	Masoretic Text (Hebrew OT)
NT	New Testament
OT	Old Testament
s.v.	*sub verbo*, under the word
vol(s).	volume(s)
v	verse
vv	verses

Modern English Versions

NASB	New American Standard Bible
NIV	New International Version
NRSV	New Revised Standard Version

Print Conventions for Translations

Bold font	NIV (bold without quotation marks in the text under study; elsewhere in the regular font, with quotation marks and no further identification)
Bold italic font	Author's translation (without quotation marks)

Behind the Text:	Literary, cultural, or historical background information average readers might not know from reading the biblical text alone
In the Text:	Comments on the biblical text, words, phrases, grammar, and so forth
From the Text:	The use of the text by later interpreters, contemporary relevance, theological and ethical implications of the text, with particular emphasis on Wesleyan concerns.

Old Testament

Gen	Genesis
Exod	Exodus
Lev	Leviticus
Num	Numbers
Deut	Deuteronomy
Josh	Joshua
Judg	Judges
Ruth	Ruth
1—2 Sam	1—2 Samuel
1—2 Kgs	1—2 Kings
1—2 Chr	1—2 Chronicles
Ezra	Ezra
Neh	Nehemiah
Esth	Esther
Job	Job
Ps/Pss	Psalm/Psalms
Prov	Proverbs
Eccl	Ecclesiastes
Song	Song of Songs / Song of Solomon
Isa	Isaiah
Jer	Jeremiah
Lam	Lamentations
Ezek	Ezekiel

Dan	Daniel
Hos	Hosea
Joel	Joel
Amos	Amos
Obad	Obadiah
Jonah	Jonah
Mic	Micah
Nah	Nahum
Hab	Habakkuk
Zeph	Zephaniah
Hag	Haggai
Zech	Zechariah
Mal	Malachi

(Note: Chapter and verse numbering in the MT and LXX often differ compared to those in English Bibles. To avoid confusion, all biblical references follow the chapter and verse numbering in English translations, even when the text in the MT and LXX is under discussion.)

New Testament

Matt	Matthew
Mark	Mark
Luke	Luke
John	John
Acts	Acts
Rom	Romans
1—2 Cor	1—2 Corinthians
Gal	Galatians
Eph	Ephesians
Phil	Philippians
Col	Colossians
1—2 Thess	1—2 Thessalonians
1—2 Tim	1—2 Timothy
Titus	Titus
Phlm	Philemon
Heb	Hebrews
Jas	James
1—2 Pet	1—2 Peter
1—2—3 John	1—2—3 John
Jude	Jude
Rev	Revelation

Apocrypha

Bar	Baruch
1—2 Esd	1—2 Esdras
1—2 Macc	1—2 Maccabees
3—4 Macc	3—4 Maccabees
Sir	Sirach/Ecclesiasticus
Tob	Tobit
Wis	Wisdom of Solomon

OT Pseudepigrapha

1 En.	*1 Enoch (Ethiopic Apocalypse)*
2 Bar.	*2 Baruch (Syriac Apocalypse)*
4 Ezra	*4 Ezra*
Pss. Sol.	*Psalms of Solomon*
Sib. Or.	*Sibylline Oracles*
T. Ash.	*Testament of Asher*
T. Jos.	*Testament of Joseph*
T. Sim.	*Testament of Simeon*

Josephus

Ant.	*Jewish Antiquities*
J.W.	*Jewish War*

Philo

Decalogue	*On the Decalogue*
Leg. 1, 2, 3	*Legum allegoriae* I, II, III
Posterity	*On the Posterity of Cain*
Virtues	*On the Virtues*

Apostolic Fathers

1–2 Clem.	*1–2 Clement*
Did.	*Didache*

Other Ancient Sources

Aristotle
Rhet.	*Rhetoric*

Augustine
Nat. Grat.	*Nature and Grace*

Hippolytus
  Haer.   *Refutation of All Heresies*
Nag Hammadi Codices
     2 Apoc. Jas. V.4 *(Second) Apocalypse of James*
     Trim. Prot. XIII,1 *Trimorphic Protennoia*

Secondary Sources: Journals, Series, and Reference Works

APOT	*The Apocrypha and Pseudepigrapha of the Old Testament* (see Charles)
BAR	*Biblical Archaeology Review*
BDAG	*A Greek-English Lexicon of the New Testament and Other Early Christian Literature* (see Bauer)
BDF	Blass, Debrunner, Funk
JSNTSup	Journal for the Study of the New Testament: Supplement Series
LCL	Loeb Classical Library
NHL	*The Nag Hammadi Library* (see Robinson)
NTS	*New Testament Studies*
TDNT	*Theological Dictionary of the New Testament* (see Kittel)
ZPED	*The Zondervan Pictorial Encyclopedia of the Bible* (see Tenney)

Greek Transliteration

Greek	*Letter*	*English*
α	*alpha*	*a*
β	*bēta*	*b*
γ	*gamma*	*g*
γ	*gamma nasal*	*n* (before γ, κ, ξ, χ)
δ	*delta*	*d*
ε	*epsilon*	*e*
ζ	*zēta*	*z*
η	*ēta*	*ē*
θ	*thēta*	*th*
ι	*iōta*	*i*
κ	*kappa*	*k*
λ	*lambda*	*l*
μ	*mu*	*m*
ν	*nu*	*n*
ξ	*xi*	*x*
ο	*omicron*	*o*
π	*pi*	*p*
ρ	*rhō*	*r*
ρ	initial *rhō*	*rh*
σ/ς	*sigma*	*s*
τ	*tau*	*t*
υ	*upsilon*	*y*
υ	*upsilon*	*u* (in diphthongs: *au, eu, ēu, ou, ui*)
φ	*phi*	*ph*
χ	*chi*	*ch*
ψ	*psi*	*ps*
ω	*ōmega*	*ō*
`	rough breathing	*h* (before initial vowels or diphthongs)

Hebrew Consonant Transliteration

Hebrew/Aramaic	*Letter*	*English*
א	*alef*	'
ב	*bet*	*b; v* (spirant)
ג	*gimel*	*g; gh* (spirant)
ד	*dalet*	*d; dh* (spirant)
ה	*he*	*h*
ו	*vav*	*v* or *w*
ז	*zayin*	*z*
ח	*khet*	*ḥ* or *kh*
ט	*tet*	*ṭ*
י	*yod*	*y*
כ/ך	*kaf*	*k: kh* (spirant)
ל	*lamed*	*l*
מ/ם	*mem*	*m*
נ/ן	*nun*	*n*
ס	*samek*	*s*
ע	*ayin*	'
פ/ף	*pe*	*p; f* (spirant)
צ/ץ	*tsade*	*ṣ*
ק	*qof*	*q*
ר	*resh*	*r*
שׂ	*sin*	*ś*
שׁ	*shin*	*š*
ת	*tav*	*t; th* (spirant)

BIBLIOGRAPHY

Adamson, James B. 1976. *The Epistle of James.* New International Commentary on the New Testament. Grand Rapids: Eerdmans.

Alexander, Patrick H., and others. 1999. *The SBL Handbook of Style for Ancient and Near Eastern, Biblical, and Early Christian Studies.* Peabody, Mass.: Hendrickson.

Aune, David. 1991. Oral Tradition and the Aphorisms of Jesus. Pages 211-65 in *Jesus and the Oral Gospel Tradition.* Edited by H. Wansbrough. JSNTSup 64; Sheffield: JSOT Press.

Baasland, E. 1982. Der Jakobusbrief als neutestamentliche Weisheitsschrift. *Studia theologica* 36, 119-39.

Barclay, William. 1976. *The Letters of James and Peter.* Rev. ed. The Daily Study Bible Series. Philadelphia: Westminster.

_____. 2003. *Letters to the Philippians, Colossians and Thessalonians.* Louisville, Ky.: Westminster/John Knox.

Bauckham, Richard. 1999. *James: Wisdom of James, Disciple of Jesus the Sage.* New York: Routledge.

Bauer, William, William F. Arndt, and Frederick W. Danker. 2000. *A Greek-English Lexicon of the New Testament and Other Early Christian Literature.* 3rd ed. Chicago: University of Chicago Press.

Benefiel, Ron. 2004. *Languages of Holiness.* Paper. See Appendix A.

Bengel, J. A. 1877. *Gnomon Novi Testamenti.* 7th ed. Edingburg: T&T Clark.

Blaiklock, E. M. 1975. Ships. Pages 410-15 in vol. 5 of *ZPED.* Grand Rapids: Zondervan.

Blankenship, Peter. 2007. Paper on James 1:26-27, 4:11-12. Mount Vernon, Ohio: Mount Vernon Nazarene University.

Blomberg, Craig L., and Mariam J. Kamell. 2008. *Exegetical Commentary on the New Testament: James.* Grand Rapids: Zondervan.

Bray, Gerald, ed. 2000. *James, 1-2 Peter, 1-3 John, Jude.* ACCS 11. Downers Grove, Ill.: InterVarsity.

Brosend II, William F. 2004. *James & Jude.* New Cambridge Bible Commentary. Cambridge: Cambridge University Press.

Bruce, F. F. 1982. *The Epistle to the Galatians: A Commentary on the Greek Text.* Grand Rapids: Eerdmans.

Bunker, Evan. 2007. Paper on James 1:19-21. Mount Vernon, Ohio: Mount Vernon Nazarene University.

Carpenter, William Boyd. 1903. *The Wisdom of James the Just.* New York: Whittaker.

Charles, R. H., ed. 1973. *The Apocrypha and Pseudepigrapha of the Old Testament.* Vol. 2. Oxford: Clarendon Press.

Chester, Andrew, and Ralph P. Martin. 1994. *The Theology of the Letters of James, Peter, and Jude.* New Testament Theology. Cambridge: Cambridge University Press.

Conybeare, F. C., and St. George Stock. 1995. *Grammar of Septuagint Greek with Selected Readings, Vocabularies and Updated Indexes.* Peabody, Mass.: Hendrickson.

Corrington, Gail Paterson. 1990. Philo on the Contemplative Life: or, On the Suppliants. Pages 134-55 in *Ascetic Behavior in Greco-Roman Antiquity: A Sourcebook.* Edited by Vincent L. Wimbush. Minneapolis: Fortress.

Davids, Peter H. 1982. *The Epistle of James.* The New International Greek Testament Commentary. Grand Rapids: Eerdmans.

_____. 1989. *James.* New International Biblical Commentary. Peabody, Mass.: Hendrickson.

Deasley, A. R. G. 1972. The Idea of Perfection in the Qumran Texts. PhD diss., University of Manchester.

Dibelius, Martin. 1975. *James: A Commentary on the Epistle of James. Hermeneia.* Revised by Heinrich Greeven. Translated by Michael A. Williams. Philadelphia: Fortress.

Doerksen, Vernon. 1983. *James.* Everyman's Bible Commentary. Chicago: Moody.

Eller, Vernard. 1962. *Brothers in Ebullience?* Letter originally published by The Christian Century Foundation, Chicago, Ill., in *The Christian Century,* October 17, 1962. Online at: http://www.hccentral.com/eller1/cc101762.html

Elliot, John H. 1981. *A Home for the Homeless: A Sociological Exegesis of 1 Peter, Its Situation and Strategy.* Philadelphia: Fortress.

Epictetus. *The Discourses* as Reported by Arrian (Book II). 1946. Translated by W. A. Oldfather. Vol. 1. LCL. Cambridge: Harvard University Press.

Etheredge, Melissa. 2007. *I Need to Wake Up.* Song for the documentary *An Inconvenient Truth.*

Evans, Louis H. 1957. *Make Your Faith Work: A Letter from James.* Westwood, N.J.: Revell.

Heiligenthal, Roman. 1990. *ergazomai, ktl.* Pages 48-49 in vol. 2 of *Exegetical Dictionary of the New Testament.* Edited by Horst Robert Balz and Gerhard Schneider. Translated by Virgil P. Howard and James W. Thompson. Grand Rapids: Eerdmans.

Hengel, Martin. 1974. *Judaism and Hellenism, Studies in Their Encounter in Palestine During the Early Hellenistic Period.* Translated by John Bowden. Philadelphia: Fortress.

———. 1989. *The 'Hellenization' of Judaea in the First Century After Christ.* Translated by John Bowden. Philadelphia: Trinity Press International.

Hippolytus. 1995. Refutation 5.11.1, *Ante-Nicene Fathers.* Vol. 5. Edited by Alexander Roberts and James Donaldson. Peabody, Mass.: Hendrickson.

Hodges, Zane C. 1994. *The Epistle of James: Proven Character Through Testing.* The Grace New Testament Commentary. Irving, Tex.: Grace Evangelical Society.

Hubbard, David A. 1980. *The Book of James: Wisdom That Works.* Waco, Tex.: Word.

Hurley, Amanda Kolson. 2002. The Last Days of James. *BAR* 28, 6:32.

Jeremias, Joachim. 1964. *grammateus.* Pages 740-42 in vol. 1 of *TDNT.* Grand Rapids: Eerdmans.

Jewett, Robert. 1970-71. "The Agitators and the Galatian Congregation," *NTS* 17, 198-212.

Johnson, Luke Timothy. 1995. *The Letter of James.* Anchor Bible 37A. New York: Doubleday.

———. 1999. *The Writings of the New Testament: An Interpretation.* Rev. ed. Minneapolis: Fortress.

———. 2004. *Brother of Jesus, Friend of God: Studies in the Letter of James.* Grand Rapids: Eerdmans.

Josephus, Flavius. 1981. *Josephus: Complete Works.* Translated by William Whiston. Grand Rapids: Kregel.

Kee, Howard Clark. 1995. *Who Are the People of God? Early Christian Models of Community.* New Haven, Conn.: Yale University Press.

Kent, Homer A., Jr. 2005. *Faith That Works: Studies and the Epistle of James.* Rev. ed. Winona Lake, Ind.: BMH Books.

Kierkegaard, Søren. 1978. *Journals and Papers.* Vol. 6. Translated and edited by H. V. Hong and E. H. Hong. Bloomington, Ind.: University Press.

Kittel, Gerhard, and Gerhard Friedrich, eds. 1964-76. *Theological Dictionary of the New Testament.* 10 vols. Translated and edited by G. W. Bromiley. Grand Rapids: Eerdmans.

Kroeger, Catherine Clark, and Mary J. Evans. 2002. *The IVP Women's Bible Commentary.* Downers Grove, Ill.: InterVarsity Press.

Lactantius. 1995. Of the Manner in Which the Persecutors Died. *Ante-Nicene Fathers.* Vol. 7. Edited by Alexander Roberts and James Donaldson. Peabody, Mass.: Hendrickson.

Laws, Sophie. 1980. *A Commentary on the Epistle of James.* Harper's New Testament Commentaries. San Francisco: Harper and Row.

Lemaire, André. 2002a. Burial Box of James the Brother of Jesus. *BAR* 28, 6:24-33.

———. 2002b. Epigraphy—and the Lab—Say It's Genuine. *BAR* 28, 6:28.

Lightfoot, J. B., and J. R. Harmer, eds. and trans. 1984. *The Apostolic Fathers: Revised Greek Texts with Introductions and English Translations.* Grand Rapids: Baker.

Lohse, Eduard. 1985. *The New Testament Environment.* Translated by John E. Steely. Nashville: Abingdon Press.

Luther, Martin. 1863. *The Prefaces to the Early Editions of Martin Luther's Bible.* Edited by T. A. Readwin. London: Hatchard.

———. 1960. *Word and Sacrament I.* Luther's Works. Vol. 35. Edited by E. Theodore Bachmann. Philadelphia: Muhlenberg.

Malina, Bruce. 2001a. *New Testament World: Insights from Cultural Anthropology.* 3rd ed. Louisville, Ky.: Westminster/John Knox.

———. 2001b. *The Social Gospel of Jesus: The Kingdom of God in Mediterranean Perspective.* Minneapolis: Fortress.

Martin, Ralph P. 1988. *James.* Word Biblical Commentary 48. Waco, Tex.: Word.

McCartney, Dan G. 2009. *James.* Baker Exegetical Commentary on the New Testament. Grand Rapids: Baker Academic.

Meeks, Wayne A. 2003. *The First Urban Christians: The Social World of the Apostle Paul.* 2nd ed. New Haven, Conn.: Yale University Press.

Meeks, Wayne A., and Robert L. Wilken. 1978. *Jews and Christians in Antioch in the First Four Centuries of the Common Era.* Missoula, Mont.: Scholars Press.

Metzger, Bruce M. 1971. *A Textual Commentary on the New Testament.* 3rd ed. New York: United Bible Societies.

Meyer, Rudolf, Karl Ludwig Schmidt, and Martin Anton Schmidt. 1967. *paroikos, ktl.* Pages 841-53 in vol. 5 of *TDNT.* Grand Rapids: Eerdmans.

Michel, Otto. 1965. *huios, katiooimai.* Pages 334-35 in vol. 3 of *TDNT.* Grand Rapids: Eerdmans.

Moo, Douglas J. 2000. *The Letter of James.* Pillar New Testament Commentary. Grand Rapids: Eerdmans.

Nystrom, David P. 1997. *James.* The NIV Application Commentary. Grand Rapids: Zondervan.

Perelman, Chaïm, and Lucie Olbrechts-Tyteca. 1969. *The New Rhetoric: A Treatise on Argumentation.* Translated by John Wilkinson and Purcell Weaver. Notre Dame, Ind.: Notre Dame University Press.

Philo. *Special Laws.* 1950. Vol. 7 of LCL. Translated by F. H. Colson. Cambridge: Harvard University Press.

_____. *Apology for the Jews.* 1954a. Vol. 9 of LCL. Translated by F. H. Colson. Cambridge: Harvard University Press.

_____. *On the Virtues.* 1954b. Vol. 8 of LCL. Translated by F. H. Colson. Cambridge: Harvard University Press.

Reicke, Bo. 1964. *Epistles of James, Peter and Jude.* Anchor Bible 37. Garden City, N.Y.: Doubleday.

Rengstorf, Karl Henrich. 1964. *didaskō, ktl.* Pages 134-65 in vol. 2 of *TDNT.* Grand Rapids: Eerdmans.

Riegel, S. K. 1977-78. Jewish Christianity: Definitions and Terminology. *NTS* 24, 410-15.

Robbins, Vernon K. 1996. Making Christian Culture in the Epistle of James. *Scriptura* 59:341-51.

Robinson, James M., ed. 1981. *The Nag Hammadi Library.* New York: Harper and Row.

Ropes, James Hardy. 1973. *A Critical and Exegetical Commentary on the Epistle of St. James.* International Critical Commentary. Edinburgh: T&T Clark.

Rudolph, Kurt. 1984. *Gnosis: The Nature and History of Gnosticism.* Translated by R. McL. Wilson. Edinburgh: T&T Clark.

Salmond, S. D. F. n.d. *Epistle to the Ephesians.* Vol. 3 of *The Expositor's Greek Testament.* Edited by W. Robertson Nicoll. Grand Rapids: Eerdmans.

Serrão, C. Jeanne Orjala. 1996. Holiness and Sexual Ethics in Paul: An Analysis of the Use of Social Sciences in the Study of the New Testament. PhD diss., The Claremont Graduate University.

Shanks, Hershel. 2003a. Cracks in the James Bone Box Repaired. *BAR* 29, 1:20-25.

_____. 2003b. Ossuary Update: The Storm over the Bone Box. *BAR* 29, 4:26-39, 83.

Shields, Jannai. 2007. Paper on James 1:15-18. Mount Vernon, Ohio: Mount Vernon Nazarene University.

Tamez, Elsa. 1990. *The Scandalous Message of James: Faith Without Works Is Dead.* Translated by John Eagleson. New York: Crossroad.

Taylor, Mark E. 2006. *A Text-Linguistic Investigation into the Discourse Structure of James.* London: T&T Clark.

Taylor, Mark E., and George H. Guthrie. 2006. The Structure of James, CBQ 68, 681-705.

Taylor II, Neil. 2007. Paper on James 2:14-17. Mount Vernon, Ohio: Mount Vernon Nazarene University.

Theissen, Gerd. 1978. *Sociology of Early Palestinian Christianity.* Translated by John Bowden. Philadelphia: Fortress.

The Septuagint Version of the Old Testament with an English Translation and with Various Reading and Critical Notes. n.d. Samuel Bagster and Sons Limited. New York: Harper and Brothers.

Trimorphic Protennoia 13, 35. 1981. Translated by John D. Turner. Pages 461-70 of *NHL.* New York: Harper and Row.

Vaage, Leif E. 1990. Musonius Rufus on Training. Pages 129-33 of *Ascetic Behavior in Greco-Roman Antiquity: A Sourcebook.* Edited by Vincent L. Wimbush. Minneapolis: Fortress.

Varughese, Alex. 2009. Personal e-mail, 8/14/09.

Wachob, Wesley H. 2000. *The Voice of Jesus in the Social Rhetoric of James.* Cambridge: Cambridge University Press.

Wall, Robert W. 1997. *Community of the Wise: The Letter of James.* Valley Forge, Pa.: Trinity Press International.

Wallace, Daniel B. 1996. *Greek Grammar: Beyond the Basics: An Exegetical Syntax of the New Testament.* Grand Rapids: Zondervan.

Wesley, John. 1955. Sermon XLIV: The Use of Money. Pages 309-27 of *Wesley's Standard Sermons.* Works of Wesley 2. Edited by Edward H. Sugden. Grand Rapids: Francis Asbury Press of Zondervan.

_____. 1979. *The Works of John Wesley.* 3rd ed. 10 vols. Edited by Thomas Jackson. Repr. Grand Rapids: Eerdmans, 1872.

_____. 2003. *Parallel Commentary on the New Testament.* Compiled and edited by Mark Water. Chattanooga, Tenn.: AMG Publishers.

Wesley, John, and Charles Wesley. 1868. *The Poetical Works.* Edited by G. Osborn. London: Wesleyan Methodist Conference Office.

Wessel, W. W. 1953. An Inquiry into the Origin, Literary Character, Historical and Religious Significance of the Epistle of James. PhD diss., University of Edinburgh.

Wuellner, W. H. 1978. *Der Jakobusbrief im Licht der Rhetorik und Textpragmatik, Linguistica Biblica* 43, 5-66.

Zodhiates, Spiros, ed. 1992. *The Complete Word Study Dictionary: New Testament.* Chattanooga, Tenn.: AMG Publishers.

Web Sites

http://www.bib-arch.org/news/forgery-trial-news.asp
http://www.ccel.org
http://www.ccel.org/j/josephus
http://www.dickenschristmascarol.com
http://www.earlyjewishwritings.com/text/philo/book37.html
http://www.earlyjewishwritings.com/testtwelve.html
http://www.earlyjewishwritings.com/wisdom.html
http://www.hccentral.com/eller1/cc101762.html
http://www.newadvent.org/fathers/250102.htm
http://www.royalty.nu/Africa/Egypt/Cleopatra.html

INTRODUCTION

A. The Importance of the Letter of James

James belongs to a subdivision of the NT labeled the general or catholic (= universal) epistles. These books are so called because their audience is usually a group of churches or the church as a whole. They are important because they offer "a non-Pauline witness to the beliefs and practices of the first Christian communities" (Bray 2000, xxi). Although there are other non-Pauline books, this is the only collection that has "never been associated in any way with the great apostle to the Gentiles" (Bray 2000, xxi).

The General Epistles were profoundly influenced by Jewish thought. They emphasize the importance of works—practical demonstrations of faith. The ancient church fathers who interpreted these letters understood such works as primarily "self-sacrifice [life, suffering], generosity [almsgiving and hospitality] and humility" (Bray 2000, xxii-xxiii).

The book of James is full of advice on how Christians should live. Thus, some say it contradicts Paul's gospel of grace and faith, and they question its place in the canon. However, this commentary will show that James' and Paul's thoughts are complementary, not contradictory. Actions demonstrate the saving work of faith that has taken place in the lives of individuals and communities.

21

The earliest surviving comments on the book of James are from the early third century in the writings of Origen (ca. 185-254) and the pseudo-Clementine *Epistles to Virgins* (Ropes 1973, 1). After Origen, James became widely accepted as part of the NT in the eastern, Greek-speaking church.

No ancient Western text of James survives. The third-century *papyrus 20*, found in Oxyrhynchus, Egypt, is the earliest Greek manuscript with sections from James. The best and earliest complete copy of the letter appears in the fourth-century Codex Alexandrinus manuscript (B), also from Egypt. James was one of the last books to gain admission into the canon of Scripture. This may have been due to the growing resistance of the increasingly Gentile membership of the church to Jewish-Christian traditions.

James was marginalized by Martin Luther during the Protestant Reformation. In an early preface to the NT, he called it "an epistle of straw" (1960, 362). Luther's fight was against the "rules and ritual" of the Roman Catholic Church in the 1500s and in favor of "faith and experience."

Luther disliked James because "it contradicted Paul's teaching on faith-righteousness" (2:14-26) and because it lacked any "gospel character." That is, it did not "show the Christ" (Johnson 1999, 507). Luther, however, agrees with the core of James: "For where works and charity do not abound, there the belief is not right; the Gospel does not apply, and Christ is not rightly known" (Luther 1863, 79).

Since longstanding Christian tradition would not allow him to exclude books from the canon, Luther did "the next best thing." He placed James, along with Hebrews, Jude, and Revelation, at the back of his German Bible and did not list them in the table of contents. "Both Luther's formulation of the theological problem and his criticism of James from a Pauline perspective remain compelling today, in fact, James-viewed-through-Paul is (lamentably) still the norm" (Wachob 2000, 32).

Luther, a German, former Roman Catholic monk, rejected James in the 1500s. But Søren Kierkegaard, a Lutheran Danish philosopher of the 1800s, wrote four complete discourses and nine shorter passages on James.

There can be no argument that his favorite verse in his favorite book of the Bible was James 1:17: "Every good and every perfect gift is from above, and cometh down from the Father of lights, with whom is no variableness, neither shadow of turning." It is significant that one of the first two discourses he ever published and his last discourse were expositions of this very verse. (Eller 1962)

Kierkegaard rejected the cold formality of the Lutheran Church of Denmark. He insisted that if Christianity mattered, it should make a difference in the way one lived.

Kierkegaard "is probably the only person who is on record as having regarded the first chapter of the letter of James as his favourite portion of Scripture" (Bauckham 1999, 1).

Although James was written in Greek, its thought-world is Jewish. For James there can be no true faith that does not affect the way one lives. In contrast to the Greek division of the person into body and mind (or body, mind, and spirit), Jews held a unified view of the person. Thus, what one really believes can be seen in what one does.

Ossuary of James, Brother of Jesus

The cover story of the November/December 2002 issue of the *Biblical Archaeological Review* was a World Exclusive: "Evidence of Jesus Written in Stone: Ossuary of 'James, Brother of Jesus' Found in Jerusalem." The discovery of the limestone bone burial box made international headlines.

The discovery could provide the first archaeological evidence for the existence of Jesus. On the side of the ossuary is an inscription in clear Aramaic letters: "James, son of Joseph, brother of Jesus." The exact location of its discovery is unknown, but probably near Jerusalem.

The practice of gathering the bones of a deceased person after the flesh had decayed was observed for a relatively short period in Israel (first century B.C. to A.D. 70). Paleographic evidence and the type of box suggest a date between 20 B.C. and A.D. 70.

The names of James, Jesus, and Joseph are all common names from this period. But the presence of all three names in the inscription increases the chances that this box might have been the burial box of James. The identification of James as the *brother* of Jesus is quite unusual. It seems to indicate that the brother was one of great consequence. Usually a man was identified only by his father's name.

Scholars remain divided on whether or not the inscription is authentic. (See Lemaire 2002a; Lemaire 2002b; Shanks 2003a; Shanks 2003b; Shanks 2008 in http://www.bib-arch.org/news/forgery-trial-news.asp, accessed 11/03/2008).

B. Historical/Cultural Context

The letter of James reflects the issues and theology of early Jewish Christians. Paul wrote much of the NT to Gentile or Gentile-Jewish communities. Most of the Gospels reached their canonical form after Paul. Thus, this early Jewish-Christian voice is not often so clearly heard either in the NT or in the church today.

Resurrection was a point of conflict between two major Jewish groups of the early first century A.D. The Pharisees believed in resurrection; Sadducees did not. We might expect James to have addressed the issues of the death and resurrection of Jesus or Christians. But he does not.

James contains nothing that is traditionally called the *kerygma*: the proclamation of Jesus' life, death, and resurrection. Nor does he mention the church and its growth in the first century. Robbins observes,

> The epistle exhibits one of the many ways in which Christians during the first century renamed certain Jewish practices, modified both Jewish practices and beliefs by using different language, and introduced new rules designed to nurture their own particular groups in various places throughout the Mediterranean world. (1996, 349)

James mentions Jesus specifically only twice. But he alludes many times to his sayings as recorded in the Gospels. When he uses the title "Lord," it is not always clear whether he means the Lord God or the Lord Jesus. He sometimes conflates the two but makes distinctions at other times.

James is concerned about the breakdown of unity, love, and charity within the church. The tests of faith were breaking the church apart as people yielded to pressure. James calls for internal unity and charity and offers a prophetic denunciation of the corrupt, rich elite. But he refuses to engage in hatred and violence toward them.

In contrast to Paul's writings, James' letter lacks an emphasis on mission or evangelism to outside groups. James' concern is for those in his community alone.

James reflects the strong Jewish life-ethic that was a major contribution of Jewish Christianity. We define this as: "Christians who were Jews and *expressed themselves* in the thought-forms of the Semitic world from which they came" (Riegel 1977-78, 415; see Martin 1988, xlii-xliii).

C. Authorship

In Jas 1:1 the author identifies himself simply as James, a "servant" or slave "of God and of the Lord Jesus Christ." He gives no personal or biographical information nor claims any apostolic status. His self-introduction implies that he was someone whose authority was clearly known to his audience.

The NT mentions several people named James: the son of Zebedee (Mark 1:19), the son of Alphaeus (Mark 3:18), the brother of Jesus (Mark 6:3), the younger (Mark 15:40), the father of Jude (Luke 6:16). Of this group James, "the Lord's brother" (Gal 1:19) was the most recognized leader in the early Christian Church.

- The Gospels indicate that James and the other siblings of Jesus did not believe in him during the days of Jesus' earthly ministry (Matt 12:46-50; John 7:1-5; 19:25-27).
- Paul specifically mentions James as one of those to whom the risen Jesus appeared (1 Cor 15:7).

- On this basis, Paul perhaps identifies James as, not only "the Lord's brother," but also as one of "the other apostles" (Gal 1:19; 1 Cor 15:7).
- Paul also includes James alongside Peter and John as one of the "pillars" of the Jerusalem church (Gal 2:9).
- Two passages in Acts portray this James as a mediator of the Jerusalem Council and head of the Jerusalem Church (15:13-21; 21:18-26).
- In Jude 1, the author identifies himself as the brother of James.
- Beyond this NT data, most of what we know about James comes from Josephus' *Antiquities of the Jews* and Eusebius' *Ecclesiastical History.*

Although the authorship of James was widely disputed among the early church authors, the letter had general acceptance in the early church. Eusebius of Caesarea (ca. 260-339) lists the Epistle among the disputed books that were familiar to most Christians. He reports that there was doubt in his day about the book's authenticity because few early writers make reference to it. However, he identifies James as one of the seven "General" epistles, frequently used in many churches (Bray 2000, xvii).

The text of James indicates that its author was fluent in Greek and may have used the LXX as his OT scripture. He was deeply influenced by Jewish Wisdom literature (e.g., Job 5:11; 34:29; Pss 18:6; 21:9; 34:13; 39:1; 102:4, 11; 103:8; 111:4; 140:3; 141:3; Prov 3:34; 10:12; 27:1; and Eccl 7:9; Sir 5:11; 15:11-13).

The influence of the Jewish wisdom tradition is not limited to the noted quotations or allusions. It is seen in

the way in which the spirit of OT and Jewish Wisdom traditions imbue the entire letter, so that it would be fair to characterize the ideology of this homiletical letter as very much a part of the sapiential tradition, yet with strong "alternative wisdom" leanings. (Brosend 2004, 10)

Conventional wisdom focuses on how things work in one's current reality (You reap what you sow). Alternative wisdom, however, invites readers to see things differently (i.e., God is gracious, and may spare us from some of the consequences of our unfortunate sowing).

That the author wrote in excellent Greek is a problem for many scholars. They assume that James, the brother of Jesus, would likely have been a Galilean, without much education in Greek. Some scholars further insist that this and other characteristics indicate that someone wrote the letter under the assumed name of James (pseudonymous). Martin hypothesizes that a Hellenistic Jewish editor in Antioch reworked James' original text. This would account for the good Greek grammar and style (1988, lxiii-lxix).

Other commentators point out that "a hard-and-fast distinction between Hellenistic Jews in the Diaspora and non-Hellenized Palestinian Jews is artificial." Thus, "the authorship of James by a Palestinian Jew is easily conceivable." Three centuries of Greek influence in Israel make it "inappropriate to call Diaspora Judaism Hellenistic Judaism, as though Palestinian Judaism were not Hellenized" (1999, 22).

The evidence of Hellenism does not exclude the idea that James, the brother of Jesus, as a Palestinian Jew could have written the letter. The main question that remains for some concerns James' level of education.

The Legend of St. James

In his *Ecclesiastical History*, church father Eusebius of Caesarea (ca. 260–339) includes a

passage from a now-lost work by Hegesippus, a Christian writer who lived in Palestine in the second century. Hegesippus said that James was holy "from his mother's womb," never drinking wine, eating meat or bathing himself and kneeling in prayer so often "that his knees became hard like those of a camel." He was therefore called "the Just" and, in Greek, *Oblias,* "Bulwark of the People."

After the death, resurrection, and ascension of Jesus,

James became the leader of the early Christians in Jerusalem. Preaching that Jesus was the Christ, or Messiah, he won many converts, including some from the ruling classes. According to Hegesippus, his preaching alarmed the scribes and Pharisees, who ordered him to stand at the Jerusalem Temple before a large crowd and retract his statements. James went to the top of the Temple, but instead of recanting, he confirmed that Jesus was indeed the Christ.

Then, according to Hegesippus,

They [the scribes and the Pharisees] went up and threw down the just man, and said to each other, "Let us stone James the Just." And they began to stone him, for he was not killed by the fall, but he knelt down and said, "I entreat thee, Lord God our Father, forgive them, for they know not what they do." And one of them, who was a fuller, took the club with which he beat out clothes and struck the just man on the head.

And thus he [James] suffered martyrdom. And they buried him on the spot, by the temple, and his monument still remains by the temple.

Hegesippus' account of James' death is probably exaggerated. But the legend is based on the historical fact of James' pious reputation as a man of prayer. A similar account appears in the first-century Jewish historian Josephus' account (*Ant.* 20.9.1; see http://www.ccel.org).

D. Audience

James greets *the twelve tribes in the Diaspora* (1:1). Although this phrase may be used metaphorically to include all Christians, other indicators in the letter suggest James was addressing Jewish Christians who lived outside the land of Israel. James' quotations from OT and Jewish intertestamental literature seem to identify his audience as humble and poor (1:9) people living in the midst of prevalent moral filth and evil (1:21).

Acts 15:13-21; 21:18-26 and early Christian tradition identify James as the head of the church in Jerusalem. Although James addresses his letter to Jewish Christians of the Diaspora, he was intimately acquainted with the needs and trials of Jewish Christians in Judea. By the end of the 60s, the church had spread north to Syria, across the vast area of Asia Minor (modern Turkey), to Greece, Rome, and perhaps as far as the Iberian Peninsula (today's Spain and Portugal). Many of the families of converted Diaspora Jews had lived outside of Judea for centuries (some since the Babylonian exile).

Some Jewish families, like Paul's, may have earned or bought Roman citizenship. But most lived as noncitizens, subject to the whims of the authorities. Although they may not have been specifically targeted for persecution, they suffered from their lack of status and power within their communities. Their distinctive dietary and ritual laws made them stand out as unusual, even strange. Even those who lived in Judea were subject to the caprice of the Roman authorities who occupied Palestine in the first century.

Peter uses two words to describe the social situation of first-century Diaspora Jews: temporary residents/refugees (1 Pet 1:1; 2:11, *parepidēmois*) and resident aliens/strangers (1 Pet 2:11, *paroikous*). Elliot defines this second word as "strangers, foreigners, aliens, people who are not at home, or who lack native roots, in the language, customs, culture, or political, social, and religious allegiances of the people among whom they dwell" (1981, 24). In both secular and biblical literature it "implies social separation, cultural alienation and a certain degree of personal deprivation" (Elliot 1981, 25).

In classical Greek the *paroikos* was "a resident alien, who has his domicile with or among the natives, having no civic rights" or "national rights" (Meyer, Schmidt, and Schmidt 1967, 842). In the LXX and so-called intertestamental Jewish literature, it "denotes the state, position or fate of a resident alien, 'dwelling abroad' without civil or native rights" (Meyer, Schmidt, and Schmidt 1967, 842). Resident aliens may be distinguished from homeless, begging strangers. But they "came with strings attached: political and economic exploitation, continued disdain and suspicion by the citizenry, and competition and envy from those below him" (Elliot 1981, 26).

Robert Wall views James' Diaspora designation as "metaphorical." He suggests that they are

> believers, even those living in Palestine, who are cut off from social and religious support systems. . . . In this sense, many members of the Palestinian working-class poor—including the first readers of James—were "homeless," in the homeland but without a home. (1997, 12)

Although these Jewish Christians considered themselves within the Jewish tradition, they were suspect and different from adherents to mainstream Judaism.

James uses "twelve tribes" rather than the more general terms "Israel" or "people of God." "While unnatural as a reference to the church, the phrase is a natural way of referring to Israel outside the land" (Bauckham 1999, 14). In using the "twelve tribes" terminology, James includes the whole nation of Israel. He corrects the common misconception that the northern tribes had disappeared by the first century A.D. (Bauckham 1999, 15).

According to the text, these readers gather in a **synagogue** (2:2), and elders lead the community (5:14). In addition, there are five quotations from the OT (Lev 19:18; Exod 20:14/Deut 5:18; Exod 20:13/Deut 5:17; Gen 15:6; Prov 3:34) and many allusions. James contains Jewish idioms like **Father of the lights** (1:17) and **Lord of Sabaoth** (5:4).

Other Jewish features include emphasis on keeping the Law (2:10; 4:11-12) and belief in one God (2:19). We find an absence of warnings against idolatry as compared to Paul's letters to Gentile churches. James says almost nothing about tensions between Jews and Gentiles in the church, and "when Gentiles are mentioned, the word clearly refers to people who were pagans" (Bray 2000, xxi-xxii).

E. Date

There is no consensus among scholars on either the date or authorship of James, as these are closely related. Ropes and Laws date James in the first third of the second century. They presuppose the author wrote pseudonymously, because "James of Jerusalem was a very considerable figure in the tradition of early Christianity" (Laws 1980, 42). Ropes dates James between A.D. 75 and 125, by "a Christian teacher in some half-hellenistic city of Palestine, in the period of quiet after the destruction of Jerusalem in 70 A.D." (1973, 49).

The characteristics Ropes sees in the author and audience include:
1. "Greek-speaking Jewish Christians in Palestine"
2. "settled conditions among Jewish neighbors"
3. no crises, no missionary passion
4. writes "later than Paul, of whose formulas he disapproves" and
5. a type of Christianity showing "extraordinary intellectual isolation." (1973, 48-49)

External evidence indicates that the date cannot be later than 150, since Origen believed the book was written by James, an apostle.

Two nineteenth-century scholars working independently, Massebieau (1895) and Spitta (1896), dated the writing before the time of James. They believed the book was written by a pre-Christian Jew and later Christianized "by the simple addition of two interpolations, one at 1:1 and one at 2:1"

(Davids 1982, 3). Some early twentieth-century scholars similarly considered James a non-Christian work of Jewish origin. But they dated it after the time of James the Just (after A.D. 62; see Table 1, Davids 1982, 4).

Davids and Martin consider the primary author of the letter to have been James, the brother of Jesus and head of the church in Jerusalem (Davids 1982, 2-22; Martin 1988, lxii-lxxvii). Davids offers seven reasons why the evidence favors an early date and James the Just as the book's author:

1. the indirect external evidence (allusions to James in early church fathers)
2. the self-designation of the author (lack of exalted titles)
3. its strong Jewish influence
4. the use of the "preliterary tradition of the words of Jesus"
5. the situation of the churches addressed
6. the lack of reference to the issue of "the reception of the gentiles"
7. the lack of explicit Christology (1982, 21-22). He suggests a date between A.D. 40 and 49, before the Jerusalem Council of Acts 15.

Both Davids and Martin acknowledge that some of the evidence does favor a later date. These include:

1. external evidence (late attestation of James)
2. James is written in good Koine Greek
3. its similarities with the Apostolic Fathers and
4. possible interaction with Paulinism (Davids 1982, 22; Martin 1988, xxxiii-lxxvii)

They explain these inconsistent features by suggesting that the book was edited by a Hellenistic Jew in the second half of the first century (Davids 1982, 22; Martin 1988, lxxiii-lxxvii; Martin cites as evidence 2 Apoc. Jas. 44:13-17 from Nag Hammadi [1988, lxxii]).

We accept the traditional view that James, the brother of Jesus, was the author of this letter. But we also consider it likely that his original letter was revised by a later Hellenistic Jewish Christian sometime in the early second half of the first century.

Tradition from the end of the fourth century dates the book of James between A.D. 40 and 62. James was the head of the church in Jerusalem during this era. The precise date of James' martyrdom is unknown. But it occurred sometime between A.D. 62 and 70.

The letter aptly reflects the known social, political, and religious conditions of Palestine during the period when James led the church in Jerusalem. This historical period was marked by political and social instability and famines, which only increased the despair of the poor. Zealot activity increased during this time, recruiting from the poor farmers.

A Historical and Social Sketch of James' Time

In A.D. 37, Emperor Caligula gave the northern Transjordan to Agrippa I. By A.D. 41 he ruled all the lands once had under his grandfather, King Herod the Great. During this time Caligula demanded that a colossal statue of himself be erected in the Jerusalem temple. Only the murder of Caligula in A.D. 41 avoided violent conflict.

Agrippa I, a shrewd ruler, appeared as a devout Jew to the Jews and a Hellenistic prince to the Gentiles. He followed his grandfather's example, building many Greco-Roman buildings. He also "humored the Pharisees, persecuted the Christian community in Jerusalem, had James the son of Zebedee executed, and had Peter thrown in prison (Acts 12:1-4)" (Lohse 1985, 46). His spectacular death in A.D. 44 is recorded both in the NT (Acts 12:21-23) and in Josephus (*Ant.* 19.8, 412).

When Agrippa I died, he left behind one son, Agrippa II, and three daughters under the age of sixteen (Bernice, Mariamne, and Drusilla). Josephus' claim that the people of Caesarea and Samaria (Sebaste) "cast such reproaches upon the deceased as are not fit to be spoken of" (*Ant.* 19.9, 413) gives some indication of how hated Agrippa I was.

The advisers of Emperor Claudius persuaded him not to send Agrippa II into this troubled situation (Josephus, *Ant.* 19.9, 413). Thus, the kingdom of Agrippa I came under the direct Roman rule of the governor of Syria, with Roman procurators of Palestine reporting to him.

By A.D. 48, Agrippa II ruled parts of Palestine. During the 50s his rule included large parts of northern Palestine. He was the King Agrippa to whom Paul pled his case (A.D. 59). Agrippa's devotion to Rome led him to appoint and depose Jewish high priests capriciously, earning the hatred of the Jews. He unsuccessfully tried to quell the developing rebellions of the 60s.

Adding to the political instability was the great famine of A.D. 46-48 when many poor Jews migrated to find better situations for their families (Theissen 1978, 35). During the reign of Claudius (A.D. 41-54), "there were failures in food supplies generally within the empire" (Theissen 1978, 40).

Robbers (resistance fighters) were prevalent during the first century. They drew their recruits from farmers no longer able to pay their taxes, those in deep debt, and the poor. Both Agrippa I and Agrippa II boasted of defeating these groups (Theissen 1978, 35). Jewett points out that

> there was a resurgence of "zealot" activity in Judaea under the governors Tiberius Julius Alexander (c. A.D. 46-48), who crucified two insurgent leaders, sons of Judas the Galilean (Jos., *Ant.* 20.102), and his successor Ventidius Cumanus (c. A.D. 48-52), during whose period of office disorder increased (*Ant.* 20.105-36; *War* 2.223-46). Zealot vengeance was liable to be visited on Jews who fraternized with Gentiles, and Jewish Christians who shared table-fellowship with their Gentile brethren were exposed to

such reprisals. If Gentile Christians could be persuaded to accept circumcision, this (it was hoped) would protect Jewish Christians against zealot vengeance. (1970-71, 198-212)

Jewish Christians were tempted to fight back against both of their oppressors: the Gentiles and the Jews. They were in a difficult and delicate situation in Palestine, Syria, and Asia Minor.

The poor represented a huge percentage of the population. They were looking for support and relief from the burdens placed on them by the rich. The Qumran community was a reaction to a society "in which the rich had a built-in advantage in the struggle for possessions" (Theissen 1978, 37). The dire economic situation in Palestine may also explain the communal arrangement that characterized the Jewish sectarian community known as the Essenes (described in Josephus, *J.W.* 2.8.3).

The unrest of this period continued throughout James' lifetime. The fourth-century church historian Eusebius characterizes the era just before James' death as one of "anarchy, which was caused by the fact that Festus had died just at this time in Judea, and that the province was thus without a governor and head" (2.23.2 [http://www.newadvent.org/fathers/250102.htm, accessed 11/3/2008).

James 1 refers to trials. In vv 9-11 James begins his comparison of the poor and the rich, claiming that the rich fade away *in his or her way of life.*

James 2 forbids favoritism within the community. The rich should not be favored because they exploit the poor! James' call for the community to feed and clothe those in need perhaps reflects on the ideal community of the 30s described in Acts 2:42-47.

James 3 warns of harboring bitter envy and selfish ambition and ends with encouraging the readers to be peacemakers. This could be a corrective to the allure of the terrorists/resistance fighters, who were recruiting from the poor and disenfranchised.

James 4 continues on this theme, addressing the problem of desires and coveting what one cannot have. It encourages the readers to ask God for what they need rather than fighting.

Finally, James 5 warns the rich of their coming misery because of the sin of oppression. He exhorts the community to be patient and to pray, because the prayer of a righteous person is powerful—more powerful than their rich oppressors!

James levels stinging eschatological denunciation in line with the strongest words of Jesus (Luke 6:24-26). His church is the church of the poor. Jewish piety shines through, but it is coupled with fervent eschatological expectation. Yet for all his sympathy for the poor, James refuses to join the Zealots (resistance fighters). He demands that Christians give up the world.

The letter of James fits well as a reminder of the moral implications of the Jewish Christians' faith. Within the church, the generosity of the 30s (Acts 2) appears to have worn off. The letter seems to indicate a period when the community structure and the care for the poor in the earliest days of the church attested in Acts no longer existed. Under financial pressure, believers held to orthodox belief but grasped their possession tightly. This may have led to a proliferation of schemes to gain financial security (see Jas 4:13-17) and a love for or faith in the ways of the world.

A date in the late 40s to early 60s allows enough time for the changes in the church's social structure from that reflected in Acts 2 in the early 30s. I consider this era the probable historical period reflected in the letter.

F. Location

According to Christian tradition, after Jesus' resurrection, James lived out his life in Jerusalem. He played a mediating role in the Council of Jerusalem in A.D. 49 (Acts 15) and led the Jerusalem church from A.D. 40 to 62/69.

The Hellenistic Jewish Christian who may have edited James' letter probably lived in Palestine or Antioch in Syria. If his redaction took place after A.D. 70, he may have lived in one of the other large Roman cities with substantial Jewish communities. Devout Jews tended to remain as close to Jerusalem as possible after its destruction.

The letter of James is too general and the salutation too vague for certainty as to the location of its first readers. They may have lived in Jerusalem. But it is more likely that they lived in large Roman cities in Syria and Asia Minor. Meeks and Wilken observe that

> the Jews of Antioch were inevitably drawn into the growing conflict between Jews and Romans in Palestine (Caligula's order that his statue be placed in the temple in Jerusalem). The Jews refused to be intimidated, and when the governor went to Jerusalem to carry out the order, Jews lined the roads to protest his action. The initial impetus for this protest, which succeeded in persuading Petronius to delay, according to both Philo and Josephus, probably originated in Antioch. (1978, 4)

They add that "in the same year, Malalas reports, mobs in Antioch attacked Jews, killing many and burning synagogues. . . . Both Kraeling and Downey find a local disturbance in 40 CE perfectly credible" (1978, 4). This indicates that much of what was happening in Palestine to Jews and Jewish Christians was also a concern for the Jews in Syria. Recall that after Agrippa I, Palestine came under the supervision of the governor of Syria.

G. Form and Genre

James begins with the traditional salutation of a Greco-Roman letter. It lacks, however, the typical prayer or thanksgiving that follows the greeting in Paul's letters. And it has no closing greeting or benediction. It clearly is a literary epistle, intended for publication to a wide audience. It is certainly not a personal letter like Paul's Epistle to the Galatians.

Literary epistles characteristically: (1) "reflect the *Sitz im Leben* [life situation] of its place of publication, not that of its 'recipients' . . . and (2) the form of the epistle will differ from that of the actual letter, especially in its lack of personal detail" (Davids 1982, 24-25). Thus, some scholars describe James as a "word of exhortation" (sermon) with an added salutation.

Bauckham calls James an "encyclical [circular letter] addressing any Jewish Christian community anywhere in the Diaspora. . . . It is unlikely to have been occasioned by any specific exigencies" (1999, 27). James reflects his context in Jerusalem. He was in "constant contact with Jewish pilgrims from the Diaspora," keeping him well informed of Jewish Christians there (Bauckham 1999, 26).

Form critics identify two types of material in James: "(1) oral discourses . . . and (2) sayings, including proverbs, which may be joined into series of sayings" (Davids 1982, 23). The oral discourses have the character of diatribes. Ropes emphasizes the Hellenistic origins of diatribes (1973, 10-16). But Wessel demonstrates that

> the features of the diatribe are in fact the features of the Jewish synagogue homily . . . dialogue (including such features as rhetorical questions, questions, and answers, and an imaginary opponent); the direct address of the auditor (e.g., "my brethren"); variety in subject matter; and harsh speech. (Davids 1982, 23; citing Wessel 1953, 71-112)

This fits the synagogue context of James better than the Hellenistic description. Ropes acknowledges some differences between James' diatribes and the extant Greek versions (1973, 15). James would have been familiar with synagogue sermons. And he almost certainly had delivered some himself in Jewish-Christian communities.

The technical designation for the rhetorical style of James is "paraenesis"—exhortation and confrontation on issues of right and wrong. James was not telling his readers anything new. He encouraged them to follow what they have been taught and to keep that faith pure. His Epistle discusses standard Jewish wisdom topics (testing, wisdom, wealth, speech, generosity, and action) that are important to a "pure and faultless" religion (1:27).

Some scholars (e.g., Dibelius 1975, 5-6) see very little structural organization in James. But it is apparent that the themes in ch 1 reappear throughout the rest of the book. Chapter 1 appears to introduce and anticipate what James intended to discuss at length in the rest of the Epistle. Davids says that "the major block of material in the book takes up the themes in reverse order" (1982, 25). Scholars differ as to how heavily James was influenced by the Jewish wisdom tradition. "Older works viewed James as wisdom literature, but the pattern of Jewish wisdom literature hardly fits the type of exhortations, the connected oral discourse and the radical tone of the epistle" (Davids 1982, 24).

James "breathes a different atmosphere" in relation to the Wisdom literature of the OT. "Some of the ideas, however, of Proverbs, Ecclesiasticus and Wisdom are found repeated in James" (Ropes 1973, 18-19). The Wisdom of Jesus Sirach (Ecclesiasticus) "offers better parallels [than Proverbs], but it is doubtful whether the common view that James unquestionably used it can be maintained" (1973, 19).

The similar topics in James and Sirach include the tongue, wisdom as a gift of God, praying with a divided heart, uncertainty of life, blaming God, humans made in the image of God and given dominion over the animals, and the eclipse of the sun as well as changes in the moon (Ropes 1973, 19).

Bauckham refers to the genre of James as "wisdom paraenesis" (1999, 29). He sees James

> as a disciple of Jesus the sage . . . a wisdom teacher who has made the wisdom of Jesus his own, and who seeks to appropriate and to develop the resources of the Jewish wisdom tradition in a way that is guided and controlled by the teaching of Jesus. (Bauckham 1999, 30)

H. Outlines of James

James is an exposition of early Jewish-Christian piety. It gives practical advice on how to live a life that is pleasing to God in a situation requiring extraordinary patience and perseverance. Because of the proverbial or aphoristic nature of James, scholars rarely agree on an outline. All acknowledge Jas 1:1 as the opening greeting, Epistle introduction, inscription, or salutation. Beyond that, agreements are few (see Wachob 2000, 54-55; Bengel 1877; Wuellner 1978; Baasland 1982; Davids 1982, 27-28; Johnson 1995, 167-347; Taylor and Guthrie 2006, 681-705).

Bauckham considers most modern attempts to analyze the organization of James as a reaction to Dibelius (1921, rev. 1975, 5-6). Dibelius identified James as incoherently ordered paraenesis (Bauckham 1999, 61). The description of the audience as the twelve tribes of Israel led to Bauckham's discovery of an original and persuasive structural outline. He divides his exposition into the twelve units, "signaled by strong formal indicators of opening and closure." Most commentators have noticed these but have not given them sufficient value (Bauckham 1999, 63-64).

This outline fits the type of literature found in James and acknowledges the important indicators of opening and concluding oral discussions. I have adopted Bauckham's outline in this commentary, with some variations in titles and with the addition of a few subunits.

I. Content Summary

The theme of James is salvation by obedient faith, which the author links to his definition of pure and undefiled religion. James is the only NT book to define "religion." For James, true religion is practical: *to visit orphans and widows in their affliction and to keep oneself unspotted by the world* (1:27).

A most important issue in the book is the nature and value of trials. James affirms that trials develop character and bring it to maturity. Those with mature character obey the Law. Mature believers treat everyone equitably, with all due respect. They also take action to correct wrong situations and do the right thing.

The most difficult aspect of self-discipline, and the one that shows the true extent of our maturity, is controlling our speech. James says that no one can tame the tongue—it takes a change of nature only God can effect. When persons are changed, then their behavior changes. The most obvious evidence is in the way we use our tongues.

James sounds a typical Jewish prophetic warning against rich oppressors before he reiterates the value and purpose of patience in suffering. These rich oppressors don't pay their workers justly, much less charitably. They may be living in luxury now. But James warns that misery awaits them in the future.

James closes his epistolary treatise with a series of instructions. Christians should pray when they are in trouble and request prayer when they are sick. The Christian tradition of anointing the sick with oil originated with Jas 5:14. James understands healing to include not only recovery from physical illness but also divine forgiveness. Prayer by mature Christians is extremely effective.

The final words of this sermon-letter deal with love and reconciliation. The community is to care for those who have "wandered from the truth" and gently bring them back.

J. Major Theological Themes in James

Although James' focus is on practical Christianity, it is based, like his actions, on his theological convictions. Several themes are particularly prominent. James' theology is implicit, not overt. He presents no systematic theology.

Theology

For James, God is unique (2:19; 4:12). He is the Creator of human beings and all living creatures (1:18). He is the giver of all good gifts (1:17), including the perfect Law (2:11). He is the "Judge . . . who is able to save and destroy" (4:12). God gives wisdom generously to all who ask (1:5). God tempts no one and is not tempted by evil (1:13). God is not fickle and undependable, subject to unpredictable changes (1:17). Those who believe God and do what he says can be called friends of God (2:23). Those who have preferred the world are enemies of God (4:4).

God defines righteousness (1:20). He chose the poor to be rich in faith and love and to inherit his kingdom (2:5). God gives grace to the humble and comes near to those who come near to him (4:6-8). God is the absolutely powerful Lord of Hosts (heavenly armies), who hears the cries of the oppressed and administers justice (4:4). He is compassionate and pities those who endure suffering, even the righteous rich, like Job (5:11).

Christology

Christology in James is more difficult to determine. James uses the name and title "Lord Jesus Christ" only twice in his letter (1:1; 2:1). Although he knew Jesus as his half-brother, this title reveals that James had come to understand him as also his Lord, the Messiah of Israel, even his God.

James 2:1 refers to **the faith of our glorious Lord Jesus Christ.** It is unclear whether this faith refers to the beliefs held by Jesus or what one believes about Jesus. The second option (as an objective genitive) defines what makes a person a Christian (see Blomberg and Kamell 2008, 106; Davids 1982, 106; and Ropes 1973, 186-87). The first option (as a subjective genitive) refers to the personal faith Jesus espoused (Johnson 1995, 220; see the commentary on 2:1).

Most commentators understand the genitive phrase, **the one of glory,** as a description of Jesus (Blomberg and Kamell 2008, 106-7; Davids 1982, 106-7; Ropes 1973, 186-87; Johnson 1995, 220-21). Its precise meaning, however, is ambiguous (see the commentary on 2:1).

Blomberg and Kamell suggest two possibilities. One is "a description or qualitative genitive, that is, 'our glorious Lord Jesus Christ' (see Jas 1:25; 1 Co 2:8)" (see Ropes 1973, 186-87). The other is "appositional, so that Christ is equated with the *shekinah* glory of God, the 'localized presence of Yahweh'" (2008, 106). Davids notes that the LXX uses *doxa* to translate the Hebrew *kābôd.* The Hebrew term means "'the luminous manifestation of God's person' particularly in his bringing salvation to Israel" (1982, 107; citing S. Aalen).

Johnson comments that "*doxa* is frequently found as shorthand for the resurrection of Jesus (see Luke 24:26; Acts 22:11; John 17:5; 1 Cor 2:8; 15:43; 2 Cor 4:6; Phil 2:11; 3:21; Col 1:11; Heb 2:7; 1 Pet 1:11)" (1995, 221). These variations on the second option would indicate the existence of a remarkably high Christology early in the development of the church.

Shekinah, *Kābôd*, and Glory

Shekinah appears in OT passages that speak of God dwelling in the tabernacle or among the people of Israel (e.g., Exod 25:8; 29:45-46; Num 5:3; Ezek

43:9). It describes the palpable manifestation of God's presence among his people. Jewish rabbis often used the word as a roundabout way of referring to God.

Kābôd is God's visible and invisible splendor or majesty (lit., his "weightiness" or "heaviness"). It is not quite synonymous with *shekinah*, which has more to do with the indwelling presence of God. In English, it is common to translate both as "glory." Glory, however, is an attribute of God. Since James was written in Greek, it is difficult to determine which Hebrew term the author had in mind. If James was thinking of the incarnation, then *shekinah* might be appropriate. If he was thinking about the splendor of God, then *kābôd* might fit better. (E-mail from Alex Varughese, 8/14/09)

James emphasizes that favoritism was not part of the faith (2:1), which reflects the teaching and practice of Jesus here on earth. According to 3:9, Christians **bless the Lord and Father.** But it is unclear whether James refers to both Jesus (Lord) and God (Father), refers only to God as both Lord and Father, or even equates Jesus with God.

The eschatological understanding of Christ appears to underlie 5:7-9, where James refers to **the appearing** [*parousia*] **of the Lord** and to "the Judge . . . standing at the door." Elsewhere in James, God is obviously the Judge (4:12). But in this context, James seems to recognize Jesus as the Judge of the end times.

In 5:14-15 the use of "the Lord" is ambiguous. Do Christians **anoint the sick with oil in the name of** Jesus or God? James adds that the Lord will raise the sick and forgive their sins. Such actions were characteristic features of the earthly ministry of Jesus (see the commentary on 5:14-15).

"Grace" appears twice in only one verse (4:6). This immediately follows James' denunciation of those who want to have friendship with the world as adulteresses. God gives greater grace because he understands the human condition. But God gives this grace only to the humble, for he continues to resist the arrogant.

"Sin(s)" appears six times in James (1:15; 2:9; 4:17; 5:15, 16, 20). The Greek *hamartia* is translated "sin" in twenty-one of the twenty-seven NT books. It refers to missing the mark or goal of our lives, that is, faithful obedience to God. It is an "offense in relation to God with emphasis on guilt" (Zodhiates 1992, 130). *Hamartia* as a departure from the divine standard of uprightness identifies specific sins, the state of being sinful (Rom 8:21, 24), and sin as a destructive evil power (Rom 5:12, 21; BDAG, 50-51).

In 1:15 James refers to sin using the metaphors of reproduction and aging. One's desires conceive and give birth to sin. But when sin is fully grown, it gives birth to death. James warns his audience not to blame God for temptation. Sin comes from a person's own desires, not from God. The fault is completely that of the person who sins.

James 2:9 calls favoritism sin. It is sinful because it violates the law of God. Here James calls sinners **transgressors** (*parabatai*), emphasizing his understanding of sin as the breaking of God's law.

In 4:17, James moves beyond sins of commission, which defy God's law. He stresses that the failure to fulfill God's law, sins of omission, are equally evil. For James, sin involves breaking God's law, whether by an overt act of rebellion or by the benign neglect of full obedience.

In chs 1—4 James refers to sin in the singular, defining it and explaining its origins. In ch 5, he explains the affect of sins (*harmartias*) on persons and communities. In James' mind, sins and sickness are closely related (5:15-16). He urges his readers to **confess** their **sins** [*hamartias*] **to one another and pray for** mutual healing, physical and spiritual (5:16).

This holistic view of healing is consistent with his Jewish worldview. Jews viewed persons as wholes, not compartmentalized into body and soul; or body, soul, and spirit. It is also consistent with James' view that "works" (actions) testify to who one is and what one believes at the deepest level. On this view, unconfessed sins might be expected to bring on illness.

James' closing sentence (5:20) encourages the faithful to bring sinners back from their **wandering way.** The result will be salvation from death and the hiding of a multitude of **sins.** Here this applies to both the person and the community. It is not just an ultimate eternal-death issue for individuals.

Salvation

Salvation in James has been a topic of considerable discussion. It is significant that the first time James employs the term **to save** (*sōsai*, 1:21) he says, **Receive the implanted word which is able to save your souls.** Those who caricature James as espousing "salvation by works" have not read his letter closely enough. James emphasizes from the outset that it is by receiving of **the implanted word** or the gospel (see on 1:15) that one is saved.

In 2:14, James asks, "Can such faith save him?" not simply, **Can faith save him?** The grammar indicates that there is an impotent faith, which does not lead to actions. Such professing believers have not truly received the gospel. Their so-called faith is unable to save them, because it is not really faith, just empty profession.

James 4:12 insists that God is "able to save and destroy." He alone is the Lawgiver and Judge. Once again, the focus is not on "salvation by works," but on God, who alone can save.

James 5:15 brings out the close relationship between physical healing and salvation from sin. The same root verb (*sōsei*), used earlier referring to the salvation of one's soul, is used here to describe both bodily healing and forgiveness.

James closes his letter by encouraging the community to pursue straying sinners and restore them to the community. James 5:20 indicates that salvation from death refers to both physical and spiritual death.

Law

Law is important to James. His first mention of law in 1:25 describes it as "perfect" and liberating. James carefully identifies the law to which he refers as "the perfect law that gives freedom" from sin. This is no endorsement of legalism. James 2:12 indicates that humanity is judged by God according to "the law that gives freedom."

In Jas 2:8-10 the law is described as "the royal law." He defines its essence as "Love your neighbor as yourself." Leviticus 19:18, cited here, is the NT's most frequently quoted passage from the Pentateuch (Matt 5:43; 19:19; Mark 12:31, 33; Rom 13:9; Gal 5:14).

This "royal law" is the one that those who showed favoritism were violating. James reminds his readers that one must keep all the Law and if one stumbles in one (i.e., the royal law), then one is guilty of breaking *the* law of God. James had in mind the Law as a whole, the central intention of the entire Mosaic corpus (Davids 1982, 117; see the commentary on 2:8-10).

Jesus said that all the Law and the Prophets depended on two commandments: love God completely and love your neighbor as yourself. Paul claimed that the observance of Lev 19:18 "is the fulfillment of the law" (Rom 13:10), for in it "The entire law is summed up in a single command" (Gal 5:14). James seems to be saying much the same thing.

In Jas 4:11 "law" is used without further description. But the context referring to slandering and judging one's brother or sister seems to point again to the royal law of loving relationships between human beings. By immediately identifying God as the Lawgiver, James seems to refer again to "the royal law" in 2:8.

Word

Word (*logos*), James claims, regenerates and saves. James 1:18 refers to "the word of truth" by which we are generated to be firstfruits of God's creatures. This is in contrast to humanity's own desires that generate sin and lead to death.

James 1:21-23 describes the gospel as "the implanted word that has the power to save your souls" (v 21 NRSV). This "implanted word" appears to parallel the embodied and enacted law of freedom or royal law. James challenges his readers to be doers of the word and not just hearers. Word and law in James are closely related. But James does not say that law saves or regenerates. That is the work of the implanted word or the gospel.

Trials/Temptations

Trials/temptations in James come from the same Greek root (*peirasmos*). Interpreters must determine which English word is the appropriate translation based on the context alone.

In 1:2 and 12, James refers to trials in the sense of the ordinary troubles that come as a part of human life. These troubles develop within believers the endurance that brings them maturity of character. So he urges his readers to be thankful for such troubles. Enduring these trials will eventually bring positive results.

But in 1:13-14, James uses the verbal root of this same word (*peirazō*). Here he cautions his readers not to attribute temptation to evil as coming from God. In v 13, James insists that "God cannot be tempted by evil" and "does not tempt anyone." The addition of the word "evil" (*kakōn*) changes the nuance of the experience from troubles to temptations.

Temptation for James comes from a person's own desires. They are not sent from God to test the strength of one's faith. Troubles and temptations are part of the normal human condition. But neither is sent by God, although each could be used to promote spiritual and personal maturity.

Wealth and Poverty/Humility

Wealth and poverty/humility are significant issues for James' readers, because of their social and religious context. He identifies with the poor. In 1:9-11 he contrasts the humble and the rich. He understands the world in a way that contradicts conventional wisdom. The humble enjoy a high status; the rich, low.

Immediately following this paradoxical claim, James pronounces a blessing on those who are enduring trials. This is because they will receive "the crown of life" (v 12). He implies that the trials and troubles of the humble/poor bring about spiritual maturity. The apparently easy life of the rich does not allow them to develop spiritual and personal maturity or the crown of life.

In 2:2-6, James uses an illustration of how differently the community treats rich and poor visitors to their synagogue. He reprimands the participants for favoring rich people. James reminds them that God chose the poor of the world "to be rich in faith" and heirs of the kingdom God promised.

Again he overturns the common perception of the relative status of rich and poor. Their practice of showing favoritism has caused the community to dishonor those God has chosen. The rich people to whom they offered deferential treatment were the ones who were oppressing the Jewish-Christian community.

James includes in 5:1-6 a strong indictment of the rich. He considers the rich greedy people, who got their wealth through corrupt ways and by oppressing others. He warns that God has heard the cries of the oppressed and will bring the greedy rich down. Their corrupt wealth will testify against them in the last days.

James' understanding of wealth and poverty arises from his understanding of the royal law: love your neighbor as yourself. Humble/poor people share what they have with others. The greedy rich (whether or not in the community) are those who hoard their belongings and send the hungry and naked out into the cold with an empty blessing instead of the necessities of life.

James sees no distinction between the social gospel and the true gospel. He agrees with Jesus' teaching in Matt 25:40: "whatever you did for one of the least of these brothers of mine, you did for me."

Faith and Works

Faith and works are at the heart of most discussions of the Epistle of James. Therefore, it is important to understand what he means by these words as related to salvation. He uses both words in 1:3-4. Here the testing of faith develops endurance, which results in a mature work. This enables one to become mature and whole. Clearly faith comes before works in this context.

In ch 2 James addresses the relationship of faith and works in his exposition of the royal law: "Love your neighbor as yourself" (v 8). He again deals first with the issue of faith. He points out that God chose the poor to be rich in faith. In 2:14 he asks what the value is of a faith that does not have works. This is followed immediately by the illustration of sending a hungry and naked brother or sister away with an empty blessing and no food or clothing. James concludes in 2:17 that faith, by itself, without works is dead.

However, James believes that one's faith is demonstrated by one's works (2:18). When one's faith does not produce actions that demonstrate one's beliefs, that faith is barren, sterile, and unproductive (2:20). He appeals to two OT illustrations of active faith. Abraham and Rahab demonstrated their faith by their actions.

James concludes in 2:26 that *just as the body is dead without the spirit, so also is faith without works dead.* James' position is that faith (demonstrated by works) brings salvation. Professed faith, however, which produces no works, is not faith at all and does not result in salvation.

In 3:13, wisdom is also demonstrated by works. True wisdom is characterized by meekness and humility. Acts of humble wisdom become visible in the way believers treat one another in the community. Whereas ch 2 emphasizes physical needs, the emphasis in ch 3 is on emotional needs that result in jealousy, divisions, and fights.

James ends his discussion of faith and works with faith. In 5:15, the prayer of faith brings physical and spiritual healing. He goes on to say that the petition of the righteous person (5:16) is strong and effective. The righteous

41

person is the one whose faith is lived out in righteous action. A righteous lifestyle demonstrates a strong faith. Prayer without faith is as worthless as faith
and wisdom without works (see 1:6-7).

Wisdom

James is often referred to as the NT book of wisdom. This is because
of its practical nature and emphasis on actions as a demonstration of who a
person really is. James 1:5 indicates that wisdom comes from God and if one
wants wisdom, all one has to do is ask for it.

Chapter 3 is James' central exposition on wisdom. Here he contrasts
earthly and heavenly wisdom. Heavenly wisdom (3:13) is demonstrated by
a lifestyle that promotes harmony and peace within the community. Earthly
wisdom (3:15) promotes jealousy, selfish rivalry, confusion, and every worthless or wicked practice. Wisdom from above (3:17) is first of all pure, peaceful,
patient, a team player, merciful, impartial, genuine, and produces good fruit.

Speech

Speech or controlling one's tongue is a significant issue in James. It is
closely related to wisdom, with its main exposition also in ch 3. James first
addresses this issue in 1:26-27 in his discussion of true religion. Those who
cannot control their tongues have a useless religion.

His discussion of speech in ch 3 is in the context of his discussion of
teachers. The vehicle of the teacher's activity is speech. And, therefore, the
teacher's words will be judged more harshly than others.

In 3:2-5, James notes how difficult the tongue is to control. Even though
it is so small, it has great impact—for good or for ill. Verses 6-8 identify the
fiery tongue as a world of evil in our bodies. Humans have tamed wild animals.
But they seem unable to tame their own tongues.

James notes the incongruity of the same mouth pronouncing both blessing and cursing (3:9-10). He implies that if we allow God really to control our
being, if we really have faith, then blessing and helpful speech will naturally
flow from our mouths (3:11-12). Only God is able to tame our tongues. Our
faith is demonstrated by what comes out of our mouths.

Prayer

James' view of prayer offers insight into his view of God. God wants
his children to be all they were created to be. So in 1:5-6, James encourages
his readers to ask God for wisdom and to believe wholeheartedly that God
is generous and able to give what is asked. Those who doubt that God can or
will give his children what they ask for will certainly receive nothing from the
Lord (1:7).

In 4:2-3, James explains why one might not receive what one needs from
God. First, one must come boldly to God, asking for what one needs. Second,

one must request only what will bring one closer to God and promote spiritual maturity and goodness in one's life. When one asks for things to waste on one's own pleasures, God will not answer that prayer.

Prayer is also a community activity (5:13-16). When members of the community suffer or are sick, they are to call the elders of the church to pray over them. James' readers are to confess their sins to one another and pray for one another.

James may have understood prayer as a time of communion and union with God. But his instructions on prayer are thoroughly practical in nature. When something is needed—whether physical, emotional, or spiritual—Christians are to pray and ask God for what they need.

James is not ashamed to petition God for anything. He encourages his readers to follow the example of Elijah, who was just like them. Elijah prayed for God to control the weather so that unbelievers would come to understand who God was. God answered his prayer.

Wholeness

Wholeness is an important concept in James' letter. He understands humans as unified beings. They may be made up of different parts, but their parts are so interrelated that each affects the other. For salvation to be complete in James' view, it must affect the whole person—it must bring wholeness to the personality.

In 2:10, James uses the term "whole" (*holon*) referring to the Law. For James the law of God is consistent and summed up in the royal law: "Love your neighbor as yourself."

In 3:2-3, James uses the term "whole" again, in his discussion of the necessity of controlling one's tongue. One who is able to do so is able to control or guide his or her whole body. Nevertheless, this is merely a hypothetical possibility. Unaided humans are unable to control their tongues. Only God has the power to do that.

In 5:13-20, James does not use the word "whole." But he nonetheless emphasizes that physical, emotional, mental, and spiritual wholeness are found only in communities that pray for one another, encourage one another, and constructively confront one another.

James paints a picture of a community in dynamic relationship with each other and with God. Sometimes one is suffering, sometimes cheerful, sometimes sick or weak, and sometimes wandering away. In all these situations, there is an appropriate community response that brings wholeness to the person and to the community.

Eschatology

In ch 5, James addresses end-times concerns. It is clearly not a dominant issue in his Epistle. His main focus is on living life here and now so that one is ready for the last days.

In vv 1-5 he warns the greedy rich that their hoarded wealth will become worthless and actually destroy them ("eat your flesh like fire," v 3). In contrast, he urges humble brothers and sisters (vv 7-9) to be patient as they wait for the appearing of the Lord. They are to be patient and to strengthen their hearts and their resolve to do right, *because the appearing* [*parousia*] *of the Lord is near.*

COMMENTARY

I. GREETING: JAMES 1:1

BEHIND THE TEXT

The author of James does not identify himself beyond his name and his relationship to **God and . . . the Lord Jesus Christ** (see Introduction). The use of **Christ** as if it were **Jesus'** surname and not a title reflects the influence of Hellenism (Davids 1982, 63).

The author refers to himself as a *doulos,* **a servant** or ***slave.*** Today, we think of servants as voluntarily serving others, versus slaves forced to serve masters/owners. In the first century, a *doulos* belonged to a lower social and economic group. This group "constituted the greatest number but possessed the fewest goods." They were "identified not by parentage, birthplace, or occupation, but by the one(s) in whose service [they] stood" (Brosend 2004, 32-35).

James' phrase **servant of God** has a dual background. It certainly reflects the sociological understanding of the identity of a *doulos*, one who stood in a relationship of service to another. But as a traditional Jewish Christian, James must also have seen himself among Israel's other servants of God. This title placed him in the company of Moses, the servant of God (Num 12:7); God's servants the prophets (Jer 7:25; 25:4); and Isaiah's servant of Yahweh (52:13—53:12). James' identification of himself as the **servant . . . of the Lord Jesus Christ** reflects the early Christian practice of identifying their leaders as standing in a special relationship to Christ (Rom 1:1; Phil 1:1; Titus 1:1).

James addressed his readers ambiguously as "the twelve tribes in the Dispersion" (NRSV). This seems to indicate an audience of Jewish background, perhaps Jewish Christians living in Syria, Rome, Greece, or Asia Minor. Many Diaspora Jews had lived outside Judea for centuries, some since the Babylonian exile. Jewish Christians of the Diaspora were familiar with the trials of Jewish resident aliens outside Palestine (see Introduction, "Audience").

Some Jewish families, like Paul's, may have earned or bought Roman citizenship. But most lived as noncitizens, subject to the whims of government authorities. Even when they were not specifically targeted for persecution, they suffered from a lack of status and influence within their communities. Their distinguishing dietary and ritual laws made them stand out as strange. Even Palestinian Jews were subject to the caprice of the Romans who occupied first-century Palestine (see Introduction, "Audience").

IN THE TEXT

■ **1** Verse 1 follows the customary pattern of the letter openings in the NT. These generally conform to the conventions of ancient Greco-Roman letter writing. Authors identified themselves by name and title, named their addressees, and closed with a salutation. Here James offers only his name. There is no personal or biographical data as in some of Paul's letters.

The English name **James** (*Iakōbos*) is from *Jacomus*, the Latin rendering of the OT name Jacob (Hebrew *yaqôb*). Thus, "a number of modern European languages now have two male names from the same linguistic root" (Blomberg and Kamell 2008, 47). If the writer of this letter was James the brother of the Lord (Matt 13:55; Mark 6:3), as ancient tradition assumed, the lack of mention of his special relationship with Jesus remains a mystery.

An explanation may be found in the self-description that follows. Instead of mentioning his family relationship to Jesus, James preferred to use a strong word (*doulos*, **slave**) describing his relationship with God and with the Lord Jesus Christ. Apparently, James' personal relationship with Jesus Christ as his Lord, and his submission to be his servant, is more important than his family connection. His Christian identity is defined by his servant-Lord relationship rather than his brother-brother relationship.

The term *doulos* identifies a slave bonded to another for life—a "bondservant" (NASB). James understands himself as a slave committed to the service of God and Jesus Christ. His life is completely dedicated to God.

James does not identify himself as either a leader or an apostle. In his letters, Paul used his apostolic designation when he needed to establish his authority. James' failure to identify himself as a leader may indicate that he was well known to his readers and his authority taken for granted.

James' self-identification as a servant/slave might be taken as an expression of humility. This is how John Wesley explained James' mentioning Jesus only twice in his letter: "It might have seemed, if he mentioned him [Jesus] often, that he did it out of vanity, as being the brother of the Lord" (Wesley 2003, 810).

But to be **a servant of God and of the Lord Jesus Christ** was no insignificant matter. This is the only passage in the NT in which this exact title appears. The closest parallel is Paul's self-designation as a "servant of God and an apostle of Jesus Christ" in Titus 1:1. In Jewish tradition, **a servant of God** is "a designation of privilege and honor" (Martin 1988, 4). The title was used to describe all of Israel's great leaders. James used it to distinguish himself from his readers "as a figure of authority" (Martin 1988, 4).

By combining *a slave* **of God and of the Lord Jesus Christ** as he does, James possibly equates Jesus with God. The grammar is not unambiguous, but perhaps James intended this distinction. At the very least James uses the fullest title of Jesus, calling him both Master and Messiah (**Lord** and **Christ;** Blomberg and Kamell 2008, 47).

The designation of James' addresses as **the twelve tribes scattered among the nations** is ambiguous. Literally, he calls them *the twelve tribes in the Diaspora.* We cannot be certain whether he intends a literal or metaphorical force for *Diaspora.* The Greek word order emphasizes the **twelve** tribes, not their Diaspora location. This suggests that they lived in these areas as aliens and sojourners.

Some scholars consider **the twelve tribes** a metaphor for "the Christian Church conceived of as the True Israel inheriting the rights of the ancient people of God" (Ropes 1973, 118). Others take it as a literal reference to the ethnicity and status of James' audience. Would James, the leader of the Jewish-Christian church, make a distinction between the two (see Bauckham 1999, 14-15; and Introduction, "Audience")?

James was written at a time (A.D. 40s) when the distinction between Jews and Christians was not clear, since most Christians were Jews (Brosend

2004, 31). Judaism in the early first century consisted of several varieties: Pharisees, Sadducees, Essenes, Zealots, and Christians.

According to Acts 11:26, the followers of Jesus were first called "Christians" in Syrian Antioch. This may have been intended to distinguish them from Jewish communities that did not accept Jesus as Israel's Messiah or welcome Gentile converts. This scattering (dispersion) of Jewish Christians from Judea, which led to the conversion of many in Antioch, occurred after Stephen's death about A.D. 35.

Some of the scattered Jewish Christians may have been born where they lived. But from a sociological perspective, their ethnic and religious background distinguished them from those who lived around them. Their different values and lifestyle did not meet the expectations of the cities they inhabited. They were open to ridicule, perhaps even physical and social abuse, for their beliefs and practices.

Verse 1 ends with a salutation of a single word: **Greetings.** This translates *chairein*, the infinitive of the verb *chairō*, meaning "rejoice" or "be glad." It is the standard greeting in most ancient letters. This is another reason for considering the book of James to be a letter. Since it has no standard letter closing, it is really a mixed genre (see Introduction, "Form and Genre").

This greeting was common in the first century. But it appears in no other canonical letter. It is found in two letters incorporated into Acts (see Acts 15:23; 23:26). The first of these reports the decision of the Jerusalem Council, where James presided. Perhaps this offers another reason for assuming this James was the author of the NT letter we call James.

Paul's letters commonly used a related Greek word, *charis* ("grace") combined with *eirēnē* ("peace": Rom 1:7; 1 Cor 1:3; 2 Cor 1:2; Gal 1:3; Eph 1:3; Phil 1:2; Col 1:2; 1 Thess 1:1; 2 Thess 1:2; Titus 1:4; Phlm 1:3; similarly 1 Tim 1:2; 2 Tim 1:2). This surprisingly reflects a more "Jewish-oriental . . . and Christian liturgical practice" than the standard Greco-Roman greeting in James (Davids 1982, 64).

"Why are these influences absent from a Jewish Christian letter" like James (Davids 1982, 64)? Did James lack the "creativity and mastery of Greek" of Paul? Or, did the later Hellenistic redactor of James "not think in Paul's more Aramaic terms" (Davids 1982, 64)? Or perhaps James simply adopted the convention of his time and saw no theological need to expand on this greeting as Paul did. James simply says, "Hello"! (Blomberg and Kamell 2008, 48).

II. INTRODUCTORY STATEMENTS ON THE CHRISTIAN LIFE: JAMES 1:2-27

This section introduces the letter and serves as an overview of what will occupy the balance of the letter. James' concern for proper understanding permeates his presentation of two sets of key themes (Johnson 1995, 175).

In vv 2-4 James addresses the need for perseverance in testing. This is crucial to becoming mature believers. This testing produces **joy** (*charan*, v 2), which verbally links it to the opening greeting (*chairein*).

James encourages his readers to ask for wisdom, which is a gift from God, in full confidence that God will do what he says (vv 5-8). In vv 9-11, James addresses the status of Christians, which should be one of humility whether they are rich or poor.

In v 12, James summarizes vv 2-11 before launching into the second set of topics he will address in the letter. He treats first the nature and source of temptation and particularly the temptation to become quickly angry (vv 13-18). James encourages his readers to listen and do what **the word** says (vv 22-25). Finally he describes what he understands pure **religion** to be (vv 26-27).

A. Key Themes: Perseverance, Wisdom, and Status (1:2-11)

1. Perseverance (1:2-4)

IN THE TEXT

■ **2** After the opening greeting, James abruptly changes the subject. This suggests to some scholars that James is not a real letter but "a sermon, diatribe, epitome—anything but a letter" (Brosend 2004, 34). This is based on the assumption that Paul's letters are the standard for all NT letters.

But James is a General Epistle. That is, it was written to several communities and not to one specific community as most of Paul's letters were. Bauckham calls James an "encyclical." "James makes no factual statements about his addressees at all. Everything is hypothetical" (1999, 26-27). His first readers probably understood the missive as general instructions and encouragement from their leader in Jerusalem.

James' first command after **Greetings** (*chairein*) employs a similar sounding word, *charan* (**joy**), or "**the experience of gladness**" (BDAG, 1077). The command to accept trials joyfully is an ingressive aorist imperative: *Begin to consider being joyful whenever you encounter various kinds of trials* (Wallace 1996, 719-20).

Whenever introduces a striking triple alliteration: *peirasmois, peripēsate, poikilois.* This stresses that "*every kind* of testing is to be regarded in terms of joy" (Johnson 1995, 277). The Greek verb *peripēsate* (**encounter**) emphasizes an unanticipated mishap (see Luke 10:30). James assumes his readers will **face** unexpected **trials.**

The word translated **trials** (*peirasmois*) can also be translated "*temptation, enticement to sin*" (BDAG, 793). The ancient church fathers took it to be "temptation." "To them the cure for temptation was patient endurance, which was the fruit of a spiritual wisdom that could be obtained only from God" (Bray 2000, 4).

But in the present context James intends a broader meaning of trials than temptation conveys. In v 3, *dokimion* (**testing**) refers to the "*means of testing*" (BDAG, 256) one's faith. Difficult experiences develop endurance and eventually maturity of faith and character (v 4).

During the first four centuries, *dokimion* described the process of smelting metallic ore. Extreme heat was employed to extract the impurities and produce pure metal. But James' only other use of this Greek root in 1:12-14 clearly means "temptation."

James' command to choose to be joyful when facing problems emphasizes that it is not natural or easy to look at their positive side. Nevertheless,

"Joy is the proper perspective for the test of faith" (Davids 1982, 67). Similar themes are found in Jesus' Sermon on the Mount (Matt 5:11-12; Luke 6:22-23; see also Rom 5:2b-5; 1 Pet 1:6-7). James' command likely echoes Jesus' words later recorded in Matthew and Luke. Writing at a time when no written Gospels existed, he often alludes to the oral tradition of Jesus' sayings without mentioning his name.

The Gospels indicate that James was not a follower of Jesus during his earthly ministry (see Mark 3:21; John 7:1-5; 19:25-27). Nonetheless, as an early Christian he had access to the oral and perhaps even pre-Gospel written traditions of Jesus' sayings. Despite James' earlier unbelief, Paul reports that Jesus graciously favored James with a postresurrection appearance, like that of the apostles and other faithful followers (1 Cor 15:6-7).

The pre-Gospel sources, perhaps "the apostles' teaching" (Acts 2:42), were a featured part of the daily and weekly gatherings of the earliest Christians in Jerusalem. Much like Paul, James learned the teachings of Jesus from eyewitnesses and may even have heard Jesus on occasion (Mark 3:21).

My brothers, a masculine plural in Greek (as the explicit use of "sister" in 2:15 indicates), should not be understood to exclude women. The masculine plural was often used generically to refer to a group of mixed gender. An acceptable translation is "My brothers and sisters" (NRSV).

The nominative plural used as a vocative of direct address—**my brothers**—indicates the beginning of a new topic or emphasis in Jas 2:1; 3:1; 4:11; and 5:7. This is one of several markers indicating the beginning of each of the twelve sections in chs 2—5. Dealing with trials is the first of the topics James discusses.

■ **3** Here James explains the reason why (*hoti*, **because**) his readers should begin to find joy in their problems: **because you know that the testing of your faith develops perseverance.** The testing process (*dokimion*, v 2) enables the community to endure as growing Christians. The pronoun **your** is plural, emphasizing the shared faith of the entire community (Johnson 1995, 177). Verse 3 "implies that there is something genuine that will survive the refining process" (Davids 1982, 68).

Perseverance refers to the enduring faithfulness of the readers. Because God is with them they realize they can endure any trial or problem; they can face the future with joy and confidence. **Perseverance** is "that permanent and underlying active trait of the soul from which endurance springs—'constancy' or 'steadfastness,' thought of as a virtue" (Ropes 1973, 136). For James, his readers' **faith** (*pistōs*) is like pure metal extracted and proven by **testing.**

The verb **develops** (*katergazetai*) is used only here in James. But the cognate *ergazesthai* occurs in 1:20 ("bring about") and 2:9 ("commit," NRSV). Both verbs are derived from the same noun root, *ergon* (**work** in v 4; developed in 2:14-26).

■ 4 To develop endurance one must be challenged—"let endurance have its full effect" (NRSV). **Perseverance** describes believers who face trials and remain faithful. By persisting in their faith over time, James' readers would become **mature and complete** in their faith. Literally, James writes: *Endurance must have a mature work in order that you may be mature and complete so that you lack nothing.*

The adjective **mature** or **perfect** (*teleioi*) is significant for James. He speaks of a "perfect gift" (1:17), the "perfect law" (1:25), and a "perfect man" (3:2). Applied to persons it means **mature**. James is innocent of Platonic notions of perfection as absolute flawlessness. *Teleioi* for him has the sense it does in the LXX, describing persons and things that fulfill their reason for existence (vv 3-4). As a result of being **mature and complete**, the community will not lack anything, morally or spiritually, they need to face the uncertain future with God.

Complete (*holoklēros*) is a synonym of **perfect**. It emphasizes soundness, health, and wholeness. This adjective appears only here and in 1 Thess 5:23 within Paul's prayer for the entire sanctification of his readers. There the emphasis is on the preservation of the whole (*holoklēron*) person—"spirit, soul and body"—blameless before God. Maturity does not just develop over time. Only divine cultivation effects the kind of physical, spiritual, and mental wholeness James expects. He is concerned about the entire character of the Christian. Maturity is more important than the test (Davids 1982, 69).

FROM THE TEXT

This passage encourages readers to learn from their trials. Everyone has problems. But when Christians face them from God's perspective, they can endure trials with joy. Wesley emphasizes that joy is the "highest degree of patience" (2003, 810).

Trials are an inescapable reality. "Faith does . . . provide one with the proper response to these realities: endurance. Endurance is a character trait important to James." It "is an outgrowth of faith, and itself yields maturity and completion, *telos* (perfection)" (Brosend 2004, 38). According to James, perfection is the goal and perseverance is only the way to get there.

James uses the adjective **perfect** more than any other NT writer (Davids 1982, 69). Here James depends on the Jewish apocalyptic tradition also found in the Qumran literature. This perfection is "a full-blown character of stable righteousness" and "is the virtue of the righteous man" (Davids 1982, 70).

Deasley explains that Jewish apocalyptic perfection "consisted of a fusion of the ritual and the moral, the legal and the spiritual, the outward and the inward, so intimate that neither was complete without the other" (Deasley 1972, 330-34; cited by Davids 1982, 70).

For James, perfection is not just concerned with outward actions, but with the inward condition of the person. Overemphasis on the observable actions alone leads to a legalism, in which one's spirituality is judged solely by what one does. Equally, an overemphasis on invisible, inward conditions can lead to self-absorption and a failure to appreciate that actions exhibit who one is.

2. Ask God for Wisdom (1:5-8)

BEHIND THE TEXT

Wisdom is an important genre in ancient Jewish literature. Many interpreters have identified James as a Jewish-Christian version of Proverbs (see Introduction, "Form and Genre"). At the beginning of his address to Jewish Christians living in a foreign environment, James urges them, should they lack wisdom, to ask God for it. Life in a complicated pagan world, which does not acknowledge the values and laws of God, calls for extraordinary judgment.

Proverbs 9:10 identifies the close relationship between reverence for God and wisdom: "The fear of the LORD is the beginning of wisdom, and knowledge of the Holy One is understanding." Solomon, to whom many of the proverbs are attributed, asked God for wisdom at the very beginning of his long and prosperous reign (1 Kgs 3:3-9). As long as he remained faithful to God, he was able to rule wisely. But when he became old, his foreign wives turned his heart after other gods (1 Kgs 11). Even for Solomon, wisdom was related to his relationship with God.

James' insistence that God gives generously to all is reminiscent of Jesus' teachings in the Sermon on the Mount (Moo 2000, 58). In Matt 7:7a Jesus says, "Ask and it will be given to you . . ." Jesus is not specifically speaking of wisdom, but about prayer in general. Nevertheless, James continues his quiet allusions to the Sermon on the Mount begun in v 2.

IN THE TEXT

■5 The verse beginning *But if anyone of you lacks* indicates a shift in topic. It continues the concern of v 4 that Christians should not be "lacking [*leipomenoi*] anything," repeating the same verb for **lacks** (*leipeitai*). James' focus moves from the testing and trials that develop endurance and maturity to the topic of **wisdom.** Wisdom was necessary, because without it Christians enduring trials could never reach maturity and wholeness.

James urges his readers honestly to assess their inward resources: **If any of you lacks wisdom.** He completes this conditional statement with a command: *Let that one continue to ask* for wisdom *from God.* This prayer is not to be a one-time request, but a daily petition.

Wisdom from God is needed for sound, everyday choices as much as for obviously monumental, life-changing decisions. Both are essential for achieving Christian maturity and wholeness—to become "perfect and complete" (v 4 NASB). Wisdom is indispensable for all who cannot be content merely to believe, but must decide how to live out their beliefs.

James explains that **God** is generous with the gift of **wisdom.** He **gives generously to all** whether or not deserving. God is the source of wisdom. It is not something humans can achieve for themselves.

The adverb translated **generously** (*haplōs*) means "*simply, . . . sincerely, openly*" (BDAG, 104). It occurs only here in the NT. The translation *who gives sincerely to all* is also possible. That James follows this appeal by insisting that his readers must "ask in faith, never doubting" (v 6 NRSV) suggests *sincerely* as a viable option. But the verb **gives** favors **generously** as the better translation. In Rom 12:8; 2 Cor 8:2; 9:11 and 13 the cognate abstract noun *haplotēs* means "generosity" or "liberality" (NASB).

James adds that God *does not find fault* (*oneidizontos*, **reproach** or **mock**) with those who pray for wisdom. His readers could ask without shame, assured that God would never disapprove such a request. In fact, James is certain **it will be given** to the one who asks (see Matt 7:7).

Contrary to many human advisers, God does not spend time finding fault with our lack of wisdom. Instead, he gives wisdom beyond what we ask! Christians can confidently ask God for wisdom, knowing he will give it. Davids conflates **generously** (*haplōs*) and "the parallel term" **without finding fault** (*mē oneidizontos*) to arrive at a paraphrasing translation: God gives "without hesitation or mental reservation" (1982, 73).

■**6** When we ask for wisdom to persevere in trials, we must truly want it and believe God will give it. Using the language of command, James pleads, *But let the one* who lacks wisdom *continually ask in faith, doubting nothing.* This exhortation reflects the language of Jesus in Matt 21:21 and Mark 11:23 (see Rom 4:20).

James is not explicit about what one should **not doubt.** Is it whether one wants the wisdom or direction God will give? Or, whether God is able to give that wisdom? Perhaps it is both. When one asks for such wisdom, one must be committed to acting upon it. Those who pray for wisdom must believe God will guide them to live a mature and wholesome Christian life. And they must follow God's guidance.

The word picture that follows is of a wave on the open sea in the middle of a storm: *For the one who doubts is like a wave of the sea, which is driven and blown here and there by the wind.* This wave has no direction of its own. It is completely at the mercy of the prevailing winds. This imagery is "easily analogous to situations of indecision or rapidly changing opinions" (Brosend 2004, 37).

■**7** James continues to issue commands: *For do not let that person expect he will receive anything from the Lord* (see Matt 7:8). The grammatical construction *ho anthrōpos ekeinos,* **that man,** is Semitic and indicates James' disapproval (Davids 1982, 74). Here it refers to **the one who doubts** in v 6. The word *anthrōpos* is a generic term for a human being (not *anēr,* **a male,** as in v 8). Thus, the admonition applies to both men and women.

Here **the Lord** refers to "God" (v 5), not to "the Lord Jesus Christ" as in v 1. James says that if indecisive, uncommitted people expect to receive wisdom from God, they are sadly mistaken. Response from God requires commitment to or faith in God. This is foundational to understanding James' convictions, especially about the inseparable connection between faith and works (2:14-26).

■**8** James refers to a specific example of human indecision, referring to **a double-minded man, unstable in all he does. Double-minded** is literally *two-souled* (*dipsychos*). James may have coined this word, which is not found in Greek literature before his time.

The concept of a divided person, however, existed as early as the fifth century B.C. in Plato's "twofold man" (*diplous anēr*). It was also found in Jewish Wisdom literature before James. The sage in Sir 1:28 urged his readers not to approach God "with a divided mind" (NRSV; *en kardia* [*heart*] *dissē*). Similarly *T. Ash.* 2:5 speaks of two-faced (*diprosōpos*) persons as wholly evil. The term appears often after James' time, especially in Christian literature dependent on James (see Johnson 1995, 181).

The **double-minded man** is *unsettled* or *unsteady* (see on 3:8, 16) *in all his ways.* Such persons try to manage two competing wills. They are restless because they have not fully and finally chosen whom they will serve or what they want out of life.

The necessary wisdom from God is dependent on a settled faith in God. Significantly, James opens his letter with a prayer for this wisdom (vv 5-8). And he closes it with a prayer for healing (5:14-18). This is only appropriate, "since prayer is the activity that most fundamentally defines and expresses that construal of reality called 'faith'" (Johnson 1995, 184).

FROM THE TEXT

Often this passage is taken out of its wisdom context and misapplied to all kinds of things we want. Here the assurance of the certainty of answered prayer is not so generalized. James refers only to prayers for godly wisdom. And he adds the disclaimer that even godly wisdom can be given only to those who have committed their lives to God. Those who prefer to stay on the fringes of faith and refuse to make a wholehearted decision to follow God should expect nothing from God.

In his *Concerning the Epistle of St. James*, the Venerable Bede (ca. 672–735) wrote:

> A man is double-minded when he wants to have fun in this world but also reign with God in heaven. Likewise, a man is double-minded when he seeks the approval of others for his good deeds rather than spiritual rewards from God. (Bray 2000, 9)

This English Benedictine monk's quotation may sound strange to our ears. But it reflects the understanding and time of Bede. By having "fun in this world" Bede refers to "doing one's own thing," in rebellion against God. Today, we might distinguish fun that doesn't last (worldly fun) and the fun that does (godly fun)! Scripture does not call Christians to lives of drudgery and boredom. The Christian walk with God is full of joy, peace, and excitement.

Bede importantly calls attention to another example of two-souled persons. He considered those who sought status, even within the Christian community, rather than the approval of God, to be double-minded. The Christian's single focus must be on pleasing God. Even committed Christians can be tempted by position that increases their wealth or status, even within the hierarchy of the institutional church. That person is two-souled.

Wesleyans often properly refer to holiness as "wholeness." Total devotion to God brings singleness of desire and wholeness to our personality. This is the context in which godly wisdom can be understood and appropriated. Holy people may not all be straight-A students or hold advanced degrees. The wisdom James talks about is "practical, not theoretical" (Johnson 1995, 179).

The ancient church fathers understood doubt and riches to be "the greatest enemies of true faith because in their different ways, they both contributed to human pride and arrogance" (Bray 2000, 4). Doubt contributes to the undermining of faith when we assume we know better than God. Riches contribute when we are deceived into thinking we have sufficient resources within ourselves to accomplish something.

What Does It Mean to Doubt?

What, in practical terms, does it mean to ask "in doubt"? Is it to doubt that God can give, or to doubt that one wishes to receive? Big difference. Because the focus in the passage has been on the human side of things, so likely is the answer. Indeed, there is little in the ideological or sacred textures of the letter to suggest that God's capacity is ever called into question. That is a contemporary issue, not an ancient one. The image James has in mind here is one who is not sure he or she wishes to be in a mature and complete relationship with God. The "doubt" is whether one truly wants to ask and so receive, not doubt over God's capacity to give. (Brosend 2004, 39)

3. Christian Status (1:9-11)

BEHIND THE TEXT

The social context of this statement is one in which the poor have little power and are easily taken advantage of by the rich. Many of James' Jewish Diaspora readers were probably poor immigrants and foreigners.

Theologically, however, Jewish tradition considered the poor more devout than the rich due to the situation in the second century B.C. Some of the rich Jews had compromised their Jewish lifestyle in deference to their Greek conquerors. And the poor had started the Maccabean revolt to defeat their oppressors (see 1—2 Maccabees). By the first century A.D., "poor" meant more than the impoverished; it connoted those loyal to God.

The metaphor that dominates this passage arose naturally from the geographical setting of the book. James and his readers were all too familiar with scorching heat. Much of Palestine is desert and the high plains of Asia Minor are dry and the sun is strong—even in the winter—because of the altitude.

IN THE TEXT

The theme of the poor and the rich in the community of James appears for the first time in the letter in the present section (see 2:2-4, 5-12, 15-16; 4:13-17; 5:1-6). Interpretation is complicated by uncertainty as to whether James referred to rich Christians or outsiders (see Martin 1988, 22-24; Johnson 1995, 185, 189-91). It is also debated whether v 12 concludes vv 9-11, introduces vv 13-15, or is a separate aphorism (so Dibelius 1975, 70-71, 88).

■ **9** The series of third person commands that began in v 2 continues here. But the topic changes from the double-minded to the humble vs. the rich. The passage begins with the command: ***Humble*** [*tapeinos*] ***brothers and sisters must keep rejoicing*** [*kauchasthō*] ***in their high position.*** "In the biblical tradition, the *tapeinos* are the special recipients of God's saving activity (see LXX Pss 9:39; 17:28; 33:19; 81:3; 101:18; Isa 11:4; 14:32" (Johnson 1995, 185).

The Greek verb *kauchaomai* can have either negative or positive connotations. The difference depends on what or whom one boasts in. It is translated "boasting" when the connotation is negative and "rejoice in" or "take pride in" when it is positive. With the exception of Heb 3:6 and James 1:9; 3:14; and 4:16, the term is otherwise used exclusively by Paul in the NT.

James, in good Jewish tradition, believes the humble are in a better position to understand what it means to serve God than the wealthy. Since vv 9 and 10 are a single sentence in Greek, the designation *adelphos*, **brother** or **sister,** seems to indicate that both the **humble** and the **rich** are part of the Christian community.

James appeals to the apocalyptic tradition of judgment as a "reversal of status" (Davids 1982, 75; Brosend 2004, 40). This is promise for the poor and threat for the rich. If this is the point of vv 9 and 10, it is not new. It continues the tradition that celebrated the loyalty to God of the poor during the Maccabean revolt, while the rich sold out to the Syrians. The rich were like the "two-souled" persons (v 7), whose efforts to preserve their status and power led them to compromise.

■ **10** The verb **take pride** is not explicit in Greek. The NIV fills in the ellipsed verb from the first half of the sentence in v 9. Just as the lowly boast in their high position in Christ, so the rich should boast in their lowly state. Interpreters disagree whether the rich are Christians as are the poor **brothers** in v 9 (Adamson 1976, 61-62).

Rich brothers must boast in their humiliation (*tapeinōsei*). The Greek term for **humiliation** or **low position** is not the usual antonym of "high position" (*hypsei*) found in v 9. We might expect *agenēs* ("lowly things") as used in 1 Cor 1:28. But *tapeinōsei* is from the same root as the word describing the humble (*tapeinos*) brother in v 9.

The rich tend to imagine they will live forever, while the poor are inescapably aware of the fragility of their lives. James' figure of speech reminds both that everyone dies: **he will pass away like a wild flower.** This **flower** (*anthos*) refers to the insignificant blossoms that appear on hay or grass. It is the first part of the plant to wilt and die from the summer's scorching heat (see v 11).

Some scholars doubt that James considered the rich (*plousios*) to be Christians, since they **will pass away** (Davids 1982, 77). In the first-century context, the rich were widely identified with greed and apostasy. Other scholars consider both lowly and rich Christians. That the lowly are exalted and the rich fade away should be understood in terms of apocalyptic eschatology (Brosend 2004, 41). One's status as rich or poor is not ultimately significant.

■ **11** James' use of aorist tense verbs (***rose, withered, fell, was destroyed***) seems unexpected in English. But these appear to be gnomic aorists, indicating that the author quotes a familiar proverb. English convention calls for a present tense translation of proverbial sayings, which are normally in the past tense in Greek.

The proverb begins, **For the sun rises with scorching heat** (*kausōni*). This rare Greek word occurs only twice in the NT (here and in Luke 12:55). Seven of the ten times it appears in the LXX, it refers to the hot desert winds. In Palestine, sirocco winds blow night and day for three to four days at a time during the spring and fall (Davids 1982, 78).

The proverb describes the results of the burning sun and the dry hot wind: ***it dries up the grass and its flower falls off and the beauty of its appearance is lost.*** This phenomenon is seen dramatically in Palestine where "the sun rises and the anemone and cyclamen droop and wither" (Davids 1982, 77).

James applies the proverb to the lives of the rich. In this way the proverb is no longer merely a wisdom observation. It becomes a prophetic prediction of what is going to be (Johnson 1995, 186). Thus, it will also be with the **rich; their *way of life will wither away.*** The word translated ***way of life*** (*poreiais*) refers to one's life "***journey***" or "***conduct***" (BDAG, 853). This echoes the language of the Psalms (68:24), Proverbs (2:7; 4:27), Prophets (Isa 8:11; Hab 3:6), and intertestamental wisdom (Sir 1:5; see Adamson 1976, 65).

The rich may seem to have enough assets to insure their long and lasting influence. But their "beautiful" assets are temporary and have no eternal value (see 4:13-16). The rich and their comfortable way of life will finally **fade away** or "***disappear***" (BDAG, 616 s.v. *marainō*). This Greek verb describes both the withering of plants and the dying of humans. James' reference to scorching heat may also allude to the fiery torments awaiting the rich at the *parousia* (see 5:1-6; Dibelius 1975, 87).

The proverb and the comparison with the rich include two Semitisms (Hebrew expressions): **the beauty of its appearance** (*hē euprepeia tou prosō-pou*) and **his way of life** (*en tais poreiais autou,* **in his journeys**). These may indicate that the proverb was originally learned in Aramaic or Hebrew and translated overly literally into Greek.

FROM THE TEXT

Verse 9 is one of the few times the Bible encourages boasting. It is significant because it is rare. Pride is included in the traditional list of the seven deadly sins. So Christians are aware of the need to be humble. But there needs to be a balance. Those with excessively low self-esteem need to recognize that they are gifted and valuable children of God.

Humility is not pretending to be less than we are. To denigrate one's gifts and hide them away behind false humility is as damaging to the Christian community as pretending to be more than we are in false and foolish pride. The boasting James encourages here is in what God has done in and through us, not in what we have done in our own strength.

Those with earthly power and abundance tend to rely on their own abilities, rather than on God. They must understand that what they build in their own strength will fade away and disappear. Only that built by Christ will stand (1 Cor 3:10-15). The rich and successful need "to examine their lives in view of the reality of their eventual deaths and to explore the choices they make each day not as meaningless but as filled with life and death significance" (Brosend 2004, 44).

Christians should

overlook the present circumstances in which it is the rich who boast (as in 4:16 and Ps 49[48]:7) and see life from an eschatological perspective. In this perspective the one who really has the exalted position and who is really rich is the Christian, the poor person. (Davids 1982, 76)

This was a message of comfort to most of James' first hearers. But how are the vast majority of affluent Western Christians to respond to this message? There is a timely warning for all who may depend on their resources and talents rather than on God.

Commentators remain conflicted on whether or not the rich in this chapter are Christians. If the rich here are believers, James urges them to take pride, not in their wealth or accomplishments, but in their "identification with Christ and his people, a matter of 'humiliation' in the eyes of the world" (Moo 2000, 66).

James is stating "*basic principles* concerning the human condition before God" (Johnson 1995, 191). In James' situation, it was probably hard to imagine that a rich person could be a Christian. This echoes Jesus' statement that "it is easier for a camel to go through the eye of a needle than for a rich man to enter the kingdom of God" (Matt 19:24; Mark 10:25; Luke 18:25).

Rich Western Christians find it easy to look down with sympathy on the poor, who make up two-thirds of the modern world and are becoming an increasing majority in the church. The poor are not unworthy or insignificant or to be pitied. The wealthy should look up to them from their lowly position in God's eyes. The poor should take pride in their lofty status in God's eyes. The church must help the poor realize that God has gifted them and made them a part of his church. "Christians must always evaluate themselves by spiritual and not material standards" (Moo 2000, 69).

Women and Christian Status

Women throughout the world have been prone to the temptation to denigrate themselves and should perhaps take special note of James's words. It is easy to see that boasting about human status comes from one's pride, but it is often assumed that excessive humility is a sign of spirituality and comes from God. This is quite wrong. To underestimate the significance of life and status in Christ, to assume that although we have that life and status we are still insignificant nobodies, is as likely to lead to spiritual death as the assumption that human status does have spiritual significance. (Kroeger and Evans 2002, 775)

B. Key Themes: Temptation, Anger, Listening and Doing, and Pure Religion (1:12-27)

1. God Does Not Tempt Us (1:12-18)

BEHIND THE TEXT

Verse 12 uses the metaphor of a **crown** (*stephanos*). Usually made of laurel wreaths, these were as familiar to first-century audiences at athletic competitions as trophies, medals, and championship rings are to today's. This **crown** identified the athlete as the winner of the competition. James, like Paul (1 Cor 9:24-27; Phil 3:12-14; 2 Tim 2:5; 4:8), compares the Christian life to a competition in which everyone who perseveres will win the prize.

Most first-century Jews believed that God would bless those righteous people who fulfilled the Law in visible and tangible ways. God would curse evil people, perhaps with poverty, childlessness, or sickness. It was popularly believed God was responsible for everything that happened to people, even their temptations. James challenges this belief and presents God as the one who gives good gifts.

Jewish tradition had two orthodox ways to deal with this problem. One was to blame the devil as the source of temptation. Another was the "Jewish teaching on the evil impulse in man which allows him to keep the responsibility squarely on the individual" (Davids 1982, 79). James seems to prefer the latter explanation.

IN THE TEXT

■ **12** James opens the second section of the letter with a restatement of his thesis. His list of new topics begins with a phrase common in the Jewish wisdom tradition: ***Blessed is the man who*** (*makarios anēr hos*) . . . (see Pss 1:1; 32:2; 34:8; 40:4; 65:4; 84:5, 12; 94:12; 112:1; Prov 8:34; Isa 56:2; Jer 17:7). It is characteristic of "stock language" used in apocalyptic Judaism and Christianity (e.g., Rom 4:8; Davids 1982, 79). The beatitudes in Matt 5 similarly use ***blessed*** (*makarioi*—the plural, rather than the singular; compare Rev 1:3).

James uses the word for a male person (*anēr*), rather than the generic word for persons (*anthrōpos*). Why? His macarism would seem to be applicable to both genders. Did he have a specific person in mind? Did this "stock language" use *anēr* with the same meaning as *anthrōpos*?

The man is blessed ***who perseveres in temptation, because after he has proven faithful, he will receive for himself the*** **crown** [*stephanon*] ***of life, promised those who love God.*** Successfully enduring temptation validates his true character. Those who prove genuine will ***receive the wreath of life***

61

promised those who love God. James restates v 2, repeating the same words for **temptation** (*peirasmon*) and **approved** (*dokimos*) used there (Blomberg and Kamell 2008, 26).

James contrasts the faithful survivor of temptation with the **two-souled** person in v 7, who will not receive anything from God. Enduring temptation/ testing shows that his faith is wholly in God. He is not double-minded!

■ **13** Another third person command follows immediately: *Let no one being tempted say, "I am being tempted by God." For God is not tempted by evil and he tempts no one!*

The word for temptation in vv 12-14 is from the verb *peirazō*, which means "**put to the test**" or "**tempt**" (BDAG, 792-93; see v 2).

> "Testing" could work for both instances in 13*a*, but v 14 so emphasizes the psychological dimension of temptation—its being rooted in human desire—that the reading of *peirazomenos* as "being tempted" virtually is demanded. (Johnson 1995, 192)

Does James' meaning shift subtly from vv 2 and 12 to vv 13 and 14? Or, does v 14 simply eliminate the earlier ambiguity? A consistent English translation throughout helps readers catch the connections and play on words.

God is **not tempted by evil** [*kakōn*] ("*bad, evil . . . wrong*"; BDAG, 501). Literally, he is **without temptation** (*apeirastos*; only here in NT). The emphatic addition of the superfluous *autos* (**himself**) in the last part of the verse emphasizes that **God** tempts no one. He has nothing to do with evil.

■ **14** How then does temptation occur? James answers: *But each person is tempted by his or her own desire and is dragged away by being enticed.* All are tempted by their own desire (*epithymias*), which lures and traps them into doing wrong.

Desire is not necessarily evil. The Greek does not add the specific adjective **evil**. *Epithymia* is qualified as good or bad by its object, whether good or bad. It is appropriate to translate *epithymias* here as **evil desire**, since it drags and entices us away from God (Johnson 1995, 193). This negative connotation of desire as a "*craving*" or "*lust*" for what is forbidden or inordinate is common in the NT (BDAG, 372; see Rom 7:7-8; Gal 5:16; 2 Pet 1:4).

The participle **being dragged away** (*exelkomenos*) can refer to being physically dragged off. Here, it refers metaphorically to being morally seduced (Latin: *seducere*, "to lead away"). The Greek verb **being enticed** (*deleazomenos*) continues the imagery. It has the literal sense of luring with bait. Here it refers to seducing someone to choose the wrong (Johnson 1995, 193).

■ **15** Then (*eita*), as a transitional adverb, closely joins vv 14-15. The consequence of being caught in temptation's trap (v 14) is the birth of **sin** (*hamartia*). James shifts metaphors as he continues, *Then the desire, after it has* *conceived, gives birth [tiktei] to sin. And sin, after it has been brought to full term, gives birth [akokyei] to death.*

Sin (*hamartia*) appears here in James for the first time (see 2:9; 4:17; 5:15, 16, 20). It means any departure from "either human or divine standards of uprightness" (BDAG, 50). In the NT, *hamartia* may refer to specific sinful acts, to the state of being sinful (Rom 8:21, 24), and to Sin personified as a destructive evil power (Rom 5:12, 21; BDAG, 51).

The verbs used metaphorically in this verse normally describe human conception and birth. The imagery is sexual—conception by the woman, followed by two nearly synonymous verbs describing a woman giving birth. Within this figurative context, the participle **having been fully formed** (*apotelestheisa*) means "brought to term" (Johnson 1995, 194). James personifies **desire** (*epithymia*, a feminine noun) as a seductress, who entices her unsuspecting prey and "conceives a bastard child by him" (Davids 1982, 84).

Tragic imagery brings the verse to an end. Ironically, **sin gives birth to** [*apokyei*] **death**! John Wesley notes that desire itself is not sin. But acting on that desire is sin (2003, 812). And sin, when it has had its way, brings the inevitable consequence of spiritual death.

■ **16** The generic *adelphoi* addresses James' first hearers as his **beloved brothers and sisters.** He loves (*agapētoi*) these fellow Christians dearly. Thus, he commands them, **Do not be deceived** (wander away in 5:19). This verse serves as a transition to the quotation in v 17 (Davids 1982, 86). Paul's similar command in 1 Cor 15:33 also introduces a quotation.

James' Christian friends need to understand that sin comes from their own desires, and not from God. Given the contemporary options, James' silence suggests that he is equally unwilling to blame the devil for human disobedience. (See the comments on v 12.)

Sin is not something forced on people. To avoid sin, they need to understand its development. In the absence of desire, sinful or not, there can be no temptation. But James does not recommend the Stoic or Buddhist pursuit of life without desire. Christians, instead, must learn to seek the strength God gives to create boundaries that will keep them out of situations in which desires can give birth to sin.

■ **17** Some commentators think the original form of this quotation was a pagan proverb. It may have been: "'every gift is good and every present perfect' (roughly equivalent to 'don't look a gift horse in the mouth')" (Davids 1982, 86). Davids speculates that James altered the secular proverb grammatically by adding **is from above,** in keeping with much Jewish and Hellenistic thought (Davids 1982, 86). But without a clear source, this assumption is "both moot and unhelpful" (Johnson 1995, 195).

Every good gift [*dosis agathē*] *and each perfect present* (*dōrēma teleion*) are examples of synonymous parallelism, referring to the same thing. These gifts *come down from the Father of the lights.*

The *Father* (1:27; 3:9) *of the lights* refers to God as the Creator of the sun, moon, and stars (Gen 1:3, 14-17). Jews recognized the Creator God as the source of life and all good things. God is ultimately responsible for everything good and perfect in our lives.

The terms in the phrase *no change or shadow of turning* are NT *hapax legomena* (occurring only once). Thus, it is not surprising that there are several scribal variations in the surviving manuscripts of James (see Davids 1982, 87; Johnson 1995, 196-97). The author's basic meaning, however, is clear enough. The phrase **shadow of turning** ("shadow due to change," NRSV; "shifting shadow," NASB) emphasizes that there is no change in the character of God.

This is not an affirmation of divine inflexibility. Only because God changes his mind may sinners repent and be forgiven (see Gen 6:6; Exod 32:12, 14; Deut 32:36; Judg 2:18; 1 Sam 15:11, 35; 2 Sam 24:16; 1 Chr 21:15; Pss 90:13; 106:45; 110:4; Jer 18:8, 10; 26:13, 19; 42:10; Hos 11:8; Joel 2:13-14; Amos 7:3, 6; Jonah 3:9, 10; 4:2). James' point is that God is not fickle, but infinitely dependable. There is not even a shadow or hint of inconstancy in God's character.

■ **18** This verse is the opposite parallel to v 15. The Father, *after he willed it, gave birth to us by the word of truth, so that we might be a kind of first fruits of his creatures.* The opening aorist participle, *having willed it* (*boulētheis*), is emphatically placed at the beginning of the Greek sentence. God *wills to act graciously in behalf of his people!* The various translations are instructive: **He chose,** "In the exercise of His will" (NASB), and even "In fulfillment of his own purpose" (NRSV). God does not act willy-nilly, but deliberately and graciously.

In his talk about God, James transcends the human categories of gender: The reference to God as "the Father of lights" in James 1:17 is paralleled by the reference to mothering, giving birth in James 1:18, and it is hard to see this parallel as anything other than deliberate. (Kroeger and Evans 2002, 777)

James uses *apokyeō* ("*give birth to*," BDAG, 114; see v 15) instead of the more general verb *gennaō* ("*beget*," "*become the father of*"; figuratively, "*bring forth, produce, cause*" (BDAG, 194) or the narrowly "feminine" word for giving birth (*tiktō*) used in v 15.

James' description of the Father giving birth (*apekyēsen*) to his children represents "one of the most striking female images for God in the NT" (Johnson 1995, 197). He **gives us birth** *by means of* **the word of truth.** In the OT Wisdom literature, Wisdom is often personified as a woman. In Prov 8, Wisdom was with God before the creation of the earth. Both the Hebrew and

Greek (LXX) words for Wisdom are feminine nouns (*hokmâ* and *sophia*). If James is a wisdom book or influenced by the OT wisdom tradition, **truth** may function as his equivalent for Lady Wisdom. If so, James may imply that **desire** is a seductress, the mother of Sin and sinners. But Lady Wisdom (= **truth**) is the legitimate mother of faithful believers.

That **word** is in the dative case indicates that human beings were generated *by means of* **the word of truth** (*logōi alōtheias*; see Ps 119:43; 2 Cor 6:7; Eph 1:13; Col 1:5). God spoke and it happened echoes the first chapter of Genesis. It also associates the Gospel of John with the wisdom tradition reflected in James. It is through the Word that all things were made (John 1:3). In James, however, the phrase refers not to the preincarnate Christ but specifically to the gospel as **the word of truth** (see Jas 1:21-22).

The uniqueness of humanity is highlighted in that we are the ***first fruits of his creatures.*** As in Rev 8:9 *ktismatōn* is best translated, not as what God created, but as his ***creatures*** (so NASB, NRSV). The metaphorical use of ***first fruits*** (*aparchē*) reflects the offering of the first products of field or flock to God (e.g., Deut 18:3-4). The NT employs the term to the "first" in various contexts (Rom 8:23; 11:16; 16:5; 1 Cor 15:20, 23; Rev 14:4).

James is certainly aware of the order of creation days in Gen 1, making humans creatures of the sixth day. But he does not claim that humans were the first creatures God created. They are the crown of creation. Created in God's image, humans enjoy a unique status as representatives of God and stewards, responsible for the rest of creation.

FROM THE TEXT

Some early church fathers had problems with James' assertion that God does not tempt anyone (v 13). The OT reports that God tested the patriarchs. If God is not the source of testing, is he not the source of all things? The Fathers explain the apparent contradiction by insisting that James meant God does not tempt us to do evil. But he does test us for virtue (see Johnson 1995, 203-4).

This rich passage carefully explains the process by which we fall into the trap of sin. We cannot excuse ourselves by claiming, "The devil made me do it." Satan's temptations would have no allure if we had no desire. That Jesus was tempted should remind us that desire is not always sinful. That he was hungry after forty days of fasting explains why he was tempted to turn stones into bread.

But if the devil cannot take the blame for human sin, neither can God. James shifts the source of the appeal of sin from outside the human being to inside. Sin comes from personal desires; and those are different for each person.

Church manuals and disciplines offer general guidelines for behavior. These boundaries help people to see such issues from the perspective of the entire community. But we must not rely on them alone for personal boundaries. Our boundaries need to be based on our unique personal inclinations. It is inappropriate to impose the boundaries I need on others. We are all unique. If we are not setting our own boundaries, then we are not dealing with our own desires. As a result we will always find a way to get around the guidelines that have been passed down. And in the process we will miss the whole purpose of guidelines.

There is no state of grace that exempts believers from the experience of temptation. "To be sure, as one develops more and more of a Christian 'mind,' the frequency and power of temptation should grow less. But temptation will be part of our experience, as it was the experience of the Lord himself" (Moo 2000, 76).

Davids notes that v 17 ties together several lines of thought:

> What is the best gift from above . . . if not wisdom, which God gives to enable people to stand in the test? God does not change, but people fail to receive wisdom because they waver (1:6-8) and even accuse God for their own failings (1:13-15). (Davids 1982, 88)

One positive message of this passage is that God is interested in giving what is best for each of us. This gracious character of God has never changed and will never change. God is dependable. Double-minded persons are not sure of this character of God. They doubt that God has their best interests in mind. So they carry the needless burden of looking out for themselves instead of trusting God's goodness.

James assures us that those who persevere in their trust in God will be called the firstfruits of his creatures and will receive a crown of life. There is status and reward for those who love God! Desire for prominence and reward is not evil. But as with any desire, it can become evil if God is not first in our lives.

2. Be Slow to Get Angry (1:19-21)

BEHIND THE TEXT

The exact form of **quick to listen, slow to speak and slow to become angry** (v 19) is unique to James. But the ideas have

> close parallels within the biblical Wisdom tradition, and one phrase or another of the triad is quite common in a variety of traditions, from ancient Egypt to Greek philosophers (e.g., Lucian) and the *Pirke Aboth*. Sir 5:11 offers the closest parallel, "Be quick to hear, but deliberate in answering." (Brosend 2004, 49)

This section is best read within the broader wisdom context, rather than as a specific command for a specific situation.

Verses 19-21 appear to introduce the theme addressed in ch 3. The body of the letter (2:1—5:7) may be read as a midrash on the wisdom saying of Jas 1:19. The main body of James consists of three essays (chs 2, 3, and 4) on "wisdom from above," which the author introduces and summarizes in 1:19 (Wall 1997, 34-38, 192; see Brosend 2004, 86). Wall identifies 1:2-21 as the book's thesis statement and 5:7-20 its concluding exhortations.

The theme of human anger as "undesirable and destructive is clearly an ancient Jewish or Hellenistic idea" (Davids 1982, 93). It is found in Jesus' teachings (e.g., Matt 5:6, 20; 6:33).

IN THE TEXT

■ **19** James begins this section with a command, Know this! (*Iste*). The verb form could be construed as indicative ("You know this," Johnson 1995, 19-20); but we take it as an imperative. Such a series of imperative commands is characteristic of James (see 1:2, 4, 5*b*, 6, 7, 9, 13, 16). The rare occurrence of the perfect imperative form is probably best explained by the verb *oida*. It consistently uses perfect forms with the force of the present tense. **Continue to be aware of this.**

The masculine plural, **My dear brothers,** addresses a mixed gender community, consisting of both men and women (see the commentary on 1:2). This is confirmed by the use of the generic term for human beings (*anthrōpos*) later in the verse. Women are certainly not exempt from the need to control their anger!

Martin identifies the first command of v 19 as the conclusion to v 18. It is a "confirmation of what the readers already have been taught. Thus v 19*b* opens a new tack" (Martin 1988, 44). This interpretation is possible, since the conjunction (*de*), which connects v 19*a* and *b*, is awkward, if we assume the two commands go together.

Depending on how one interprets v 19, the new topic begins: **And every person must be [*estō*] quick to listen, slow to speak, slow to anger.** The present imperative verb *estō* emphasizes the need for constant vigilance in this. This initial command is followed by two parallel infinitive constructions: **quick to listen** and **slow to speak.** In the third phrase, the author shifts from an infinitive to prepositional phrase: **slow to anger** (*eis orgēn*). Since **anger** is a verbal noun, the shift from infinitives, which function as verbal nouns, is almost imperceptible in English.

James insists that everyone needs to be instantly ready **to listen** to one another. Listening quickly is not speed-hearing. To be **quick to listen** requires an ongoing commitment to hear carefully and clearly what others are actually saying, explicitly and implicitly. This requires hearing their words and sensing their underlying feelings. Such listening requires **slow** and thoughtful reflection before people decide **to speak** in reply. People too often really **listen** only after the volume of a conversation has been turned up. Then discussions tend to become arguments and anger flares quickly.

James does not exclude either the possibility or the necessity of anger. But he implies that anger is justified only after people have thought about the issues and weighed the value of anger in the situation. The reason for anger should come from reflection on "the word of truth" (1:18).

■ **20** James explains why people should delay offering verbal responses and arousing anger: *Because a man's [andros] anger does not work the righteousness of God.* James uses the Greek noun for a male person (as in 1:12), perhaps with a specific example in mind. In antiquity anger was attributed primarily to men. And anger is still associated with the higher testosterone levels in males. But what James says applies to all humans (Johnson 1995, 200). He emphasizes human **anger** as a specific kind of impatient, rash anger that comes out of a deep, settled, angry disposition.

James clarifies the contrast between *man's anger* and *God's righteousness.* A man's anger does not *produce* the righteous life that God desires. James used *work* (*ergazetai*) terminology earlier in 1:3-4. In both passages, *ergazomai* "takes on the meaning of *katergazomai*" in 2 Cor 7:10, that is, "'bring about/produce'" (Heiligenthal 1990, 48).

Anger in the Greek Texts

There are at least three different words in Greek translated as "anger" in English. Ephesians 4:26 and 31 contrast them well. In Eph 4:26 *parorgismos* ("anger," NRSV; only here in the NT) has an apparently neutral sense. It seems to refer to the sudden emotion arising from exasperation at someone or some situation, not a settled disposition: "Do not let the sun go down on your anger" (NRSV).

In Eph 4:31 Paul uses two other words, "rage and anger" (*thymos* and *orgē*). They are often used together in the LXX, the NT, and nonbiblical Greek (Salmond n.d., 348). "Rage" (*thymos*) has the sense of a passionate outburst of anger, wrath, or indignation, similar to *parorgismos* (BDAG, 461). Its connection to *orgē* seems to indicate that it is a violent reaction that comes out of deep-seated, unresolved anger and resentment.

The term for **anger** used in Jas 1:19 is *orgē* (**wrath**). This is more a deeply settled disposition than merely an occasional provocation. NT texts employ it to refer to God's settled disposition toward sin and sinners, a righteous anger (John 3:36; Rom 1:18; 12:19; Eph 5:6; Col 3:6; 1 Thess 2:16; Heb 3:11; 4:3; Rev 11:18). But James specifically insists that human anger (*orgē*) does not produce or bring about righteousness. So when James uses this term in reference to human beings, it is a uniformly negative word. It reflects "a state of intense displeasure" (BDAG, 461 s.v. *thymos*)—a settled disposition of selfish resentment.

The **righteousness** [*dikaiosynēn*] **of God** (*theou*) can be interpreted several different ways. Davids identifies four options: "(a) God's righteous standard, (b) the righteousness God gives, (c) righteousness before God, or (d) God's eschatological righteousness" (1982, 93). The meanings are not mutually exclusive.

We must avoid interpreting James in light of Paul's usage in his letters (e.g., Rom 1:17; Johnson 1995, 200). In the immediate context the meaning appears to be that a human outburst of anger does not meet the standard of what God considers right or God approves. Angry outbursts are not the kind of life God desires for his people. A righteous life for James requires one to listen intently and to respond cautiously—slow to speak retaliatory words or get angry (v 19).

■ **21** Therefore (*dio*) furnishes a direct inference from what precedes to the exhortation that follows: **get rid of . . . and humbly accept** (see Rom 1:24; Gal 4:31; 1 Pet 1:13).

In this verse, removing **moral filth,** pictured as soiled clothing, may precede the central command. We could translate the adverbial participle *apothemenoi* indicating antecedent time: *After you take off . . . , receive . . ."* Because the participle is an aorist, the taking off of *all filthiness and malice* must occur before one receives *the implanted word.* But the participle could be read as an adverbial participle of attendant circumstance. Since its main verb is an imperative, it would be translated as an imperative: "rid yourselves" (NRSV).

The NT employs the verb *apotithēmi* ("take off") to introduce a list of vices Christians must abandon when they are converted (Eph 4:22, 25; Col 3:8; 1 Pet 2:1; see Rom 13:13; Heb 12:1). Other first-century Christian and Jewish literature (*1 Clem.* 13:1; Philo, *Posterity* 48) also used this verb to introduce vice lists.

Moral filth or *filthiness* is the basic word for "a state of moral defilement or corruption" (BDAG, 908 s.v. *rhyparia*). It is used in the NT as a noun only here. But the idea is found in Zech 3:3-4 where "Joshua is stripped of his 'filthy garments' and clothed in rich apparel by an angel" (Johnson 1995, 201). James will use the idea again in 1:27 where true religion is "to keep oneself from being polluted by the world."

Evil (*kakia*) is a general word for "the quality or state of wickedness" (BDAG, 500). In the context of anger and a list of vices (as in 1 Pet 2:1), it is probably best translated as *malice* (Davids 1982, 94).

James continues his exhortation, urging his hearers: *in meekness receive for yourselves the implanted word.* So after the excess moral filthiness of their pre-Christian past is thrown off, believers are to **receive . . . the implanted word.** The aorist imperative **receive** suggests that this occurs in one's conversion, not repeatedly.

Meekness is important to James as the attitude of the righteous poor (*tapeinos*, 1:9). It also is the rhetorical antonym of assertive **anger** (vv 19-20). The command to **receive** indicates that the **implanted word** is a gift, not something earned by throwing off the moral filthiness.

Receiving the word of God or the gospel is a repeated NT description of conversion (Luke 8:13; Acts 8:14; 11:1; 17:11; 2 Cor 11:4; 1 Thess 1:6; 2:13). But the expression **receive the implanted word** appears nowhere else in Scripture. In light of James' use of "the word of truth" in v 18, there can be little doubt that the **implanted word** refers to the gospel (Johnson 1995, 202). Believers receive the **implanted word** by accepting and acting on the gospel at their conversions (Davids 1982, 95). The gospel takes root in them by means of "the word of truth" (v 18), through which the Father gave birth to them.

The adjectival participial phrase **which is able to save your souls** adds that the **implanted word** has the power to save. The word **can** translates *dynamenon*, the verbal root of the most common Greek word for **power** (*dynamis*: "**power, might, strength, force**"; BDAG, 262). James, like Paul, frequently uses power language to contrast the impotence of humanity with the mighty ability of God (see 4:2 and 2:14 vs. 4:12).

All that James meant by **save your souls** (*psychas*) is not clear. But it clearly has an eschatological meaning (see 1:12; 2:12-13; 3:1; 5:5, 7; Johnson 1995, 203). In Jewish thought, **souls** do not refer to an intangible part of human beings, separate from their bodies. Often, the best translation is **lives.** Since it refers to human persons in their wholeness, the NIV paraphrase seems to capture the force here: **which can save you.**

Salvation is a process that begins with the planting of the gospel seed when one is converted. But it will only be complete at harvesttime, at "the Lord's coming" (5:7-8). James does not claim that believers are already saved. A favorable response to the gospel **can save** only those who remain faithful to the end by continuing to put their faith into action.

FROM THE TEXT

Verses 19-21 emphasize the need to remember to listen first and to make sure we understand the situation before we speak words in anger. Impatient and rash words may only make matters worse and destroy relationships.

This passage comes immediately after James' discussion of how sin develops from human desires. Desires for status or always to be right can lead to sinful anger. Instead we are to receive the gospel and its lifestyle-altering demands on us with humility. Receiving the implanted word of truth gives us life, if we allow that word to transform us and finally demonstrate the power of God to save us.

Humans live in a sinful world. Thus, they tend to become angry and say things that do not produce God's righteousness in their lives. But the miraculous truth is that when we accept what God wants to do in our lives, God has the power to save us! God can enable us to overcome sin and do the right thing.

3. Listen and Do (1:22-25)

BEHIND THE TEXT

Polished metal was used as mirrors by first-century people. Such mirrors were not as clear as modern mirrors. But they were the most convenient means of representing what a person looked like.

Verse 24 was probably a common proverb of the human tendency to forgetfulness. It would be comparable to our saying, "If he didn't have his head screwed on, he'd probably forget it."

James refers to his audience as hearers rather than readers. Like the vast majority of people in the first century, the early Christian community was primarily an oral/aural community. Letters were sent to the churches and the author expected them to be read aloud to the assembled community. This is because written copies were very expensive. The Torah and other religious writings were copied by scribes onto papyrus or prepared animal skins. Most people would hear the OT or writings of the apostles read to them from a single copy owned by the community.

IN THE TEXT

■ **22** In Greek, this verse begins with a command: *And you* [plural] *must always be* [*Genesthe, Become*] *doers of the word and not just hearers, who keep misleading themselves.* The expression *doers of the word* here is a Semitism, because the "phrase in classical Greek would mean a wordsmith or poet" (Johnson 1995, 206). This is definitely not the meaning here. Here, James probably paraphrases the teaching of Jesus (see Matt 7:21-25; Luke 6:46-48; 11:28; Rom 2:13). He commands believers not simply to hear what God commands, but to heed it. The present imperative emphasizes that obedience to the word God speaks is an ongoing commitment, not just a one-time activity. True believers constantly do God's will.

James explains that those who **merely listen** and do nothing are *misleading themselves.* The word for *misleading* (*paralogizomenoi*, **deceive**) is also found in Col 2:4. There the Colossians were being deceived by attractive but false arguments.

71

The word *monon,* **merely (*only* or *just*),** suggests a parallel in 2:24. There James addresses in detail the intimate connection between faith and works. The contrast between hearing and doing is "one of the most widespread in ancient moral instruction" (Johnson 1995, 206-7).

■ **23** Hearers and doers of the **word** belong to two distinct categories. Those who only hear do not change their lifestyles to obey what God says. The doers hear the word and conform their lifestyle to that **word.**

James uses a proverb of forgetfulness to illustrate what he means: *Because if anyone is a hearer of the word and not a doer, this one has become like a man who sees the face of his natural being in a mirror.*

James uses the masculine word for *man* (*andri*) not because his message applies only to males. He creates a word picture for his hearers, not a general statement about male forgetfulness.

Instead of the usual word for the physical act of looking (*blepō*), James employs *katanoeō,* a verb that means "**consider, contemplate**" (BDAG, 523). This verb can refer also to spiritual reflection or moral self-examination (Johnson 1995, 208). As he looks in a mirror, a man catches more than a glimpse of his physical reflection. *His natural being* (*tēs gemeseōs autou*) is literally "his origin" or "his birth" (Johnson 1995, 207). His physical appearance betrays his ethnicity, his ancestry, his identity.

■ **24** The metaphorical use of "mirror" governs James' thought in vv 23-25. The proverb of forgetfulness (v 23) continues: *For he sees himself and goes away and immediately forgets what sort he was* (what he looks like). The verbs of seeing and forgetting are gnomic aorists (past tense in form with a timeless force), characteristic of verb tenses in Greek proverbs. In English we translate these aorists as present tense since that is expected for English proverbs.

This man should have looked at himself for the purpose of doing something about his appearance, not just admiring himself. His seeing (*katanoeō;* see v 23) was done in haste. There was no contemplation aimed toward doing anything about what he saw (Adamson 1976, 82).

"The momentariness and lack of real effect is the point of the parable, not a comparison with a different type of mirror or a different way of seeing" (Davids 1982, 98). The mirror was there so people could use it to improve their appearance. This man does not take advantage of it.

■ **25** James uses a stronger verb for seeing here than in v 24. *Parakypsas* originally meant "to bend over" to get a closer look (John 20:11). James recommends the example of *the one who looks closely into the perfect law.* The one **who looks intently** into something takes the time really to contemplate what is there—even the things that are beneath the surface. Close self-examination calls for change.

Here *law* (*nomos*) occurs for the first time in James. He uses it in an absolute sense (2:9, 10, 11; 4:11) and describes it in 2:8 as "the royal law." Here it is **the perfect law, the law of freedom.** James calls it **perfect** (*teleion*), like the gifts God gives (1:17; see 1:4). The association of **law** and **freedom** is found in both Jewish and Hellenistic literature of the time (Johnson 1995, 209).

The **law** replaces the mirror in James' application of the analogy. This suggests that James understands law to include more than a list of dos and don'ts. The Law includes moral example. Torah, the Hebrew word for **law**, may best be translated **instruction.** The Law teaches us how we should live—by precept and example. This, in turn, gives us the freedom to be the people God created us to be. Echoing in the background is the OT revelation: "The law of the LORD is perfect, reviving the soul" (Ps 19:7; see Pss 1; 119; Rom 7:12, 14, 16).

James adds to this stronger word for seeing. Those who **remain** with the perfect law contemplate its personal implications for their lives. They not only hear the Law but also spend time studying the Law to understand its deep meaning and practical application. This is the **law that gives freedom.**

In contrast to the forgetful person (vv 23-24) is the **doer.** James adds: **this one will be blessed in his doing.** Such people see, hear, contemplate how they will respond, and then they act. And God blesses them for this obedience. Those who have reflected on divine instruction put into practice what they learn.

The logic of this passage makes "the word of truth" in v 18 and "'the perfect law of freedom' virtually synonymous" (Johnson 1995, 214; see John 8:32, 36). One cannot get far from the grace of the gospel in James.

James promises that an obedient hearer **will be blessed in what he does** (see on 1:12; Luke 11:28). The three participles—**looks . . . remains . . . becomes**—are all Greek gnomic aorists. These past tense verbs have a timeless force. They prepare for the final future tense (*estai*): **he will be blessed.** "The sense of progression seems significant" (Johnson 1995, 209).

FROM THE TEXT

Brosend argues that vv 22-25 are the thesis statement of the Epistle of James: "When all is said, all is not done" (Brosend 2004, 51). At the least, this section, along with vv 26-27, is extremely important to the book. What we really believe becomes obvious in what we do. It is not enough just to say we believe the gospel. It must make a difference in our lives. Those who do not take time to study and reflect on the gospel and its application for everyday living are forgetful hearers.

Citizens of the twenty-first century suffer from information overload. In this digital age we hear and read and see a lot of superficial data. But do we dig deeply into the wisdom of God found in Scripture? Doing the Law is important, not just in reference to our lifestyle, but also to the security of our future salvation (Davids 1982, 54). James reminds us how easy it is to deceive ourselves that we have done something significant, just because we have talked about it. This deception of self is really about being blind to our true religious state (Moo 2000, 90). Biblical illiteracy is not just a problem of the lack of study and reflection on Scripture. It is an extremely dangerous threat to our eternal destiny.

The word picture James paints in this passage is deliberately humorous. All of us have at least once become distracted while looking in the mirror. Another more urgent matter captured our attention, and we forgot to finish making ourselves presentable. In retrospect, this may seem humorous. But at the time it was embarrassing. This points out how ridiculous it is simply to hear the word of God and not do anything about it. Yet, sadly, we have all done this as well. It is difficult to connect our alleged beliefs with our everyday behavior.

Some Protestants overemphasize salvation by faith. For them, salvation is only a set of propositional beliefs. This has blinded the eyes of some well-meaning Christians to the need to act on what they believe. The word of God was not given to "sound pretty" but to make a difference in our lives. James will become much more specific about what this means as he continues his letter.

4. Pure Religion Described (1:26-27)

BEHIND THE TEXT

"Religion" in this passage is the word for external religious practices. It refers to what people can see. First-century Christians and Jews were sometimes called atheists because they did not worship statues and idols as most Greeks and Romans did. It seemed to many Gentiles that Jews, especially those in the Diaspora, to which James' readers belonged, had no religion at all. They had no temples with images of their gods and goddesses to bring offerings to or pray to. Jews had one temple in Jerusalem, while Greeks and Romans built temples everywhere.

Within the Jewish world, outward expressions of religion meant keeping purity and dietary laws. These often created a cultural chasm, separating the Jews socially from their Gentile neighbors. When a Christian congregation included both Jews and Gentiles, these laws became a major obstacle to the unity of the community.

Some Jewish Christians thought the answer to this problem was for Gentiles to keep the traditional purity and dietary laws. In other words, they had to become Jews to become Christians. Such Jewish Christians have been called Judaizers, based on Gal 2:14.

Other Jewish Christians, like Paul and James, did not recognize Jewish purity and dietary laws as definitive of Christianity. Other issues more important than these outward forms of religion, which only divided Jews and Gentiles, reflected the core of Christianity.

The more common word for religion or worship in the NT is the verb *proskyneō*. James chose an outward, action-oriented noun for religion, *thrēskeia*, because it better fits what he is trying to say.

IN THE TEXT

■ **26** In this concluding section of James' introductory statements on the Christian life (1:2-27), he connects hearing and doing with his definition of religion: *If anyone thinks, "I am religious* [*thrēskos*]," *who at the same time does not bridle his tongue, but deceives his heart, this person's religion* [*thrēskeia*] *is worthless.* Both the adjective *thrēskos* (only here in the NT) and the noun *thrēskeia* normally describe those who observe the purity and dietary laws. The expression **keep a tight rein on his tongue** rehearses the command to be "slow to speak" (in 1:19) and anticipates the discourse on the tongue in 3:3-12.

If the one who **considers himself religious** does damage by what he says, his religious ritual is **worthless** (*mataios*)—"*empty, fruitless, useless, powerless, lacking truth*" (BDAG, 621). In wisdom contexts *mataios* can mean "foolish" vs. "wise" (i.e., idolatrous; Johnson 1995, 211).

Furthermore, if one does not recognize that what he says and how he says it reflects his true beliefs, he *is deceiving* [*apatōn*] *his heart.* Johnson translates this "*indulging his heart*," following LXX precedent (1995, 210). Such worthless religion is self-indulgent, because it does not look out for the needs of others (see 4:1-3; 5:1-5). "James sketches a supposed religion of uncontrolled speech and self-gratification . . . as idolatry" (Johnson 1995, 211).

■ **27** James defines **religion** that is *pure and undefiled before God* in positive ethical terms. Two synonyms describe the kind of worship **God our Father** accepts. *Pure* (*kathara*) can also be translated as "*clean*"; *undefiled* (*amiantos*) may be translated as "*pure*" (BDAG, 489 and 54). In the LXX both adjectives appear in discussions of ritual purity. Here both refer to moral purity, described in terms of the following behaviors: *To visit orphans and widows in their distress and to keep oneself unspotted by the world.*

James describes the conduct of truly religious persons toward *orphans and widows* as decisive. Religion must be concerned about and care for those who have no status in the community and are often desperately poor. The behavior he calls for is visiting (*episkeptesthai*) them. Elsewhere, in both the LXX (Gen 50:24; Exod 3:16; Ruth 1:6) and the NT (Luke 1:68, 78; 7:16), this Greek verb describes God's active care for his people.

The truly religious person will personally visit the outcasts and power-less in their distressing situation. It is not enough merely to give alms, however generous. And it will not do merely to send a surrogate to minister to their needs. He must go himself, see and experience their life-situation and then do something about it, to bring the necessary relief and help. True religion must manifest itself in what some call today compassionate ministries.

In addition to this, an authentically religious man will also **keep himself unspotted by the world.** An **unspotted** (*aspilon*) character is one that is "un-stained" (NRSV) and *"spotless, without blemish"* (BDAG, 144). Believers must guard themselves from moral contamination by the world. They need to set boundaries that keep them from being influenced by people and values that increase desires and give birth to sin (1:15). James uses **world** (*kosmon*) here, as later (2:5; 3:6; 4:4), to refer to all that is opposed to God's standard (*para tōi theōi*, **before God**).

Commentators emphasize that James is not exhaustively "intending to summarize all that true worship of God should involve" (Moo 2000, 96). Nys-trom generalizes James' definition of pure religion as "the control of speech, acts of charity, and resisting temptation" (1997, 96). For James, the core of what comes out of the heart of true worshippers are acts of compassion and personal purity.

FROM THE TEXT

James ties the outward perception of our religion to what we say. What we profess with our words should be consistent with what we do (1:22-25). But what we say can affect others as much as our actions. James will explain in ch 3 that speech can bless or curse others.

This is the only passage in the NT in which religion is defined. It echoes the definition in Mic 6:8, "He has showed you, O man, what is good. And what does the LORD require of you? To act justly and to love mercy and to walk humbly with your God."

Wesley comments, "If any one be ever so religious—Exact in the out-ward offices of religion. And bridleth not his tongue—From backbiting, tale bearing, evil speaking, he only deceiveth his own heart, if he fancies he has any true religion at all" (2003, 814). He adds:

> The only true religion in the sight of God, is this, to visit—With coun-sel, comfort, and relief. The fatherless and widows—Those who need it most. And to keep himself unspotted from the world—From the max-ims, tempers, and customs of it. But this cannot be done, till we have given our hearts to God, and love our neighbour as ourselves. (Wesley 2003, 814)

Wesley believed God had ordained "The Means of Grace" as the ordinary channels of conveying his grace to human souls. Among the chief of these he stressed: prayer, private and public; reading, hearing, and meditating on the Scriptures; regular participation in the Lord's Supper; Christian conference; covenant renewal; and "works of mercy," particularly visiting the poor (1979, 5:188).

Wesley considered what we call compassionate ministries today "real means of grace." They are more especially such to those who do them as expressions of love for God and neighbor. Those who neglect to share their excess with the poor, to visit the sick and imprisoned, and so forth, do not receive the grace they could. And by neglect, they lose grace they previously received.

In his sermon "On Visiting the Sick," Wesley insisted that giving money to others to minister to the needy on our behalf was no substitute for doing it ourselves. If we do not minister personally, we lose a means of grace. We miss an excellent means of increasing our thankfulness to God, who has spared us from such pain and sickness, and who gives us health and strength. And we miss an invaluable means of increasing our compassion for the afflicted, our generosity, and similar social affections (Wesley 1979, 7:117, 119).

For James, religion that has no impact on our ethical behavior is worthless and should be considered no religion at all. The gospel James preaches ("the word of truth") is powerful. It transforms lives and makes the lives of those it transforms fruitful, wise, and meaningful.

James insists that both social compassion and moral purity are needed. As Christians, we cannot isolate ourselves from the world; we are called to make a difference by our godly actions in the world. But we cannot participate in the sinful habits and patterns of the world. Although never easy, we are called to be in the world, but not a part of its sinfulness (see John 17:11-23).

James focuses on the character and spiritual health of his readers. He summarizes pure religion as "control of speech, acts of charity, and resisting temptation" (Nystrom 1997, 96). This certainly does not exhaust all the good Christians can and must do nor list every evil we must avoid. For example, he says nothing of the necessity of telling others the good news (Matt 28:18-20; Acts 1:8).

Evangelism, a constant concern in Paul's letters, seems unimportant to James' conversation with his community. He is not occupied with non-Christians in this Epistle. But if effective evangelism is to occur and its fruit remain, Christian evangelists and communities of faith must evidence the pure religion described by James.

Evangelical Christianity has sometimes forgotten the importance of such pure religion in its zeal to evangelize. Both are important; and neither works for long without the other. Blankenship comments:

When we have been Christ-followers for a while we forget who we were before our conversion. We forget that we were once like those whom we are now called to minister to. Often this leads Christians to act somewhat aloof, as though they are stepping off of a pedestal to descend into the world and aid those who are not as they are. (2007, 10)

III. THE EXPOSITION: JAMES 2:1—5:20

Having concluded his introductory statements, James begins to address the issues raised in greater depth. This exposition occupies the rest of the Epistle. It seems to be divided into twelve sections with "strong formal indicators of opening and closure" (Bauckham 1991, 64; see 64-66).

James ends ch 1 with the admonition to be doers of the word. He begins ch 2 referring to the second half of Jesus' great commandment: "Love your neighbor as yourself" (2:8). Favoritism seems to be prevalent in his Jewish-Christian community. So James shows how it fails to fulfill the commandment. To do so, he moves smoothly into the theme he is best known for: faith and works. I prefer the terms "faith" and "actions," because "works" has taken on negative connotations in English-speaking Christianity. James insists that faith is evidenced by godly actions.

James does not neglect his concern for speech and its power to do good and evil. He addresses this again in ch 3, immediately after his discussion of faith and actions. The subject of speech prepares for a discussion of earthly vs. heavenly wisdom.

The distinction between earthly and heavenly wisdom in turn transitions in ch 4 to a treatment of the need for believers to submit totally to God. Christians cannot live schizophrenically trying to follow their own wills and God's will at the same time.

James next issues two commands for committed Christians: Do not judge your neighbors and do not boast about what you will do tomorrow. Some interpreters consider this discussion of boasting as a resumption of James' advice to the wealthy in his community (see the commentary on 1:10-11), here specifically addressing rich traders. Regardless, James 5 warns the rich and comforts the poor, encouraging them to be patient in their suffering.

James reminds everyone in his Jewish-Christian communities to keep their communication honest and straightforward. Instruction on the nature and efficacy of prayer within the community of faith follows.

James does not use the regular closing found in most first-century letters. Some scholars consider 5:19-20 a kind of conclusion. It encourages the faithful to reach out to those who have lost their way and bring them back from their lives of sin.

A. Partiality and the Law of Love (2:1-13)

Chapter 2 has two parts. In vv 1-13, James deals with the issue of favoritism. He identifies its expression in Christian communities a clear violation of the second half of Jesus' great commandment. The second half of ch 2 (vv 14-26) contains James' discussion of faith and actions for which he is best known.

Although it is possible to show favoritism toward any social group, James addresses the incongruous tendency of his first-century Jewish-Christian communities to favor the rich. He identifies the rich as those who exploit the community and bring shame on **the noble name of him to whom you belong** (v 7). In the second half of ch 2, he mentions neglect to feed or clothe the needy as reflecting badly on the faith community. They cannot simply tell those in need: *Go in peace, keep warm and well fed* (v 16).

Catchwords connect chs 1 and 2, indicating the relationship between them. In 2:13, mercy boasts/rejoices (*katakauchatai*) against judgment. This points back to 1:9, where James ironically urges the lowly to boast/rejoice (*kauchasthō*) in their high position. The concepts of doubting in 1:6 and unfairly discriminating in 2:4 both use the same Greek verb (*diakrinō*). This verb is usually translated *I judge* or *discriminate* in the active voice; and, *I doubt* or *waver* in the middle voice. The Greek verb is identical. Both passages possess the same overall concern for

> making a distinction. In the one case people doubt because they waver between two options, trying to discern what is best. In the other case people

discriminate, because they make the wrong choice entirely as to how to react to two different situations. (Blomberg and Kamell 2008, 101)

1. Don't Show Favoritism (2:1-4)

BEHIND THE TEXT

James' commands in this passage are amazingly countercultural. Within the honor-shame society of the first-century Mediterranean world, it was expected and natural for persons of wealth and status to be treated better than the poor. It would challenge the rich person's status to be seated next to a person of a lower status. James seems to expand on the principle Paul enunciated in Gal 3:28: "There is neither Jew nor Greek, slave nor free, male nor female," to include, *rich nor poor.* He would have also agreed with Paul's rationale: "for you are all one in Christ."

IN THE TEXT

■ 1 James begins ch 2 with his usual address for members of the congregations: *My brothers and sisters* (see the commentary on 1:2, 19). He introduces seven of the twelve sections in his exposition in this way.

James also continues with his familiar imperatives: *you must not continue to hold together with favoritism the faith of our Lord Jesus Christ, the one of glory.* Scholars are divided on how to interpret the final string of genitives. The grammatical construction is atypical, so ancient manuscripts differ in their efforts to "correct" the text. Some place *of glory* right after *faith,* rather than after *Jesus Christ.* This would call for the unlikely translation: *the glorious faith of our Lord Jesus Christ.*

Some commentators take *faith of our Lord Jesus Christ* as an objective genitive: *faith in our Lord Jesus Christ* (Martin 1988, 59-60; Nystrom 1997, 112-15). This makes sense within Paul's letters. But James addresses different communities. Elsewhere he refers only to faith in God the Father (e.g., 2:19, 23). Johnson offers two reasons for translating *the faith of our Lord* as a subjective genitive:

First, the Christology of the letter is not such as to make "faith in Christ" natural; . . . Second, the use of Jesus' sayings throughout the composition suggests a meaning like "the faith of Jesus in God as reflected in his teaching," or perhaps "the faith that is from Jesus Christ," in the sense "declared by Jesus." (1995, 220)

The phrase *tēs doxēs—the one of glory* or *the glorious one*—is difficult to interpret. Since Erasmus in the sixteenth century, scholars have tried to make sense of this phrase. Most attach it to the **Lord Jesus Christ.** But it seems too far removed from this in Greek. Adamson suggests the translation "our glory"

(1976, 104). But "*doxa* is frequently found as shorthand for the resurrection of Jesus" (Luke 24:26; Acts 22:11; John 17:5; 1 Cor 2:8; 15:43; 2 Cor 4:6; Phil 2:11; 3:21; Col 1:11; Heb 2:7; 1 Pet 1:11). Thus, James is "confessing Jesus as the resurrected one" (Johnson 1995, 221; see Introduction, "Christology").

Although the grammar is rough, the meaning is clear. Communities that profess to follow Jesus Christ must not show partiality or favoritism. As will be seen, this becomes a primary expression of sin in the lives of the Christians in James' communities.

■ **2** Here James introduces a specific example of favoritism in a conditional (subjunctive) tense. The situation he describes may not actually have occurred, but it could. This is characteristic of encyclical letters sent to several congregations. James cannot address specific community problems as do Paul's letters.

James sets the scene: ***For if a gold-fingered man in splendid clothing enters into your synagogue and also a poor person in filthy clothing enters*** **. . .** The word *anēr*, referring to a male person, suggests that James has a concrete example in mind. The Jewish nature of this passage becomes obvious in the word *synagōgēn*, synagogue, describing the **meeting** or "assembly" (NRSV). The meaning **meeting place** requires the definite article, found in several good manuscripts. If James has a building in mind, it is curious that he calls it **your** synagogue. Were there enough Jewish Christians in places that they had their own synagogues?

The rich man enters their synagogue, ***gold-fingered,*** that is, with **a gold ring,** or probably many gold rings, on his finger(s). In antiquity, these were overt indications of power and arrogance (Johnson 1995, 222). His **clothes,** as well, were radiant (*lampra*, "***bright, shining***"; BDAG, 485; see Luke 23:11).

James uses extremes to communicate his message. No one would wonder what the status was of each individual. In stark contrast, the poor person comes to the gathering of believers dressed in ***filthy*** or **shabby** (*rypara*, "dirty"), foul-smelling ***clothing.*** **Poor** (*ptōchos*) stresses the man's material poverty. Nystrom describes the scope of poverty in James' culture: Nearly ninety percent of all people were impoverished; eight percent were wealthy. (See his survey of social order in the Roman world and the contrast between "the humble" and "the great in legal" terms of the time. 1997, 123-28.)

■ **3** James employs a strengthened form of the common word for "look" (*blepō*), involving the double use of the preposition *epi* (**on** or **upon**). The NIV translates *epiblepsete . . . epi* as **show special attention to.** The synagogue greeter looks intently upon the man who appears to be rich. There is no indication that the greeter even looked at the poor person.

The greeter says to the rich man, ***"You sit here on the honorable seat."*** But the poor person is greeted: ***"You stand over there."*** Not even the greeter wants the filthy poor person to stand near him. If he wants seating space, the

82

only option is to *sit below my footstool.* The variants in this phrase within the manuscript tradition indicate that even ancient scribes found it difficult to understand precisely what James meant. Translators, similarly unsure, resort to paraphrase: **"Sit on the floor by my feet,"** or "sit at my feet" (NRSV). Tel Hum, a second-/third-century synagogue, had "a stone bench running along the walls, with a lower tier for the feet of those sitting on the bench" (Adamson 1976, 107). Perhaps this is what James envisioned: the poor man sitting two levels beneath the greeter.

In ancient times, using someone as a footstool was to humiliate him. Ancient conquerors did this to the emperors or leaders they had conquered (see Lactantius 1995, 302). Adamson comments, "To come under or to lick the shoe for the Jew meant slavish subjection and even conquest" (1976, 107). To ask a person to sit under one's footstool would be the ultimate humiliation. James' hyperbolic language makes his point.

■ 4 This conclusion to vv 2-3 poses a question: *Were you not passing judgment among yourselves; and, thus, did you not become judges with evil thoughts?* James uses the verb *diakrinō* (*"make a distinction"*; BDAG, 231) in the first part of this compound sentence. The verb contains the same root word translated **judges** (*kritēs*), the subject of the second half of the sentence.

Passing judgment or *discriminating* (NIV: **have you not discriminated**) in itself is not the problem. The issue is wrongly judging others based on appearance or status *"with evil thoughts."* Their "evil motives" (NASB) were the problem. Did the community cater to the rich man as a means of elevating its own status? It was certainly **evil** to humiliate further one already disgraced by society (on **evil** see the commentary on 4:16).

FROM THE TEXT

James clearly illustrates that God is no respecter of persons and neither should his children be (see Acts 10:34; Rom 2:11; Eph 6:9; Col 3:25). James' rejection of partiality attacked the core "values" of ancient Mediterranean culture. People expected to be treated consistent with their status, whether high or low. But "in Christ," as Paul eloquently says in Gal 3:28, such status distinctions are inconsequential. Within the redeemed Christian community, the curse of the fall no longer determined relationships between God's people. The rules of society no longer govern with whom we can be friends.

Modern societies also suffer from the tendency to show favoritism based on shallow, if not evil motives. Today's categories of distinctions are not limited to rich and poor. But economic issues are often still at the heart of such unjust distinctions. Christians have much to learn from those whom rich Western society does not recognize as our equals in wealth, influence, social class, education, intellectual ability, physical prowess, beauty, celebrity, sophistication, ethnicity, and so forth. We might do well to learn at their feet (see Robert McAfee Brown's 1984 *Unexpected News: Reading the Bible with Third World Eyes* [Louisville, Ky.: Westminster/John Knox]).

Today, people's professions, anonymity in society, attire, and wealth all stigmatize and stereotype them, making them less than whole persons and easier to generalize, categorize, and dismiss (Nystrom 1997, 137-39). We cannot assume that all people of a particular ethnicity or geographic region or profession, and so forth, are alike, as our preoccupation with demographic data tends to assume. Partiality/favoritism is not just a vice of the past; it exists today. The church needs to resist its influence in society and eliminate it within the Christian communities.

2. The Poor Are Rich in Faith (2:5-7)

BEHIND THE TEXT

This passage would resonate with James' readers at several levels. The exploitation of the poor by the rich is a common theme of the Hebrew prophets (Amos, Hosea, Isaiah, and Micah). During the Syrian oppression in the second and first centuries B.C., rich Jews adopted Hellenism because of its political and economic advantages. The poor rejected it in favor of ancient Jewish traditions (see 1 and 2 Maccabees). Consequently, in some circles within Judaism, the poor were presumed to be the most pious and loyal to God. In the Sermon on the Mount, Jesus called the poor blessed because the kingdom of God belongs to them (Matt 5:3; Luke 6:20).

Another level of approval arose from the everyday experience as immigrants and foreigners of many in James' audience. The rich and status-seekers were interested in suing newcomers in court to establish their superior status. Jewish Christians were widely persecuted by Gentiles for various reasons. They worshiped an invisible God, not represented by idols, and did so in ways Gentiles considered strange and often offensive.

Who Were the Poor?

When descriptions of the poor in the NT are grouped in terms of what they have in common, it would seem that being classified as poor was the result of some unfortunate turn of events or some untoward circumstance. Poor persons seem to be those who cannot maintain their inherited status due to circumstances that befall them and their families such as debt, being in a foreign land, sickness, death of a spouse (widow), or some personal physical accident. Consequently, the poor would not be a permanent social standing but a sort of revolving category of people who unfortunately cannot maintain their inherited status. . . . rich and poor really refer to the greedy and the socially ill-fated. (Malina 2001a, 100)

■5 James begins this section with a command: *Listen!* This is an attention-getting device like *Know this!* in 1:19 or *Behold!* in 5:11. If chs 2—5 develop the wisdom saying in 1:19, this verse refers back to the first command in 1:19 to be "quick to listen" (Wall 1997, 34-38, 192). As James calls his audience to listen, he addresses them as **_beloved brothers and sisters_** (see on 1:16, 19; emphasis added). This indicates that (1) he is addressing Christians within the community; and (2) he is treating a sensitive issue of which they should be aware.

James calls attention to the high value of *the poor of the world* in the estimate of God, employing the OT language of election. **Has not God chosen** (*exelexato*) applies the terms describing God's call of Israel as his special people in Deut 4:37; 7:7; and elsewhere. This terminology continues in the NT in reference to the messianic community (e.g., Mark 13:20; John 15:16; Eph 1:4).

James delicately addresses the issue with a rhetorical question expecting a positive answer: *Did not God choose the poor in the world to be the rich in faith and to be the heirs of* the kingdom he promised those who love him? With key terms he has just used, James' question contrasts *the poor* (*ptōchous*) with *the rich* (*plousious*). In James' paradoxical vision of divine reality, the **rich** are *the poor in the world.*

The **poor** may refer to the economically deprived described in vv 2-3. Or, James may refer to the perceived status of the Christian community in the opinion of the pagan majority: the **poor in the eyes of the world.** If the latter is his intent, *in the world* would be a dative of reference or respect (Ropes 1973, 193; Dibelius 1975, 138). Some scribes altered the text to make the literal meaning inescapable, by changing the dative to the genitive: *of the world* (Johnson 1995, 224). On either reading, conventional wisdom is turned on its head. God regards as **rich in faith** those the world despises as worthless (see 1 Cor 1:27-28).

As such they are *heirs of the kingdom* promised those who love God. The concept of *heirs* (*klēronomous*) and inheritance reaches back to the OT promise of land to Abraham's descendants (Gen 28:4; Deut 1:8; Acts 7:5). The LXX of Ps 16:5 affirms: "the LORD is the portion of my inheritance" (see Ps 37:18). In the NT the language of inheritance is frequently applied to Christians. Christians are "heirs—heirs of God and co-heirs with Christ" (Rom 8:17; see Gal 3:29; 4:7; 6:17). James uses the terms *heirs* and **kingdom** only here.

James does not use the full expression "kingdom of God," frequent in the Synoptic teaching of Jesus. But this is clearly what he intends. His **king-**

dom–language refers to the future inheritance of God's people. Only as James' communities submit to the rule of God in the *present* can they expect to participate in God's coming *future* **kingdom.** Here, as in Matt 25:34 and 1 Cor 15:50, inheriting the **kingdom** means sharing in the final hope of believers. Elsewhere in the NT, this is called the resurrection from the dead or inheriting eternal life (see Matt 19:29; Mark 10:17; Luke 10:25; 18:18; Col 3:24; Titus 3:7; Rev 21:7).

To experience this future inheritance requires a favorable decision from God in the last judgment. Recall the macarism pronounced in Jas 1:12: "Blessed is the man who perseveres under trial, because when he has stood the test, he will receive the crown of life that God has promised to those who love him." Perseverance in trials alone will not prove the genuineness of James' readers' religion (1:26-27). They must demonstrate their faith by dealing with anger (1:19-21), doing the word (1:22-25), ministering to outcasts, keeping undefiled by the world (1:26-27), and by eliminating favoritism within their communities (2:1-4).

No term for "promise," either as a noun or verb, is explicit in the LXX. But God's covenant assurances to Abraham and his descendants were understood by first-century Jews in these terms. God's commitments to Abraham were essential to Israel's faith and identity as God's people (see Exod 32:13; 1 Chr 16:14-18; Neh 9:7-8; Ps 105:6-11; Sir 44:21; Wis 12:21). The Greek term for promise (*epangelia* and its cognates), however, first appears within the biblical tradition within the apocryphal literature of Hellenistic Judaism (3 Macc 2:10-11; *Pss. Sol.* 12:6; *T. Jos.* 20:1).

For most Jews, the essence of God's promises was taken to be a share in the world to come. It was only during the second century B.C. that resurrection faith entered Jewish thought. It arose, in part, in response to the failure of this-worldly hopes for justice. During the Maccabean era, the Jews who were willing to compromise with their Greek conquerors became wealthy and influential. The pious poor who faithfully adhered to the traditions of Israel were marginalized or martyred. James' rhetorical question in 2:5 almost certainly reminded his readers of the heroic faith of the Jewish poor during the time of the Syrian invasion and the Maccabean revolt.

James' question probably also reminded them of Jesus' saying in the Sermon on the Mount that "the poor in spirit" will inherit "the kingdom of heaven" (Matt 5:3). Brosend considers James' phrasing an interpretation of the beatitude (2004, 59). Even if the Gospels were not yet in their finished written form, the oral and written traditions that were the sources of the Gospels were undoubtedly known to James.

■ **6** James restates and generalizes what he implies in his hypothetical illustration in vv 2-3: *But you dishonored the poor.* The communities have *dishonored the poor* by their favoritism.

Modern audiences might not understand James' claim. How could they dishonor someone already at the bottom of the social ladder? In first-century society, all were born with the honor of their family. Honor was not tied directly to wealth. Misfortune can cause poverty even in the best of families. Shabby clothing did not necessarily indicate these poor people were without honor.

These Jewish Christians probably knew exactly what James meant. Furthermore, he identifies the community with the poor by means of two questions. They were to consider what the rich and greedy were doing to their community.

The first question, *Are not the rich oppressing you?* uses the compound verb *katadynasteuō* (the preposition *kata* ["against"] and the verb *dynasteuō* ["hold power"]) to describe the actions of the rich. They "*oppress, exploit, dominate*" (BDAG, 516) the powerless in the Christian community. In the LXX the word characterized the outrages by the rich on the poor, widows, and orphans (e.g., Jer 7:6; 22:3; Ezek 18:7, 12, 16; 22:7, 29; Amos 4:1; 8:4). Such offenses were the antithesis of James' definition of pure religion (1:27). Why would his readers cater to those who took advantage of them and those they were to care for—"orphans and widows"?

James is fond of using hyperbole to make his point (see 2:2-4, 15-16; 3:3-6; 4:14; 5:2-6). He undoubtedly does this with his characterization of the rich. Not all rich people are heartless oppressors. James' style makes it difficult for scholars to decide whether he intended to condemn all rich people. How could any rich person possibly be a Christian, given his equation of being rich with being greedy. No philanthropic rich people appear in James!

The second question asks: *And are they not the ones who drag you into court?* The verb *drag* denotes physically moving someone from one place to another without consent. It can also be used figuratively, to attract or draw a person "**in the direction of values for inner life**" (BDAG, 318). But the violent context indicates that members of the community were being hauled into court involuntarily.

The oppression the poor were facing here was not religious persecution. They were victims of social injustice by legal decrees (Ropes 1973, 195-96). James was outraged that the "characteristic of the world's rich to oppress and humiliate the poor by 'legal' means" was taking place in the Christian community (Johnson 1995, 226).

The First-Century Meaning of Going to Court

In the first-century world, normal legal procedures were used to dishonor someone or some group perceived to be of higher, more powerful status, and recourse to such procedures was an admission of inequality. (Malina 2001a, 43)

In the first century, honorable people settled their differences outside of court.

■ **7** James continues the list of offenses by the rich in the form of questions: *Are they not blaspheming* [*blasphēmousin*] *the good name invoked over you?* Blaspheming involves injuring another's reputation—to "*slander, revile, defame*" him (BDAG, 178). Surely, the **noble name** by which the community was called is that of Christ—Christian. Were greedy Christians acting consistent with their class, betraying fellow believers and bringing shame on Christ?

Nystrom suggests, contrary to the usual assumptions about James, that *the good name* as a substitute for "Christ" indicates an early high Christology (1997, 120). To call or to invoke a name over another constitutes a statement of ownership (Deut 12:11) or special relationship (Amos 9:12; Johnson 1995, 226).

FROM THE TEXT

Standing in solidarity with the poor is at the core of the Judeo-Christian religious tradition. Both religions have suffered poverty and persecution because of their faith. Both understand that God has mercy on the powerless. This section anticipates 5:1-6, which denounces the rich even more severely and specifically names their sins.

It is difficult for the rich and powerful, even in our day, even those who are Christians, to appreciate fully just how their daily routines oppress, dominate, or exploit the poor. Perhaps, it is even more difficult for those of us who live in the affluent Western world to realize that compared to the two-thirds world, we are the rich and powerful! James invites rich Christians to humiliate themselves (1:10-11), not to expect privilege (2:1-4), and to learn from the poor how to have faith (2:5). Wesley claimed that if all Christians were more spiritually-minded, churches would be much more in tune to the needs of the poor. "A lowly state is most favorable for inward peace and growth in holiness" (Wesley 2003, 815).

Some liberation theologians have claimed that the poor are the only ones who have salvation. James certainly lends credence to such radical claims. No wonder "the indigenous peoples of Guatemala make more images of James than of other better known saints" (Tamez 1990, 77)!

Moo warns against too broad an interpretation of the phrase, "Did not God choose the poor . . . ?" (v 5 NASB) (2000, 107). Interpreting the saying within its first-century context will correct the extreme positions of liberation theology about the limits of salvation. But it will also warn rich Christians.

James' statement about God's election of the poor "to be rich in faith" reminds his readers of the loyal poor of the second century B.C. It reminds Jewish Christians too prone to cater to the rich of their own recent history of oppression. However we choose to soften James' scathing criticism of the rich to make ourselves more comfortable, we must not negate his insight that the rich have a lot to learn from the poor in matters of faith.

The class system of the first century was a pyramid with a small, upper class on the top. The economic system was not able to generate much profit. So the rich got richer by depriving those at the bottom of the pyramid. In other words, the poor generated the wealth of the rich who oppressed them. In the final analysis, James' "call is not for impartiality (which as we shall see is often quite partial in favor of the elite) but for partiality and action on behalf of the poor" (Brosend 2004, 66).

Brosend suggests that Jas 2:6 calls for more than simply patronizing the poor. We must assist them in such a way as to restore their lost honor (2004, 70). Ministry to the poor must elevate their dignity and create ways for them to determine their own destinies and make their own living. Paternalistic relationships, which do not allow people to develop and become the persons God has created them to be, are not what James has in mind.

James' diagnosis of the rich is as controversial today as it was in the first century. But James is abundantly clear: If we are to take the Bible seriously, we must consider the difficult sayings as well as the easy ones.

3. The Law of Love (2:8-13)

BEHIND THE TEXT

This section contains several references to Jesus' sayings and OT texts probably familiar to James' readers. He assumes his readers know and follow what Jesus called the great commandment: "Love the Lord your God with all your heart and with all your soul and with all your strength and with all your mind" (Luke 10:27). This commandment summarizes the first four of the Ten Commandments.

The second commandment, "Love your neighbor as yourself" (2:8; Matt 5:43; 22:39; Mark 12:33; Luke 10:27; Rom 13:9; Gal 5:14), summarizes the next six commandments. It is clear that James is addressing person-to-person relationships. He even cites two of the Ten Commandments dealing with human relationships (in v 11). Jesus had earlier commented on these same commandments in his Sermon on the Mount (Matt 5:21-30).

Murder and adultery are probably the most extreme imaginable sins against a fellow human being. The extreme nature of murder is obvious to modern people. It is the ultimate sin against a fellow human, because it ends a life. Jesus broadened this command against murder to include anger, insult, and defamation of one's brother or sister (vv 21-22).

During the first century, adultery was considered more than a moral failure affecting relationships with one's spouse and family. The male adulterer was guilty of stealing the property of the woman's husband, that is, the fertility of his wife. Adultery made it impossible for the husband to know whether or not the children his wife bore were his. Again, Jesus expands the definition of adultery to include looking at the opposite sex with lust (vv 27-28).

Brosend reviews three insights from socio-historical anthropology that are helpful here. First, the rich were extremely rich; and most people were desperately poor. And "the wealth of those at the top was only available through the deprivation of those at the bottom—the rich prospered on the backs of the poor, slave or free" (2004, 65). James simply takes for granted that the rich gained their wealth at the expense of others. They are greedy. This perspective makes it difficult for his readers to consider the rich truly Christian.

Second, first-century people assumed that there was a fixed amount of wealth. In a limited goods society, the only way to obtain more was to take it away from someone else. The people at the top "took it by force—force of arms, force of law (enforcing usurious loans resulting in the confiscation and consolidation of landholdings), and force of taxation at rates that often exceeded fifty percent" (Brosend 2004, 65).

Third, for most people "living in the first-century Mediterranean world, life was unimaginably precarious and fragile. The daily challenge was not to climb another rung up the ladder of success but simply to find or earn enough to eat to survive (Mt 6:11)" (Brosend 2004, 66).

IN THE TEXT

■ **8** James' emphasis in this verse is on *fulfilling* the royal law. The usual Greek word for keeping or observing the provisions of the Law was *tēreō* (used in v 10; see Matt 23:30). James uses instead the verb *teleō*, which means to "*carry out, accomplish, perform, fulfill*" (BDAG, 997; compare Luke 2:39 and Rom 2:27). His choice of verbs emphasizes doing exhaustively what the Law requires. A still different Greek verb (*plēroō*) refers to fulfilling the Law elsewhere in the NT (Matt 5:17; Luke 24:44; John 15:25; Rom 8:4; 13:8; Gal 5:14).

The first reference of **the royal law** is to the law God spoke to Moses. James' quotation of the command to love from Lev 19:18 embodies the spirit of the entire OT legal corpus (Nystrom 1997, 121; Davids 1982, 114). Leviticus contains God's instructions to Israel's priests as to what God expects in worship.

Leviticus 19 begins with the famous command, "Be holy because I, the LORD your God, am holy." In this context God commands, "Do not pervert justice; do not show partiality to the poor or favoritism to the great, but judge your neighbor fairly" (19:15). Verse 34 adds, "The alien living with you must be treated as one of your native-born. Love him as yourself, for you were aliens in Egypt."

Johnson plausibly suggests that since "kingdom" (*basileias*) is used in v 5, **royal law** (*nomon . . . basilikon*) may mean the "law of the kingdom." That is, "the law articulated or ratified by Jesus 'the glorious Lord'" (Johnson 1995, 230). Moo agrees that the royal law probably refers to Jesus as king. James may suggest that "completing the sum total of God's will for his people takes place in accordance with conformity to the central demand of that law, love for the neighbor" (2000, 112). Jesus was summarizing the whole law in the great commandment.

James' quotation of Jesus' second commandment uses the future tense of the verb as a command. This is the standard form used for OT commands such as the Ten Commandments (e.g., Matt 5:43; 19:18-19; 22:39). Both verbs in Jas 2:8 (***are fulfilling*** and **are doing**) are in the continuous present tense. Thus, loving one's neighbor as oneself must be a lifestyle. This is ***doing well.***

Not surprisingly, Jesus seems to influence James' use of **law** more than Paul. James uses the word **law** in each of these expressions: **the perfect law,** *the law of freedom* (1:25), **the royal law** (2:8), the *law of freedom* (2:12), and the **whole law** (2:10). Each time it means simply **law** (as it does standing alone in 2:9, 11; and 4:11). James uses different adjectives to intensify the word **law,** not modify it. The <u>royal</u> law (emphasis added) is not to be understood in opposition to some "other" law. "'Law,' above all, is what members of a community 'do'" (Brosend 2004, 69).

■ **9** James contrasts loving one's neighbor with ***showing*** favoritism toward people based on their status in society (see 2:1, 9; Lev 19:15). Loving one's neighbor and showing **favoritism** are mutually exclusive in James' mind. For James, love is an action verb. To discriminate against someone because of economic status—or any other accident of birth—is a sin. For first-century people, even one's economic status was almost always an accident of birth.

In Greek, the clause translated **you sin** is more than meets the eye in English. The word **sin** here is not a verb but a noun. James says that if you ***are showing favoritism, you are working/performing*** [*ergazesthe*, see the commentary on 1:20] ***sin*** (see the commentary on 1:15; 4:17). This verb prepares for James' discussion of faith vs. works (*erga*), which follows in the next section of the Epistle (2:14-26).

Those who give the wealthy preferential treatment are ***committing sin*** because they are violating the law calling for loving one's neighbor. A causal present participle explains the reason: *since you are being convicted* [*elencho-menoi*] *by the law as transgressors"* (see v 11). The verb *elenchō* means *"convict* or *convince* someone," to point out a wrong-doing (BDAG, 315). In light of the Law, to **show favoritism** is exposed as a **sin.**

"Since breaking Lev. 19:15 clearly reveals that Lev 19:18*c* is not being kept, the law itself exposes and convicts the sinner" (Johnson 1995, 231). It becomes obvious in the bright light of the Law that those who **show favoritism** have become *transgressors.* That is, they have overstepped or violated the "the royal law."

John Wesley sees this verse as referring to Exod 23:3: "And do not show favoritism to a poor man in his lawsuit" (2003, 814). This is not a passage James would have cited. It is true that Exod 23:2-3 advocates just and fair trials. But it also encourages witnesses not to side with the crowd or favor the poor.

■ **10** Here James applies the widely accepted Jewish principle of the unity of **the whole law** (see Deut 27:26; 4 Macc 5:20; *T. Ash.* 2:5; Philo *Leg.* 3.241; Matt 5:18-19; 19:17; 23:23; Acts 15:5; Gal 5:3). *For whoever would try to keep the whole law, but sins in one respect, has become guilty of breaking every command.*

One cannot treat the Law like a buffet line, arbitrarily choosing which laws to obey and which to ignore. Jewish nomism calls for a commitment to observe *all the law* (*holon ton nomon tērēsē*). It is a truism that failure to obey even one law makes one a "lawbreaker" (v 11; Davids 1982, 117). James' use of the traditional verb for keeping the Law may indicate he is quoting a common Jewish saying.

But James is not exercised to enforce or attack legalistic excess. It is merely to recall the community to what Jesus identifies as the central issue of the Law: love. Thus, his concern in vv 8-11 "is whether the 'royal law' of Lev 19:18 is being kept" (Johnson 1995, 232). The community could not neglect the Law's commands against partiality. To break any command was to become a sinner, standing **guilty** of breaking the whole Law (the force of the perfect tense of the concluding clause).

If **guilty** (*enochos:* "**liable, answerable**"; BDAG, 338) carries judicial force, any failure of obedience makes one liable to legal charges or penalties (Davids 1982, 116; Zodhiates 1992, 592; Laws 1980, 112). First-century Judaism debated whether breaking one command meant a person had broken every single command or the "law as a whole" (Ropes 1973, 200). James does not seem concerned about legal consequences. For him the crucial issue is the scriptural law of love. Clearly, to set it aside is to become a sinner in danger of being out of fellowship with God.

The verb *ptaiō* ("*stumble, trip*"; BDAG, 894) implies an inadvertent stumbling due to inattention. To prevent such missteps, the Pharisees constructed a fence of oral law around the Torah. Thus, they urged the faithful to do more than the Law required and less than it permitted. By playing it safe, people would not accidentally violate the Law. James does not recommend the Pharisaic approach.

■ 11 James explains the reason why (**For**) breaking the law at one point makes one "guilty of breaking all of it" (v 10). There is just one "Lawgiver" (4:12). The same God gave all of the Ten Commandments. James cites just two, from the second tablet of the Law, and in the reverse order of their sequence in the Decalogue. This sequence is also found in some manuscripts of the Hebrew Bible, in the LXX, and elsewhere in the NT (Luke 18:20; Rom 13:9). This combination of murder and adultery exemplifies the central commands of God as also found in Matt 5:21, 27; 19:18; Mark 10:19; Luke 18:20; and Rom 13:9 (Johnson 1995, 233).

James' version of the commands, **"Do not commit adultery"** and **"Do not murder,"** use the prohibitive aorist subjunctive (as in Mark 10:19 and Luke 18:20). The LXX and other NT authors, however, use the negated future tense, literally translating the Hebrew: *You will not commit adultery* and *You will not murder.* James follows Koine Greek grammar, instead of the Semitic pattern.

James applies his examples to illustrate his point about the unity of the Law (see v 10): **If you do not commit adultery but do commit murder, you have become a lawbreaker.** The two verbs for committing adultery and murdering are in the emphatic present tense. The verb in the conclusion, **have become,** is in the perfect tense. This suggests that the effects of breaking a commandment in the past has continuing consequences in the present. James does not suggest that murder is less "wrong" than adultery.

Why did James pick these two commands? Were they particularly appropriate to his first audience? Moo thinks James considered favoritism a result of anger, and thus a form of murder. Even if one is not committing adultery, one may be murdering in the broadened sense that Jesus used in the Sermon on the Mount (Moo 2000, 115). Davids notes that "Jer. 7:6; 22:3; Amos 8:4; Sirach 34:26; Testament of Gad 4:6-7, and 1 John 3:15 all associate murder with the failure to care for the poor" (1989, 74).

■ 12 James instructs his hearers: *Thus [Houtōs] speak and act in this way [houtōs]: as those who are about to be judged by God based on the law of freedom.* The adverb *houtōs* appears twice ("so . . . so," NRSV). The first refers to what has come before. James has just reminded them that if they fail to keep any part of the Law, they have broken "the whole law" (v 10). The second refers to what follows: They are to live their entire lives (comprehended in the verbs **Speak and act**) in the constant awareness that God will judge them.

The verb in the second clause is the participle *mellontes* (**being about to**). It has an "eschatological edge," with the judgment not being too far off (Johnson 1995, 233). This is followed by the passive infinitive, **to be judged.** This is a "divine passive"—God is obviously the Judge, although James does not explicitly state it (unlike my paraphrase). This usage is common throughout the NT. That God is the Judge was a self-evident part of the NT worldview. "The nature of this book demands that we see him even when he is not mentioned" (Wallace 1996, 438).

The phrase "**by means of a law of freedom**" immediately follows "**Speak and act in this way.**" This emphatic position of the prepositional phrase stresses that something is more crucial than an awareness of impending judgment. It is the knowledge that the **law** will be the basis of judgment (see Ropes 1973, 201). This is good news, since it is specifically **the law that gives freedom** (see on 1:25). John Wesley identifies the law of freedom as the gospel: "the law of universal love, which alone is perfect freedom" (2003, 814). Those who do not adhere to the gospel in word and deed will be condemned as transgressors.

■ **13** James emphasizes mercy in the midst of his discussion of the law and warning of impending judgment. *For the judgment will be unmerciful to the one who has not been merciful. But mercy triumphs over judgment.*

The participle *katakauchatai* (**triumphing**) is from the same verb root translated rejoice/boast in 1:9 (see the commentary; see 3:14; 4:16). This is basically boasting based on superior power (BDAG, 517). The present tense emphasizes the ongoing triumph of mercy over judgment. Mercy is winning. We might assume that this refers to God's mercy demonstrated in the life, ministry, and death of Jesus Christ, but James never makes this Christian conviction explicit.

The first clause of this verse may be a negative form of Jesus' positive statement in the beatitude: "Blessed are the merciful, for they will be shown mercy" (Johnson 1995, 234). It aptly summarizes Jesus' teaching in Matt 18:21-35—the parable of the unmerciful servant. James does not identify his source. But it is probably no coincidence that the NT's strongest encouragement to show mercy because one has received mercy is found only in Matthew and James. Matthew, like James, is usually identified as written primarily to Jewish Christians.

Moo understands **mercy** here to concern human interpersonal relations. This is not just about one's relationship with God. James is "making a point about the way in which the mercy we show towards others shows our desire to obey the law of the kingdom and, indirectly therefore, of a heart made right by the work of God's grace" (Moo 2000, 118). In light of the preceding context and James' social situation, Brosend adds: "the call is really not for impartiality but for partiality and action on behalf of the poor" (Brosend 2004, 66).

Neighbor Love. Despite James' lack of direct reference to Jesus Christ apart from 1:1, we find many allusions to Christ in this Epistle. One is in its emphasis on "Love your neighbor as yourself" (2:8). Although this was originally stated in Lev 19:18*b*, it is associated with Jesus' summary of the Law and the Prophets in the NT (see Matt 5:43; 22:39; Mark 12:31; Luke 10:27; Rom 13:9; Gal 5:14). Pre-Christian Jewish tradition never cites Lev 19:18*b*, but it is the OT passage most frequently quoted by NT writers (Matt 5:43; 19:19; Mark 12:31, 33; Rom 13:9; Gal 5:14; Jas 2:8).

James has twice referred to his audience as **those who love God** (1:12; 2:5). He could take for granted that as pious Jews, his readers were committed to what Jesus called the first and greatest commandment. Its charge to "Love the Lord your God . . ." was part of the Shema (Deut 6:4-9). Devout Jews recited this daily and carried a copy of it in phylacteries on their wrists and foreheads.

James' concern throughout his letter is with the second half of the great commandment. He assumes what 1 John (4:12, 20, 21; 5:2) makes explicit: The evidence of a believer's adherence to the first commandment is demonstrated in fulfilling the second. If we truly love God, we will prove this by loving our neighbor.

Mere words and emotions were insufficient expression of love. The key verb is "acted out." James was concerned that people were loved by caring for their physical and spiritual needs. Saying that one loved his or her neighbors without doing anything to meet their needs did not meet his understanding of the "love your neighbor" criteria. Words alone were empty and meaningless. They definitely would not reflect obedience to the second commandment.

Favoritism. James' concern in this passage is with the favoritism his communities were showing based on people's wealth or poverty. They were not treating everyone as equally valuable children of God. First-century people, as a rule, would "consider all persons in their society as 'equal.' Money is not the determiner of one's social standing or status ranking as it is in our [Western] society; rather, birth is" (Malina 2001a, 99). So the favoritism of James' audience probably violated both unwritten social codes and the second commandment.

Theologically, this passage reminds us that God created all human beings. Each one should be respected and treated equally. No segment of society can be ignored by the church. No human need is beyond its purview. Christians are called to minister to the physical, mental, and spiritual needs of every level of our society. This includes those considered rich, middle class, and poor.

But James gave special consideration to the poor. Although this might be perceived as reverse favoritism, he was merely "leveling the playing field." The powerless need advocates to free them from their oppression by the unmerciful powerful.

Certainly, for a variety of obvious reasons, some people are better equipped than others to understand and minister to particular groups—education, background, and experience. But all Christians are called to actively love their neighbor as themselves.

Those judged by society as outcasts and those with low self-esteem need to know that human beings are all equal before God. All have something to contribute to the community. All can actively love their neighbors, regardless of their intelligence or wealth. Those who are proud of their achievements need to understand that they can learn from those with perceived lower achievements. They are no better or worse than their neighbor. Christians need the active love of their fellow Christians and human beings. Christians need, for their own personal spiritual development, to actively love their neighbors.

Law. This passage also deals with the function of God's law in the Christian's life. Christians cannot pick and choose which of God's commands they will follow. There is no choosing behaviors based on the likelihood of being "caught." God is everywhere and knows everything. Everyone is headed for judgment and needs to understand his or her predicament. Fortunately, Christians belong to a merciful God. Because his mercy triumphs over judgment, they are saved!

Mercy. There are several apparent allusions to the teaching of Jesus in vv 14-15. Consider the prayer Jesus taught his disciples in Matthew: "For if you forgive men when they sin against you, your heavenly Father will also forgive you. But if you do not forgive men their sins, your Father will not forgive your sins" (6:14-15).

James says that *judgment will be unmerciful to the one who has not shown mercy* (v 13). These are hard sayings for those who think superficially about salvation by faith alone. But it strikes at the core of what James is saying in his letter. If there has really been a change in one's heart—if one really loves God with all one's heart, soul, mind, and strength—then that one will forgive others and will show mercy. Those who do not forgive or show mercy are living in rebellion against God and his commandment to "Love your neighbor as yourself."

James and Jesus

The only place James mentions Jesus by name in his Epistle is in 1:1. There he identifies himself as the slave of God and of the Lord Jesus Christ. In 5:8, he talks about the appearing (*parousia*) of the Lord, which is usually associated in the NT with Jesus' promised second coming. This reference is followed by several references to "lord," which are OT references, usually attributed to God the Father. James 5:14 encourages believers to anoint the sick in the name of the Lord and assures them that the Lord will raise the sick person.

James seems to make no real distinction between the Father and the Son, except in the first verse. Can we assume that, since this is the only distinction James makes between them, when James refers to **Lord** (*kyrios*) he means Jesus Christ. In many passages James uses "God" (*theos*) to refer to God the Father. But is it possible, even more likely, that he refers to God as a unity, as in the OT rather than as after the consensus of the ecumenical creeds prevailed? If this is true, does James take for granted the preexistence of Christ and his activity in the OT era? This is made explicit in the late first century Gospel of John: "In the beginning was the Word, and the Word was with God, and the Word was God" (John 1:1). Where does James stand on the way toward Nicene Christology?

B. Faith and Actions (2:14-26)

Two formal indicators (v 14) mark the beginning of the second major division of James' exposition. These consist of (1) a question: **What good is it . . . ?** and (2) a direct address: *my brothers and sisters.* James closes this division with a symmetrical comparison, summarizing the conclusion already argued (vv 12-13; Bauckham 1999, 65).

This division is classically referred to as James' treatise on "faith and works." But "works" in English-speaking Christian circles has developed a specialized and pejorative meaning. So I use the neutral term "actions." This speaks clearly to those familiar with the proverbial saying, "Actions speak louder than words." James believes the actions of Christians reflect what they truly believe. He would probably agree with the above saying. But he would add that words also reflect one's interior condition.

This familiar division on faith and actions consists of three sections:

- The first uses an illustration of one possible (but wholly unsatisfactory) response to the obvious needs of a poor person to conclude that faith without action is dead (vv 14-17).
- James begins the second section in classic diatribe style (vv 18-20). An unnamed, imaginary antagonist (**someone**: *tis*) attempts sharply to distinguish between faith and action. James responds that no distinction can be made, because one's faith is evidenced by one's actions. Thus, faith without action is useless.
- The third section (vv 21-26) gives two examples of OT personages. The actions of one man and one woman revealed their faith and resulted in their salvation.

1. Faith Without Action Is Dead (2:14-17)

BEHIND THE TEXT

This passage builds on James' earlier discussion of the royal law: "Love your neighbor as yourself." He has already argued that favoritism violates this Law (2:1-13). Here, he addresses his communities' lack of social concern for their neighbors.

James' concern for the physical needs of people reflects his debt to Judaism and the contribution of Judaism to Christianity. In contrast to Greco-Roman culture, Jews believed that the body was essential to human identity. Most Pharisees believed in bodily resurrection in the last days. If the body matters to God enough to reconstitute it in the final age, the body was important. Jews assumed that if they did not care for the bodies of their neighbors, they were neglecting their persons.

Like most Greeks, Romans, and other non-Jews, Sadducees denied the resurrection of the body. Most Sadducees held that the earthly life was all there was. Greco-Romans believed the body imprisoned the soul. The soul was thus always looking for a way to escape back to the ethereal "forms" from which it came. So the body was something to "punish" and not specifically associated with who a person was.

IN THE TEXT

■ **14** James begins by asking: **What good is it . . . ?** *What is the benefit* [*ophelos*], *my brothers and sisters, if someone says he or she has faith, but does not have actions?* This was a common question for the moralists of the day. They were concerned with behavior that shapes character rather than merely the profession of ideals (Johnson 1995, 237).

This is James' first specific reference to the potential contrast between faith and actions. The conditional (subjunctive) mood used in his first question is one indication that he is engaged in deliberative rhetoric. Another is his use of the word *benefit* (vs. disadvantage).

James attempts to persuade his audience to decide in favor of his perspective—that faith and actions are inseparable. Thus, he simultaneously attempts to dissuade them from assigning any moral value to faith without actions.

His question is rhetorical: *What is the benefit?* always expects a negative answer (see 1 Cor 15:32; Davids 1982, 120). James finds it impossible to believe anyone has saving faith who fails to reflect it in his or her lifestyle.

James uses the indefinite pronoun *tis*, **a man**, better translated **someone** in v 18. This hypothetical ***anyone*** serves as an example of all who might claim they have faith, but do nothing. The infinitive **to have** indicates that James is quoting indirectly. The person had said, "I have faith."

The subjunctive mood in the second clause—**but he or she does not have actions**—indicates that the person had not explicitly said, "I have no actions." It is only the person's lifestyle that reveals he or she has no actions.

The second question—**"Can this kind of faith save him?"**—refers to alleged faith that exhibits no actions. James does not ask whether faith in general can save. Rather, he asks: **Can faith that does nothing save?** Apparently, James distinguishes two different kinds of faith. One is merely mental assent. The other is such deeply held conviction that it affects the very core of the person's being. Such faith is obvious from one's conduct in everyday life.

James is asking an eschatological question (see v 13). Can so-called faith, which does not express itself in acts of love, save one at the final judgment? James is not the first or only voice in Scripture to require actions as evidence of faith.

The OT prophets condemned ritual piety when it was not accompanied by justice for the poor (Amos 2:4-16; Mic 6:6-8). John the Baptist required "fruit in keeping with repentance." The tangible evidence he expected involved giving clothing and food to those in need (Luke 3:7-11).

Jesus taught that "every good tree bears good fruit, but a bad tree bears bad fruit" (Matt 7:17). He warned that "not everyone who says to me, 'Lord, Lord,' will enter the kingdom of heaven, but only he who does the will of my Father who is in heaven" (Matt 7:21). His description of the final judgment identifies the criterion as actions. Eternal life and punishment are based on feeding the hungry, providing shelter, clothing the naked, visiting the sick and imprisoned (Matt 25:31-46).

Paul is often misrepresented as the champion of salvation by faith alone (Rom 3:21-28). When he actually refers to justification by faith, he has in mind the beginning of the Christian life, not its final outcome. He emphasizes the "obedience that comes from faith" (Rom 1:5; see 15:18). He insists that "God 'will give to each person according to what he has done'" (Rom 2:6; see 2 Cor 5:10). Paul's letters are full of ethical instructions on how Christians are to live.

James insists so-called faith alone is not able to save, because *it is the "word of truth" implanted by God that is "able to save their souls"* (v 18). James, no more than any other biblical witness, believes that authentic faith will transform the character and conduct of those who have it. Biblical faith is not merely mental assent or a momentary transaction to be put on the shelf until needed to secure entrance to heaven. True faith is only present in believers, "as 1:22-25 argues, if they are 'doers of the word and not hearers only'" (Johnson 1995, 238).

■ **15-16** This long sentence begins with a conditional **If** (*ean*) and the subjunctive mood, indicating a hypothetical situation: *"If a brother or sister exists [hyparchōsin] naked and lacking daily food . . ."* Such an instance of total destitution and deprivation would clearly call for immediate attention! The person's survival is at stake.

The Bible treats nakedness caused by poverty (vs. sexual exhibitionism) as evidence of extreme vulnerability. "It is associated with poverty (Rev 3:17) and shame (Gen 3:10; Ezek 16:7; Rev 3:18)" (Johnson 1995, 238; see also Matt 25:36). The expression **daily food,** in secular Greek, functioned much like the English phrase "daily bread." The lack of it showed "a poor person's need as urgent" (Ropes 1973, 206).

The use of **sister** (*adelphē*) as the female counterpart of **brother** is comparatively rare in the NT (see, e.g., Matt 12:50; 19:29; Rom 16:1, 15; 1 Cor 7:15; 9:5; 1 Tim 5:2; Phlm 2). Here it seems to emphasize that the destitute of both genders are not unknown strangers. They are members of the community. This heightens the awfulness of inaction.

James illustrates one possible, but inappropriate, response to this dire situation. This is another of his exaggerated examples, this time of what faith without action might look like. *"Were someone in your community to say to them: 'Depart in peace, be warmed and be filled with food,' but not give them the necessities of the body . . ."* (v 16). James refers to someone from the same community, who claims to be saved by faith, not an unrepentant sinner. His continued use of the subjunctive mood reminds us that he considers such a situation not only reprehensible, but incomprehensible.

The one with faith without actions gives these poor destitute brothers and sisters three superficially pious exhortations. The plural verbal forms indicate that he or she addressed several destitute persons. The exhortations were hollow because the needy had no means to fulfill them. The one with the means would not give them what they needed. Instead, empty platitudes urged them immediately to get out of sight: *Go away* (*hyagete*)!

The full command: *Depart in peace,* is a common biblical blessing. *Peace* refers to the goodness and blessedness that is given by God to those who walk according to his will (Moo 2000, 125). Here, the blessing serves as a religious cover, a pious camouflage, for the failure to meet the poor person's needs (Johnson 1995, 239). The heartless professing Christian "is telling the poor person to get his life in shape and then God will bless him" (Taylor 2007, 1). Such alleged Christian cannot plead ignorance of the need. His or her "blessing" expresses the implicit wish that food and clothing might miraculously be given the poor person, without the necessity of acting himself or herself.

James repeats the identical phrase he used in v 14: *"What is the benefit?"* Again, he expects the same "no" answer. Johnson translates the question:

"*What is the use?*" He suggests that this is a harsh question that tries to convince the readers of how inappropriate their position is (1995, 239).

Verses 15 and 16 pose the same question as v 14. But they illustrate what James means by actions. James is perfectly clear that by "works" he is not referring to doing rituals or keeping dietary and purity laws. He refers rather to obviously appropriate social intervention. The actions he calls for involve urgent care for the mental and physical needs of one's fellow believers, fellow human beings.

■ 17 James uses three different grammatical emphases to clarify his point. He is discussing a **faith . . . not accompanied by action.** This cannot be a true faith, which naturally manifests itself in social action. He adds, ***"Thus, this kind of faith, if it does not have actions, is dead by itself."***

- First, the article (*hē*) before **faith** is probably anaphoric. That is, it picks up James' earlier reference to the so-called faith of 2:14 (Martin 1988, 85).
- Second, James describes the kind of faith he has in mind as **faith** that ***does not have actions.***
- Third, he emphasizes that this supposed **faith** exists alone, all **by itself** (*kath heautēn*). Now that he has been perfectly clear, he states that this action-less faith **is dead.** "The two things which are opposed are not faith and works (as with Paul) but a living faith and a dead faith" (Ropes 1973, 207).

FROM THE TEXT

James teaches the simple truth that God created human beings as whole persons. What Christians truly think in their minds and believe in their hearts will come out in their actions. Many like to imagine that belief or faith alone is all that is necessary for salvation. But James makes it abundantly clear that only faith confirmed by appropriate subsequent actions brings final salvation.

James is not refuting the doctrine of Paul, only those who abuse it. The dead faith of those who refuse the hungry and naked is of no use to them, just as he is of no use to the poor person (Wesley 2003, 816).

The faith-demonstrating actions James calls for here are tangible expressions of obedience to "the royal law": "Love your neighbor as yourself" (2:8). Those who claim to follow Christ claim to love God and to love their neighbor. Authentic faith is evidenced by taking care of the mental and physical needs of the needy people around them. The bodily care of one's neighbors shows both the genuineness of one's love for God and love for them.

Today, many evangelical Christians judge whether people are "saved" or not by their adherence to certain defined social standards (e.g., whether they smoke or drink), by their church attendance, and by their support of a local

JAMES

2:15-17

institutional church (whether they tithe). James would probably assign such evidence of true faith to the same category as ritual actions and purity laws. He would insist: "This is not what I'm talking about!"

Individually and corporately, Christians need to ask themselves: What are we doing to meet the spiritual, mental, emotional, and physical needs of our neighbors? "If the verbal profession of faith does not come to life in acts applicable to those naked and hungry and living on the margin, *they* will die!" (Johnson 1995, 239; see 1 John 3:17-18). And what will be our destiny if we do nothing?

As individuals, Christians can make a difference in the physical lives of needy people. Corporately, Christians can make a difference in defeating entrenched systems that oppress and denigrate their neighbors, locally and in the larger global village we share with them.

Social justice is not just for far-out radicals, it is at the heart and soul of both Judaism and historic Christianity. Do Christians truly love their neighbors as themselves? If so, James says Christians must do something about the plight of those who are destitute, who have no options, and who are unable to help themselves.

2. Faith Evidenced by Action (2:18-20)

BEHIND THE TEXT

Judaism has always been an ethical religion. Its high ethical standards were one of the reasons many Gentiles in the first century were attracted to it. This was true even of males, who found the ritual of initiation to full Jewish status reprehensible. Paul is merely one example of early Christian preachers who found a welcome hearing for the gospel, in part, because he rejected the necessity of circumcision as a requirement for Gentile inclusion among God's people.

Apparently, this emphasis on believing in Jesus of Nazareth as the Messiah was misinterpreted by some converts. They misunderstood the concept of salvation by faith. Perhaps, this partially explains the conflict between Paul and the Judaizers. They could not separate keeping the purity and dietary laws from the ethical and social standards of the Torah. Paul could and did. For even though he emphasized salvation by faith, he always included ethical exhortations in his letters.

James appears to be on the same theological page as Paul, although he articulates the issue differently. James believed in salvation by faith and that it included ethical standards. James seems, however, to address different issues and a different audience from Paul. There were among his readers some who saw no correlation between what they believed and how they behaved. Perhaps they had replaced concern for the whole law with a kind of mental belief that did not affect their behavior. Gnostic ideas were already appearing during the first century. Perhaps some in the community had been influenced by Jewish Gnosticism.

Gnosticism

Gnosticism was and is a perspective that attaches itself to different religions and belief structures. The focus is on receiving special liberating or saving knowledge. How one behaves is not as important as what one knows. The early church fathers compared gnostic teaching to the many-headed Hydra (serpent or monster) of Greek legend (Hippolytus, *Haer.* 5.11.1; Rudolph 1984, 53). In other words, it was hard to pin down precisely what the gnostics believed:

1. "There was no gnostic 'church' or normative theology, no gnostic rule of faith nor any dogmas of exclusive importance" (Rudolph 1984, 53).

2. Gnostic systems attached themselves to "host" religions, so they did not have their own tradition, sacred books or stories, only borrowed ones from the host religion or a mixture of host religious ideas (Rudolph 1984, 53-55).

The name Gnosticism comes from the Greek word *gnosis,* meaning **knowledge.** Gnostics claimed to have special, secretly revealed knowledge. They were "gnostics" or "knowers, people of understanding" (Rudolph 1984, 55). This *gnosis,* according to their belief, had a "liberating and redeeming effect" (Rudolph 1984, 55). It was given by revelation "only to the elect who were capable of receiving it" (Rudolph 1984, 55). The basic ideas are that:

1. In each person there is a divine "spark" that comes from the divine world and has to be awakened or recovered (Rudolph 1984, 57). For some people this is very easy to do, because the spark glows brighter; for others it requires more effort.

2. They believed in dualism on the "cosmological and anthropological levels" (Rudolph 1984, 57). So there are good and evil gods/goddesses or heavenly beings as well as good and evil people. Good and evil forces or beings are of equal strength in pure dualism. So the question of who will win in the end remains to be determined.

3. The transcendent God is the "unknown God," and "beyond all that is visible or sensible" (Rudolph 1984, 58). Angels and other heavenly beings played an important role in the creation of the world. The gnostic creation stories explain why things are the way they are (Rudolph 1984, 58)

4. As far as gnostic soteriology (doctrine of salvation) is concerned, God/god/goddess and his or her helpers open up a way in which the soul can escape. What they escape to or by what methods is not always the same and debated among scholars (Rudolph 1984, 58).

This is where the special knowledge comes in. Those with special knowledge know how to get the God/gods/goddesses and their helpers to "reveal the things that are difficult to interpret and the things that are secret" (*Trim. Prot.* XIII, 35; Robinson 1981).

5. In gnostic eschatology (end-times beliefs), the deliverance of the heavenly soul has cosmic significance (Rudolph 1984, 59). So when a soul is liberated from its earthly body and condition, this will affect the gods/goddesses as well as the rest of the heavens.

For a fuller discussion see Kurt Rudolph, *Gnosis: The Nature and History of Gnosticism*; and James M. Robinson, ed., *The Nag Hammadi Library*.

IN THE TEXT

Verses 18-20 are among the most difficult in the NT both to translate and to understand in detail. The textual variants in the manuscript tradition indicate that ancient scribes had similar difficulties.

These verses illustrate the diatribe style of ancient rhetoric. The author invents a conversation partner, who serves as his opponent. This imaginary antagonist poses competing arguments, which allow the author to advance his argument (Johnson 1995, 239). It is difficult at times to distinguish between speakers—James and his opponent. By v 20, the speaker is obviously James. But does he begin his response to the opponent's challenge in v 18*b* with *kagō*, v 19*a* with *sy*, or v 19*b* with *kalōs*? (See Johnson 1995, 239-40; Martin 1988, 86-88; Davids 1982, 123-24; Dibelius, 1975, 154-58.)

■ **18** Although the meaning of this verse is fairly straightforward, the translation of *All'* as **But** has been disputed. It normally serves as an "adversative particle . . . indicating a difference with or contrast to what precedes" (BDAG, 44). Some scholars, however, take *alla* here as an emphatic particle, following the implied negatives in 2:14-17. Others think "the objection has disappeared from the text; only James' reply remains" (Davids 1982, 123). Since ancient Greek had no quotation marks, it is unclear where the quotation ends. As it reads in the NIV, if the antagonist is supposed to be contradicting James, he isn't! (Brosend 2004, 73-74).

The Greek text does indicate the relative emphases on **faith** (*pistin*) vs. **actions**. The straw man begins the discussion by separating the two: "**You have faith; *and* I have actions.**" James replies that a person cannot have one without the other.

James' response seems to begin with the demand that the objector show his faith without actions: **Show me your faith without deeds, and I will show my faith by what I do.** In Greek, ***by my actions*** immediately follows the verb **show**; and **faith** stands in the emphatic final position in the sentence.

Pistis is the common Greek word for **faith** or ***trust***. It can refer to true piety, genuine religion. But it can refer to what one believes, a "***body of faith***" or "***teaching***" (BDAG, 820). James insists that **faith** needs ***actions*** (*erga*), because belief in a doctrine or teaching "represents only one side of true piety" (BDAG, 820). He wants his hearers to realize that faith is more than mental assent to a body of teaching. To be genuine, one's deeply held beliefs call for appropriate action.

I translate the Greek plural noun *erga* as **actions** to avoid the pejorative connotations the traditional translation as "works" (KJV) conveys in modern evangelical Christian vocabulary. With reference to human beings, *erga* carries the meaning of actions "exhibiting a consistent moral character" (BDAG, 390). James summarizes his definition of faith evidenced by actions. Verses 14-17 offered concrete examples of what he means by "a consistent moral character."

■ **19** James directly addresses his imaginary opponent as **You** (singular). He identifies what the antagonist believes citing the traditional formula of Jewish orthodoxy from the Shema (Deut 6:4): **You believe that there is one God.**

The definite article before **God** indicates that the author meant for God to be the subject. Some ancient manuscripts omit the article, calling for the translation, **there is one God.** Most scholars, however, consider the article original and favor the translation, "God is one" (so NASB, NRSV). This makes no difference in the meaning.

James affirms the correctness of this confession of faith with **You are doing well.** His antagonist believes "*appropriately, . . . in a manner free from objection*" (BDAG, 505). But the stinging sarcasm of James' next statement indicates that such correct opinions are not enough. **Even the demons believe that** *and tremble with fear.*

The demons do not respond to their belief with reverential awe and obedient trust. Their certainty that this one God exists makes them **shudder** with fright. Ancient people often "regarded the very pronouncing of the name of a god as having the power to provoke fear and terror" (Moo 2000, 131). James' verb choice, *phrissousin,* "the involuntary reaction of the body in shaking" (Johnson 1995, 241), is particularly appropriate in this context (Moo 2000, 131).

> The point is that the knowledge of who God is does not save them; in fact, it is this very knowledge which makes them shudder . . . ! A faith which cannot go beyond this level is worse than useless. (Davids 1982, 125-26)

■ **20** Continuing in typical diatribe style, James addresses his antagonist directly, **"O senseless human being."** The word translated **man** (*anthrōpe*) is the generic term for human beings. The adjective *kenos* (**foolish**) describes him as **empty-headed,** "*foolish, senseless*" (BDAG, 539). His is not an intellectual, but a moral failure—a "stubborn, 'hard-hearted' ignorance" (Moo 2000, 132).

In Greek, the address follows James' initial question, which expects a response. He does not ask about the morality or possibility of **faith without**

deeds. He does not assume that such an empty-headed man actually wants *to know* anything. His question merely gives him the opportunity to offer scriptural evidence that actions confirm faith in vv 21-26.

The question is common to diatribe, *But do you wish to know . . . ?* Does this person **want evidence** that *faith without actions is barren?* Is he "willing to recognize" (NASB) his error? Some later scribes found the adjective *argē*, **barren** or **useless,** describing faith in the best Greek manuscripts, unusual. Manuscripts that were the basis for the KJV replace it with "dead" (*nekra*), in keeping with James' use in 2:17 and 26.

But in 1:15 James alluded to desire giving birth to sin and sin giving birth to death. In 1:18 he claimed that God birthed us as firstfruits. So the metaphors of birth and barrenness are not unexpected. James may make a subtle play on words between the Greek roots meaning action (*erg-*) and barren (*arg-*).

FROM THE TEXT

The Protestant Reformer Martin Luther (1483—1546) was troubled by Jas 2:14-20. He was fighting a battle similar to Paul's against those who insisted upon "works"—the observance of certain religious rituals to be acceptable to God. The "works" Paul resisted were Jewish purity and dietary laws imposed on his non-Jewish converts. Luther fought "works" in the form of the abuse of indulgences, purchased in exchange for punishment in purgatory. The "works" James defended were actions ministering physical care for needy neighbors, which his opponents neglected in favor of religious rituals.

Only the first edition of Luther's *Preface to the New Testament* in 1522 contained his infamous negative quotation about the book of James:

> In a word St. John's Gospel and his first epistle, St. Paul's epistles, especially Romans, Galatians, and Ephesians, and St. Peter's first epistle are the books that show you Christ and teach you all that is necessary and salvatory for you to know, even if you were never to see or hear any other book or doctrine. Therefore St. James' epistle is really an epistle of straw, compared to these others, for it has nothing of the nature of the gospel about it. But more of this in the other prefaces. (Luther 1960, 362)

Luther also writes in his *Preface to the New Testament*: "For where works and charity do not abound, there the belief is not right; the Gospel does not apply, and Christ is not rightly known" (Luther 1863, 79). His negative assessment of James was made in comparison to the exalted Christology of John, Peter, and Paul. Luther omitted his "straw" comment in all subsequent editions of his *Preface to the New Testament*. Unlike many conservative-evangelical scholars today, he did not identify the author of James as the brother of Jesus nor accept his status as an apostle.

James was fighting a battle different from Paul and Luther. His readers needed to understand that real faith produced a changed lifestyle, a change in behavior. James' opponents were paying lip service to the church's faith. They thought their confession of faith meant that nothing else was required of them. James was trying to show his readers that true faith results in godly actions.

This passage speaks clearly to our current generation. James would certainly agree with this section of a recent popular song, *I Need to Wake Up*: "I am not an island. / I am not alone. / I am my intentions, / Trapped here in this flesh and bone" (Etheridge 2007). Faith, belief, even good intentions are not enough, if they don't work themselves out in what Christians do.

The younger generation of Christians are looking at current lifestyles and actions and comparing them to what the older generation of Christians says. When Christians do what they say, their children believe them and are willing to follow their Christ. But when what Christians do contradicts what they say, their children look for their own way and denounce their parents' hypocrisy. James' message on faith and actions is as relevant and essential today as it was in the first century.

3. Old Testament Examples of Faith in Action (2:21-26)

BEHIND THE TEXT

James selects scriptural examples already familiar to his audience. Abraham and Rahab, although social opposites, both serve as examples of faith in action. Before the law of Moses was given, Abraham was justified by doing what God asked. James' appeal to Abraham is not surprising, given his generally accepted status as the father of all Jews.

But Rahab is another matter. A former prostitute, she was justified by extending hospitality to the Hebrew spies.

In Jewish tradition, Rahab was celebrated as a proselyte and a model of hospitality. . . . The story of Rahab in Josh 2:1-21 already makes clear that Rahab's deeds were an expression of *faith*. . . . Rahab's faith is also singled out by Heb 11:31, and the examples of Abraham and Rahab are combined by *1 Clem.* 10 and 12. (Johnson 1995, 245)

Hospitality was an important ancient virtue. Paul lists it among the qualifications for church leaders in 1 Tim 3:2 and Titus 1:8. In Rom 12:13, Paul includes it as one of the ways love is acted out in community. The entire concern of 3 John is with the challenges the early church faced with respect to extending or withholding hospitality.

In ancient times, receiving travelers into one's home was not just a nice thing to do. It could actually save their lives and protect them from thieves and sickness. There were public places to stay along the main roads; but they

107

were for those who were not fortunate enough to know anyone in the area. Christian and Jewish missionaries carried letters of introduction so they could stay with other believers or friends of believers along the way (Acts 9:1-2; 18:27; 22:5; Rom 16:1-2; 1 Cor 16:3, 10-11; 2 Cor 3:1; 8:23-24; Phil 2:25-30; Phlm; 3 John 5-8, 12).

James' choice of Rahab's actions, which resulted in her and her family's holistic salvation, highlighted an important loving action. The spread of Christianity depended on Christians giving hospitality to unknown Christians in their travels.

The NT uses several different words for hospitality. The most common ones are related to the root word *xenos* ("stranger"). The active verb form (*xenizō*) means **receive as a guest, entertain.** The passive voice means stay with someone (BDAG, 681). The church leaders were to be *philoxenon* (loving strangers). They were not only to receive someone as a guest but also to do it with kindness or friendliness (*philos*).

Other words associated with hospitality are occasionally used with the root meanings of "receive" as a guest—*dechomai* and *lambanō*. James uses an intensive form of the first verb (*hypodexamenē*) in his description of Rahab (v 25). These words indicate that the virtue of hospitality had to do with protection, feeding, and housing those needing these. Included were friends and strangers, but particularly strangers.

IN THE TEXT

■ 21 James introduces the example of Abraham in vv 21-24 with a rhetorical question that expects a "yes" answer. James has shown how ridiculous it is to claim to be a believer and not be involved in social ministry. Even demons are monotheists.

Here James employs the example of Abraham, the common **ancestor** (*patēr*; Gen 17:4-5) of all Jews. Most Jews considered *father* Abraham the prototypical righteous man. James reaches back into their shared Jewish understanding to legitimate his position on saving faith. He appeals to the familiar *Akedah*-narrative, the binding of Isaac in Gen 22. **Was not our father Abraham justified by actions when he offered up Isaac his son on the altar?**

The verb **Was . . . justified** is a divine passive, since God is one who **considered** Abraham **righteous for what he did.** Abraham's willingness to sacrifice his son and heir demonstrated the authenticity of his faith. The verb *edikaiōth,* **was justified,** is difficult to translate

> because of its frequent use by Paul in contexts opposing righteousness by faith and "works of the law" (Rom 2:13; 3:4, 20, 24, 26, 28, 30; 4:2, 5; 5:1, 9; 8:30, 33; Gal 2:16-17; 3:8, 11, 24) and the complex use of the

verb and its cognates in the OT (e.g., LXX Gen 38:26; Exod 23:7; Deut 25:1; Pss 50:6; 81:3; 142:2; Sir 1:22). (Johnson 1995, 242)

As with any word, this verb must be given the meaning its author intended within its own context. Verse 18 clearly indicates that faith is demonstrated by actions. They are actions that only a person with true faith and a right relationship with God can produce.

Wesley attempts to find common ground between James and Paul, explaining that James

> does not speak of the same justification. . . . [Abraham] was justified, therefore, in St. Paul's sense, (that is, accounted righteous,) by faith, antecedent to his works. He was justified in St. James's sense, (that is, made righteous,) by works, consequent to his faith. So that St. James's justification by works is the fruit of St. Paul's justification by faith. (Wesley 2003, 816)

This observation helps clarify the kind of actions to which James refers (see Heb 11:17-19). James implies that Abraham was justified *after* offering up Isaac. Does he mean that his righteousness was not obvious before? Johnson suggests translating *edikaiōth* "shown to be righteous," which is intelligible even in a post-Pauline context (1995, 242).

■ **22** James says **You** [singular] **see** as a response to the foolish person he addresses in v 20. *Blepeis*, **you see,** is better translated *you notice* or *you discover* (BDAG, 179). James uses another verb of perception (*orate,* **You see**) in v 24.

This example should help the foolish person understand that Abraham's *faith was working together with his actions; and from his actions, his faith was made mature* (*eteleiōth*, "perfect"). Faith is important, but it must always work with actions to be complete.

The two verbs, *synergei* (*was working together with*) and *eteleiōthē* (*was made mature*), take the reader back to 1:3-4. There, James states his objective to help his audience become mature/perfect (*te teleion*). James addresses Christians to help them understand what must happen in their lives if they are to become mature Christians. Verse 3 suggests one means: **the testing of your faith develops perseverance.**

■ **23** James refers to Gen 15:6 and 2 Chr 20:7 to legitimize his position. He writes, **And the scripture was fulfilled that says, "Abraham believed God, and it was credited to him as righteousness."** As a result, **he was called God's friend** (see also Exod 33:11).

In the NT, the verb translated **was fulfilled** (*eplērōthē*) frequently designates how Scripture texts were completed in subsequent events (Johnson 1995, 243). Significantly, James uses it only here. He quotes the LXX of Gen 15:6 almost exactly. It differs only in the spelling of Abraham (James uses

Abraam; the LXX, *Abram).* The quotation from 2 Chr 20:7 follows the Hebrew version rather than the Greek.

Friendship, "the essential quality and unity of friends," was a significant moral virtue in the Hellenistic world (see Johnson 1995, 243-44). James' mention of the theme anticipates 4:4, in which he defines "friendship with the world" as incompatible with friendship with God.

This verse confirms the interpretation of **was justified** (*edikaiōthē*) in v 21. Abraham's actions demonstrated his faith. That Abraham **believed God** was manifested by his willingness to sacrifice his son (see Gen 18:19). The word translated **believed** (*episteusen*) is a verb form of the noun **faith** (*pistis*). The concepts of faith and actions are intimately related for James. According to the Scriptures, **it** [i.e., his belief validated by his actions] **was credited to him as righteousness.** That is, his faithful actions showed that he believed God.

■ **24** You [plural] see introduces James' second response (see v 22). He no longer addresses his imaginary antagonist but his readers. The verb for perception here, *horate,* has a nuance slightly different from *blepeis* in v 22. Here, *horate* means "be mentally or spiritually perceptive" (BDAG, 720). Both visual verbs may have reminded his hearers of the imagery of the mirror in 1:22-25.

This time James is more to the point. He says, *that by actions a person is justified and not by faith only.* He uses the more generic word, *anthrōpos* ("person, human being"), to include everyone.

■ **25** James introduces his second example of faith accompanied by actions with *And likewise.* He compares the hospitality and protection of Joshua's spies by **Rahab the prostitute** (Josh 2; 6:22-25) with Abraham's offering of Isaac.

James poses another rhetorical question (see v 21): **was not even Rahab the prostitute** *justified by actions when she entertained the messengers* [*angelous*] *as guests* **and sent them off in a different direction?** Some ancient manuscripts replaced *angelous* with *kataskopous* (**spies**), so readers would not misunderstand Joshua's **messengers** for angels (similarly NIV). Other ancient manuscripts added *of Israel* to further clarify James' intention.

The adverbial participle *hypodexamenē,* translated **entertained** in this passage, indicates that Rahab received the Israelite spies hospitably and entertained them as guests (BDAG, 1037). Even though she knew she could have lost her life for welcoming these enemies of Jericho, she did it. Both Abraham and Rahab acted on their faith when much was at stake. Jewish tradition considered Rahab a model of hospitality (Johnson 1995, 245). Hebrews 11:31 lists her in its Faith Hall of Fame.

■ **26** James compares the way the **spirit** animates the body with how actions similarly bring **faith** to life. James uses the comparative conjunction *hōsper* (*just as*) to conclude his analogy and his argument in 2:14-26. **As the body without the spirit is dead, so faith without *actions* is dead.**

James uses the common word for body (*sōma*), usually used in contrast with spirit when the dual nature of the human person is meant. Its synonym, *sarx* (*flesh*), is used when the emphasis is on the meat that covers the bones of a human or animal, or on bodily desires. One can have a spiritual *sōma* (1 Cor 15:44), but not a spiritual *sarx*.

The word *pneuma* (**spirit**) here indicates "**that which . . . gives life to the body**" (BDAG, 832). The root meaning of *pneuma* (**breath** or **wind**) refers to the intangible and unseen dimension of life. Like the invisible wind, unseen life can move things or persons and its effects are visible (John 3:8). The spirit gives life to the body and the Holy Spirit inspires and empowers human beings to do God's will.

The point of James' comparison, of course, is that unseen **faith** makes its presence known only by the actions it moves people to do consistent with the will of God. It moves Christians to loving action (Gal 5:6). Just as we conclude there is wind when we see the leaves on the trees moving, James concludes there is **faith** only if a person exhibits that faith through actions. When the wind "dies down" we know it because the leaves no longer move. When Christians no longer act out their **faith,** James concludes that their **faith** is **dead.**

FROM THE TEXT

Through scriptural examples and an everyday analogy, James illustrates how dependent our understanding of faith should be on action. Many modern Christians think of faith as a set of beliefs to which they give mental assent. But such beliefs need not have any impact on how they live their lives. James' "point is not that deeds give life, but that they express life, 'demonstrate' that life is present. The obvious assumption is that whatever is living also acts" (Johnson 1995, 245).

The emphasis on the necessity of both faith and actions is one strength of the Wesleyan-Holiness heritage and its theology. John Wesley said, "The gospel of Christ knows of no religion, but social; no holiness, but social holiness" (1868, xxii). These words were originally spoken against solitary mysticism to urge Christians to seek the fellowship of other believers. Modern interpreters of Wesley have extended that meaning, following Wesley's own instructions and behavior, to include taking care of the poor and disenfranchised. Indeed, if someone is holy, that holiness will work itself out in holy actions and impact the community.

Problems come in this area when faith and actions are not kept in balance. When people do good things with no basis in faith, they can create dependency and low self-esteem in communities. When actions are the result of faith, people learn self-discipline and realize they can improve their situation by relying on God and his power in their lives.

Too often professing Christians fool themselves into believing all they need to do is confess their sins and accept certain articles of faith. They see no need to become involved in the lives of the poor and oppressed. They surround themselves with likeminded friends and forget about the rest of the world. These are the people James tries to awaken! Jesus called his followers to be salt and light in the world (Matt 5:13-16). We have a job to do! If Christians are not making a difference in their world, then what good are they?

Jesus said that his mission is our mission (John 17:18; 20:21-23). He came to seek and to save the lost. But he also came to heal, protect, and feed those in need. Matthew 25 emphasizes what Jesus expects of his followers: feed the hungry, give drink to the thirsty, hospitality to the stranger, clothing to the naked, care for the sick, and visit those in prison. Nowhere in the parable of the sheep and goats in Matt 25:31-46 is belief in the articles of faith identified as a criterion of judgment. Rather, professed belief is evaluated by how it is lived out in daily life.

Perhaps James used the example of Rahab because the church has refused to show hospitality to those whose outward appearance indicated that they had no ability to benefit the church. Yet Abraham and Rahab showed hospitality to those whose outward appearance mirrored the poor in the church. (Nystrom 1997, 155. See his discussion of the Jewish tradition on Rahab.)

John Wesley believed the example of Rahab was important because as a woman and a Gentile sinner she illustrated "that in every nation and sex true faith produces works and is perfected by them; that is, by the grace of God working in the believer, while he is showing his faith by his works" (Wesley 2003, 818).

C. The Tongue Reveals One's True Nature (3:1-12)

The formal indicator of direct address, "my brothers and sisters" (NRSV), marks the beginning of the third section of James' exposition. A short aphoristic statement following two rhetorical questions in vv 11-12a (Bauckham 1999, 64-65) marks its ending. The unifying theme is the role of the tongue— what one says—in revealing our true character. James links what we say with our actions. What we do in our bodies—our actions and speech—reveals our essential nature, what is at the core of our being.

In keeping with the introductory character of ch 1, this section develops the second admonition in Jas 1:19, be "slow to speak." The verb **keep . . . in** check (*chalinagōgēsai*, **bridle**) in v 2 recalls 1:26. There James describes the self-deceived who imagine themselves religious but do not "keep a tight rein on" (*chalinagōgōn*, **bridle**) their tongues. The analogy becomes explicit in 3:3, when James compares horses' **bridles** (*chalinous*, **bits**) to disciplined speech.

This section has three major subsections:

- Why teachers, who use their tongues more than most, are judged more severely than others (vv 1-2)
- The uncontrollable tongue (vv 3-6)
- The conundrum of praising and cursing coming from the same tongue (vv 7-12)

I. Teachers Are Judged More Strictly (3:1-2)

BEHIND THE TEXT

Teachers were highly regarded in the first century. According to John 1:38, "Teacher" was the appropriate translation for "Rabbi." Jesus instructed his disciples not to call each other "Rabbi" (Matt 23:8) or "teacher" (*kathēgē-tais*; Matt 23:10). He was to be their only Teacher (*didaskalos* in 23:8; *kath-ēgētēs* in 23:10).

In Jewish tradition, Rabbi was a title of honor in the Jewish schools; it indicated the person's level of competence in understanding and explaining scripture.

> The rabbis formed a closed order. Only fully qualified scholars, who by ordination had received the official spirit of Moses, mediated by succession (cf. Mt. 23:2), were legitimate members of the guild of scribes. . . . Sociologically the rabbis were the direct successors of the prophets, i.e., men who knew the divine will and proclaimed it in instruction, judgment and preaching. (Jeremias 1964, 741; Rengstorf 1964, 158)

We know that teachers were greatly respected in the first century. But there is no consensus as to their duties and responsibilities (Brosend 2004, 95). Despite Jesus' admonition in Matt 23, James does claim the role of teacher for himself (v 1: **we who teach**). In trying to determine the teacher's job description, Brosend observes that "James reproves, instructs, admonishes, and chastens, but makes no demands and puts forward no prerogative" (2004, 95).

Ephesians 4:11 and the later Christian writing, *Didache* (15:1), identify teaching as a divine office. Some scholars think teaching was the major function of pastors of the early church (Rengstorf 1964, 158).

> The leading role in Christianity was probably thought of as rabbinic or scribal in some communities (e.g. Mt. 13:52), but of course it was charismatic as well (1 Cor. 12:28). Clearly it was an office of some social rank (mentioned with prophets in Acts 13:1; cf. Did. 13:2). Thus there was

quite an impulse for those fit and unfit to press into this office. (Davids 1982, 136)

Both the Pauline and General Epistles illustrate that distinguishing true teachers and prophets from the false was an ongoing problem in the early church. The high status of teachers may have tempted the "unfit" to aspire to become teachers. The warning in this passage fits James' other warnings about status-seeking and favoritism.

Teaching in the Hellenistic context meant a systematic presentation of concepts. The ability to use words correctly to communicate God's message was of utmost importance. James warns that not many should aspire to be teachers. This was not only because of the need to have a good command of language. Even more crucial was the need for teachers' lifestyles to reflect their teaching. In fact, false teachers/prophets were identified by their actions more than by what they taught (see 2 Pet 2:13-22; 1 John 2:22-23; 4:1-13; 3 John 9-11; Jude 12-16). Due to their authoritative status and example, teachers will be judged more severely than others.

IN THE TEXT

■ I James begins his well-known treatment of taming the tongue as he began his section on favoritism in 2:1. He addresses his readers as fellow believers, "brothers and sisters" (NRSV) and issues a command. There is no clear grammatical or content transition from 2:26. His discussion of the use of the tongue continues with a new focus on teachers.

"Not many of you should *become* teachers, *my brothers and sisters, for you know that we who teach will be judged with greater strictness*" (NRSV, emphasis added). James does not say that no one should become a teacher. His warning suggests that the demands of the office are such that few are qualified to undergo the rigorous "final examination" teachers must face. Does he imply that only those with a clear calling, gifting, education, and spiritual maturity should become teachers?

James asks those seeking this high position of church leadership to reconsider, because they **will be judged more strictly.** Teachers instruct in doctrine and lifestyle, so what they say and how they live will be judged both by God and by their students.

Johnson notes that "the precise meaning of *krima* [**judgment**] here is difficult. Does it mean (. . .) that they are to be judged by a higher standard (. . .)? Or does it mean that they will be punished more severely?" (1995, 255). The teaching of Jesus seems to influence James' rationale. In Matt 23:13 and Luke 20:47, Jesus indicates that teachers will be severely punished for leading others astray. They also have the potential to be more visibly hypocritical. James may have both considerations in mind. Teachers are held to a higher standard and will be more severely punished for failing to meet that standard.

James' first person plural, *we will receive,* indicates that James considers himself one of the teachers who will be more strictly judged. As the first personal note since the greeting in 1:1, this self-reference is significant. As James begins to treat the difficult topic of disciplined speech, he wants his readers to know that he deals personally with the issue.

■ **2** In v 2*a*, James includes himself among those who sometimes fail: **We all stumble in many ways.** The NIV omits the conjunction *gar (for),* which opens the Greek sentence. This explains the precarious position of teachers: Nobody's perfect. This includes teachers. But more is expected of them. They are, after all, those who show others the way to walk.

The verb *ptaiomen* (**we . . . stumble**) figuratively describes human fallibility. None of us flawlessly lives out our lives of faith. Everyone loses one's footing, stumbles, and trips (BDAG, 894). James' verb-choice indicates that this stumbling is inadvertent, due to lack of attention to what one is doing. Such "slips" are unavoidable by those who teach. James offers teachers no license to take deliberate missteps.

James gets more specific. Nobody's perfect. And the most difficult behavior to perfect is one's speech. But teachers regularly speak in fulfilling their office. No wonder they are **judged more strictly!**

If anyone does not stumble in what he says, this man [*anēr*] *is perfect, powerful enough to bridle even his whole body.* The paraphrase **what he says** is literally *in a word.* The hypothetically **perfect man** never slips up in so much as one word.

The descriptive adjective *teleios* (**perfect**) can also mean **mature** or **complete.** It describes something that has reached a goal (*telos*). In the moral sphere, it means "completely blameless," fully satisfying what God expects (Zodhiates 1992, 1372). In 1:4 James identifies the goal of perseverance in trials: "that you may be mature [*teleioi*] and complete, not lacking anything." In 2:22 he says Abraham's faith "was made complete" (*eteleiōthē*) by his actions.

In 3:2, two colorful words describe the **perfect man** James has in mind. First, he is *dynatos.* That is, he is **able** or has the necessary *power*; second, **to keep his whole body in check** (*chalinagōgēsai*). That is, he has the strength **to bridle** himself. The Greek adjective entered English as the source of our word "dynamite." The Greek verb combines the noun *chalinos* ("**bit, bridle**"; BDAG, 1076) and the verb *agō* ("**lead, bring**"; BDAG, 16). James' readers would be familiar with bridles and their use in controlling domestic animals (Rev 14:20).

This short passage is powerful in its application. Those entrusted with leadership, interpretation of Scripture, and guiding God's people need to take their responsibility seriously. It is a sacred trust and one for which they will be held accountable. Those who aspire to this role need to be mature and complete (*teleios*).

Leadership in the church and in Christian higher education is for those who are spiritually, doctrinally, and educationally mature. New converts need not apply. Church leadership requires more than skills and abilities. It requires the honing of those skills through education and spiritual maturity. But James would emphasize that above all it requires the ability to control one's speech—to know what to say to whom, when, where, why, and how. We might call this diplomacy.

The teachers James has specifically in mind are "evidently leaders who are summoned to control and guide the course of the church's life and destiny" (Martin 1988, 104). Because of the emphasis at the beginning of this chapter on teachers, James must think of the church as a "'house of instruction' (*bēt-hammidraš*, to use the Jewish phrase of the synagogue). . . . It is primarily the teachers in the community who are causing dissension and division" (Martin 1988, 104).

When immature persons of any age are placed in positions of leadership, listeners come away embarrassed or disgusted with the leader's lack of understanding. Worse than that, leaders who lack understanding can hinder the growth and progress God intends for the church.

Doctrinal errors can be disseminated when immature teachers hear something that appeals to them, but lack the knowledge to evaluate what they hear. Relationships can be damaged when immature leaders respond to perceived threats with unguarded criticism.

As James says, not all should aspire to the lofty status of teacher! Christian teaching and leadership must be something one is gifted for, educated for, and called to. We should be "be quick to listen, slow to speak" (1:19). Even then, we must carefully and humbly listen to God, seeking continually to grow spiritually.

2. The Uncontrollable Tongue (3:3-6)

BEHIND THE TEXT

James continues his concern for controlling the "whole body" (v 2), appealing to two examples of large things managed by relatively small things: horses and ships.

Few common persons owned horses. But from time to time they would see horses owned by Roman officers and officials. They were large and high-spirited, perhaps even used in chariot racing.

James' description of ships as large and driven by strong winds indicates that he refers to seafaring ships. James' readers would have observed these large vessels. Some may even have sailed to Asia Minor in one of them. Ancient paintings and inscriptions describe these boats: "The rudders resembled large paddles attached to the stern. Some ships apparently had two such rudders" (Kent 2005, 110; see Blaiklock 1975, 410-15). To these comparisons he adds the proverb in v 5 about the small flame burning a whole forest.

Such comparisons and proverbial sayings were quite common in the Hellenistic world. James adapted these to make his point (Davids 1982, 139-40). Traditional sayings add emphasis and understanding to his argument.

The word James uses for hell (*geennēs*) is the Greek form of the Hebrew *Hinnom*. Originally, the Valley of the Sons of Hinnom was a ravine south of Jerusalem. King Ahaz (2 Chr 28:3) burned sacrifices, including his sons, in this valley. Jeremiah prophesies (7:30-34) that because Judah has worshiped idols in the Valley of the Sons of Hinnom by sacrificing their sons and daughters, there would come a day when it will be called the

> Valley of Slaughter, for they will bury the dead in Topheth [the Valley of the Sons of Hinnom] until there is no more room. Then the carcasses of this people will become food for the birds of the air and the beasts of the earth, and there will be no one to frighten them away. (Jer 7:32-33)

In later Judaism *Hinnom* (*Gehenna*) became associated with the final judgment as a place of fire and punishment in the next life. In Jesus' day the valley was the city garbage dump, which was continually burning. The NT refers to *Gehenna* (in Matt 5:22, 29, 30; 10:28; 18:9; 23:15, 33; Mark 9:43, 45, 47; and Luke 12:5) as a place of final judgment usually accompanied by fire. It is regularly translated "hell."

IN THE TEXT

■ **3** Scholars are divided on the original text. Some Greek manuscripts begin with *ei de* (**When** or ***But if***); others with *ide* ("***look! see!***" BDAG, 466). Some scholars (e.g., Ropes 1973, 229) defend *ide*, given the similar commands in vv 4 and 5 (*idou . . . idou*). The consensus, however, is that the original text was most probably *ei de*.

But if we are able to put horses' bits into their mouths so that they obey us, indeed we are guiding their whole body. These **bits** compel horses to obey their riders. In English, **bits** refers to the metal parts of bridles, which are inserted into horses' mouths in the sensitive space between their teeth. Bridles are the sets of leather straps that hold the bit in place. Thus, the English translation **bits** makes better sense than "bridles." Greek uses *chalinos* for both. The infinitive *peithesthai* (**to obey**) preceded by *eis to* (**in order to**) identifies the purpose or result of placing a bit in the horses' mouths: **so that they** obey the rider.

■ **4** James turns from horses to large sailing ships. He begins with the attention-getting command, **Look!** (*idou*). These ships are characterized as **so large** as to require **strong** [*skērōn*, "**hard, harsh, unpleasant**"; BDAG, 930] **winds** to move them. James emphasizes the relative sizes to heighten the wonder. The pilot is able to control a large boat in an extremely hostile environment with only the **smallest** [*elachistou*] **of rudders** (BDAG, 314).

James cites Hellenistic oral proverbs in common use (see Behind the Text above). Some of the vocabulary in vv 3-4 is not found elsewhere in the NT or in biblical Greek.

> The twin figures of the control of horse and of ship are frequently found together in later Greek writers . . . In some of the instances the point of the comparison is the smallness of the instrument which controls so great a body. James is evidently acquainted with the forms of current Greek popular thought. (Ropes 1973, 231; for specific citations, see Johnson 1995, 256-58)

■ **5a** Here James compares (**Likewise**) the **small** size of the **tongue** with the rudder of a boat. The comparison is inverted, since it is the tiny tongue that needs to be controlled because the consequences of what it says can be enormous. Nevertheless, by controlling this **small part,** a man is "able to keep his whole body in check" (v 2).

Martin acknowledges that the imagery of the bit and the horse and the rudder and the ship

> do not correspond exactly with the tongue and its relationship to the human body. The bit and the rudder control the larger bodies, but the tongue does not control the human body. However, if we assume that the body is the church congregation then we have a point of agreement because all three instruments . . . [are] exercising influence over the larger body of which they form a significant part. (1988, 111)

The Greek word *glōssa* literally means **tongue,** the "**organ of speech.**" But by metonymy, **tongue** may encompass "**a body of words and systems that makes up a distinctive language**" (BDAG, 201). James exploits the ambiguity of the term to imply both meanings. The **tongue** represents the entire complicated communication process. Physically, speech requires lungs, larynx, palate, teeth, and lips; to say nothing of the antecedent intellectual processes. In the broadest sense, however, communication involves not only what we say but how we say it—intonation and body language.

James adds that the tongue **makes great boasts.** "The phrase is here used in the sense not of an empty boast, but of a justified, though haughty, sense of importance" (Ropes 1973, 232). In the ancient world, rhetoric, the art of persuasive speech, was central to the entire educational process. Without the tongue, speech was impossible. Some scholars note that boasting is usually associated with sin. James stresses the power of the tongue, the evil it can do, and the need to control it (Davids 1982, 140).

■ **5b** James introduces a fresh analogy in the second half of v 5. The relationship between tongue and body (v 2) works better here. He begins with the same Greek command that introduces the example of the large ships in v 4. **Consider** [*idou*] **how small** [*hēlikon*] **a flame is able to burn how great** [*hēlikēn*] **forest.** James' wordplay suggests that he quotes a common proverb. "The structure *hēlikon . . . hēlikēn* gives balance and symmetry to the expression" (Davids 1982, 140; see 140-41 for ancient parallels). The adjective *helikos* is ambiguous. It can mean either "*how small*" or "*how large*" (BDAG, 436). Some later manuscripts changed the first *hēlikon* to the clearer *oligon*, which means "*little, small, short*" (BDAG, 702).

Nystrom acknowledges the Hellenistic parallels but concludes that the background for this saying is found in Jewish literature. The wisdom tradition especially has much to say about the destructive power of the tongue, at times associating the tongue with images of fire. Few disasters in the ancient world were more feared than fire, as the ancients possessed precious few resources to battle them, even in urban centers. (1997, 177)

■ **6** Although the meaning of this verse is generally clear, the structure of the second clause of the verse is "notoriously difficult" (Johnson 1995, 259; see Davids 1982, 141; Martin 1988, 113). Nystrom comments that

the first portion of verse 6 contains five terms in the nominative case but only one verb in the indicative (*kathistatai*) . . . The difficulty is to know how best to assign the verb. In addition, the text is marked by a number of variant readings, which has led some commentators to surmise that the text as we have it is corrupt. (1997, 178; see Ropes 1973, 234, and Adamson 1976, 158-64).

Most modern commentators (e.g., Davids, Martin, Johnson) attempt to make sense of the Greek as it stands. Davids suggests one possible solution. The first phrase, **And the tongue** [is] **a fire,** is a "nominal sentence." Greek often leaves the verb "to be" unexpressed. The third nominative noun, "**the world of wickedness,**" stands in apposition to the predicate noun **fire** (1982, 142). This is the approach of the NIV translators.

Another possible translation is suggested by James' Jewish heritage and audience. The noun **fire** may function as the adjective **fiery.** This is uncommon in Greek but frequent in Hebrew grammar. The alternate translation would be: *And the fiery tongue is a world of wickedness in our members* (*melesin*, **parts of the body**).

James connects the example of the destructive flame that burns a whole forest with the power of the tongue. He uses *kosmos*, usually translated **world** or *"universe"* (BDAG, 561). But *kosmos* can also refer to the orderly arrangement of the world, thus, **ornament** or *"adornment"* (BDAG, 561). This is the source of the English term "cosmetics." Johnson insists that

> James' meaning is only to be grasped in the light of 1:27 and 2:5 where *kosmos* and God are opposed, in light of 4:4 where the same verb (*kathistēmi*) is used for those whose choice of "friendship with the world" has "established" them as an enemy of God. (1995, 259)

To describe this **world** James chooses *adikias*, **wickedness** (from the negative prefix *a-* and the adjective *dikaios*, **right** or **just**, thus **injustice** or **unrighteousness**). In the LXX (see Gen 6:11; 1 Sam 3:13, 14; Ps 11:5; Zech 3:9), this term describes "the neglect of the true God and His laws and . . . adherence to the world or to idolatry" (Zodhiates 1992, 84; see Rom 1:18; 2:8; 2 Thess 2:10, 12; 2 Pet 2:15).

The second part of this verse is a series of adjectival participles, which describe *the fiery tongue.* This grammatical structure, frequent in Greek, creates an unintelligibly long sentence in English. Most translations make a separate sentence out of the participial phrase. A more literal translation might be: *which corrupts the whole body, inflames the circular course of nature, and is inflamed by Gehenna* (*geennēs* [hell]; see Behind the Text above).

The first participle, **corrupting** (*spilousa*), literally means *"stain, defile"* (BDAG, 938). The NT always uses it metaphorically in the moral sense (see Jude 23). So *the fiery tongue* **corrupts,** making *the whole body* impure. The Greek word for **body** (*sōma*) denotes **the whole person,** not just the physical. James may have intended to include the communal body, the church (Martin 1988, 104).

The second and third participles are from the same verb, *phlogizō.* The first is in the active voice; the second, passive. This allows James to connect his description of the tongue with its means of destruction—**setting on fire** (BDAG, 1060).

The *fiery tongue* sets on fire the **course of** . . . **life,** one's natural existence. This is related to the potter's wheel. It probably indicates a circular track, a circle of life from birth to death. So the *fiery tongue* not only morally **corrupts the whole person** but its effects follow a person to his or her grave.

The wicked and corrupt tongue that causes so much destruction in one's life is **set on fire** by the fires of **hell** itself (see Behind the Text above). James has painted a dramatic and ominous picture of what the uncontrolled, fiery tongue can do to a person and the surrounding community. A smooth translation would be: *It corrupts the whole person, sets the course of one's existence on fire, and has been set on fire by hell itself.*

James' reference to Gehenna as the ultimate source of evil is noteworthy. (1) This is a singular, if clear and understandable, figure, for the prison now stands for the imprisoned (perhaps as a warning to living people as well), and (2) the evil in a person, already spoken of as the world or evil impulse, is now traced for the first time to its ultimate source in Satan. (Davids 1982, 143)

James probably understood hell as a place where evil beings are tormented or imprisoned (see Behind the Text on 3:3-6). This develops the vague Hebrew idea of Sheol (the place of the dead) to another level, dividing it into a place for the righteous and a place for the evil.

FROM THE TEXT

Human beings are unable to control the smallest part of their body, the tongue. Nystrom ties this section to the first two verses:

The first two analogies are not quite precise (the tongue does not control the body in the fashion that a bit controls a horse or a rudder a ship), but the meaning is plain enough. The church is controlled by those in leadership roles. Thus, just as the rider directs the horse and the pilot the rudder, so the Christian teacher must be under the direction of the proper authority. (1997, 176)

Human beings can control large, spirited animals and imposing seagoing ships. But like a small spark in a dry forest, they cannot control their speech. The only way for the fiery tongue to be controlled is to put out the fire. Only God can do that. He is the one who changes persons at the very center of their beings.

As the chapter proceeds, James explains that what comes out of one's mouth arises from the core of the person. Jesus said that "the things that come out of the mouth come from the heart, and these make a man 'unclean'" (Matt 15:18). The "heart" refers to the intersection of the mind and will, not the emotions. First-century readers believed the center of human emotions to be in the bowels.

One may try to tame one's tongue, unaided by God. But sooner or later, the bitterness, anger, and ugliness of the inner core will spill out. The only way for the tongue to be "controlled" is for the person to be cleansed from bitterness and anger. The Holy Spirit can accomplish this in the lives of Christians, as they surrender themselves unreservedly to God. The Spirit remains the guardian of their thoughts and warns them, should they try to allow the bitterness, anger, and ugliness back into their lives.

3. Praising and Cursing from the Same Tongue (3:7-12)

BEHIND THE TEXT

This passage begins with echoes of Gen 1:20-24 in the LXX. All the Greek names for animals, except the marine animals, are the same as in the LXX. These wild creatures are seldom domesticated: wild animals, birds, reptiles, and marine animals.

Deadly poisons were well-known. History records that emperors and kings were especially wary of being poisoned by family members and enemies. Cleopatra (d. 30 B.C.) experimented with poisons to determine which were the most painless. Tradition says she died from the venomous bite of an asp (http://www.royalty.nu/Africa/Egypt/Cleopatra.html).

The plants James mentions among his examples are all native to the Mediterranean region of Asia Minor. Today, in modern Turkey, travelers will see miles of olive trees. And then suddenly, miles of grapevines or fig trees appear. In the Lycus River Valley of Turkey, hot mineral springs are still found at Hierapolis; and cold fresh water wells, near Colossae. Barclay estimates that in the first century the Jewish population of Asia Minor numbered as high as 50,000 (2003, 93). James' first readers may have been among them.

IN THE TEXT

■ **7** This verse seeks to answer the question implicit in v 6: "How do we know that the tongue is lit by a cosmic force?" (Johnson 1995, 260). A long, complex sentence begins here and continues through v 8.

For every species [*physei*] *of wild animals* [*thērion*] . . . *is tamed and has been tamed by the human race* (*physei*). The repetition of *physis* gives symmetry and balance to the original saying.

James does not use *zōon*, which refers to "a living creature, wild or domesticated" (BDAG, 431), for *wild animals.* He emphasizes that humanity has tamed and was commanded to tame (Gen 1:28) the specifically *wild animals*. But it cannot tame the tongue.

James names three types of wild animals: *birds, reptiles, and marine animals.* His intention was to mention exhaustively all types of wild animals. The terms for *birds* and *reptiles* are common in biblical Greek. But the word for *marine animals* (*enaliōn*) occurs only here (see Philo, *Decalogue* 54; Johnson 1995, 261).

James uses both the present and the perfect tenses—*is being tamed and has been tamed*—to describe the taming of these animals. The present tense emphasizes that the taming is still in progress; the perfect, that such animals were tamed in the past and remain tame. His hyperbole emphasizes the notable exception: no one, past or present, has succeeded in taming the tongue (v 8). Thus, the control of the tongue must come from some "cosmic force," whether the fires of Gehenna (i.e., Satan; v 6) or God himself (Johnson 1995, 260).

■ 8 Verse 8 returns to the human **tongue,** which no one **can tame.** Verse 6 describes the tongue as a destructive flame from hell. Here, James describes it as **a restless evil, full of deadly poison.**

In v 6, the evil is **wickedness** (*adikias*), which prefers the world over God and impedes the worship of God by others. Here James uses the more general word for **evil** (*kakos*) (BDAG, 501). Even if a society would not agree that unfaithfulness to God was harmful, it would certainly agree that *kakos* was.

The tongue is **an unstable** (*akatastaton*; see relevant comments on 1:8 and 3:16) **evil.** It is **restless** and unpredictable. It surfaces when least expected and can shoot off in all directions. It is not mildly inconvenient; it contains a poison that will eventually bring death (*thanatēphorou*; see Ps 140:3; Rom 3:13). It is a "'poison on the lips' that leads to violence between humans" (Johnson 1995, 261). Obviously, this kind of evil needs to be tamed. But no one has been able to do it.

The repetition of *akatastatos* (**unstable**), used first in 1:8, suggests that James may refer to the **double-souled** person introduced there (Brosend 2004, 91). This fits the context of v 9 and the role of ch 1 as an introduction to the entire Epistle. But instability and chaos are universal characteristics of evil, prevalent in first-century society (Serrão 1996, 124).

Johnson considers **restless evil** to fit the context of the tongue as untamed and a raging fire, rather than referring specifically to the double-minded person. He takes *de* at the beginning of this verse as the strong adversative **But.** It contrasts the ability of humans to domesticate wild animals and their total inability to discipline the tongue (Johnson 1995, 261).

The taming of the tongue is something only God can do. Augustine (*Nat. Grat.* 16 [XV]) and Wesley (2003, 818) agree. Other scholars associate this with incurable human imperfection (see 3:2), discounting the possibility of any solution in this life (Moo 2000, 161; Ropes 1973, 240).

■ 9 James transitions from the destructiveness of the tongue to its duplicity. With the same **tongue** we both **bless** God and **curse** humanity. The Greek word for **tongue** in v 9 is only implied from v 8, linking it closely with what precedes. James considers the duplicitous tongue totally incongruous. How can we **praise our Lord and Father** and at the same time *curse people* made in God's likeness?

The word for **praising** (*eulogoumen*), sometimes translated "bless" (NRSV), is what humans do when they speak well of God or others. It is commonly used in Jewish prayers: "The blessing formulary begins: 'Blessed are you Lord God'" (Johnson 1995, 261). Some manuscripts replace **Lord** with God, which fits better with the following phrase, *made according to the likeness of God*. But **Lord,** as the harder reading, is to be preferred as more likely original.

Here the verb *eulogeō* means to **praise** or "bless" (NRSV) in the sense of speaking well of another. It is used in happy, temporary situations. This verb is from a different root than *makarizō* (**bless**). In the Beatitudes (Matt 5:1-12), the *makarioi* ("blessed") enjoy a constant state of being blessed by God's presence with them, even in suffering (see Jas 1:12, 25; 5:11). The fleeting character of such praise coheres with the instability of the tongue.

Cursing (*katarōmetha,* **we curse**) is to wish ruin to befall another (Mark 11:21; Luke 6:28; Rom 12:14). James notes the inconsistency of humans praising God and praying for disaster to befall those made in God's image. Human beings are a reflection of God on earth. Why would one both **bless** God and **curse** his image? The phrase **made in God's likeness** (*homoiōsin*) refers to Gen 1:26-28 (LXX). God created humanity according to God's **image** [*eikona*] **and likeness** (*homoiōsin*).

James' first person plural verbs, **we praise** and **we curse,** seem to imply that he is among those who speak inappropriately. Does he actually place himself with those whose practice falls short of their profession? Or, is this merely a rhetorical **we,** identifying him with his hearers? It is unclear whether this is a confession or a rhetorical strategy. But it is clear from the following verses that this kind of duplicitous speech should be impossible. It does not occur in nature.

■ **10** James continues to address the feasibility of **praise and cursing** coming from **the same mouth.** He leaves the metaphor of the tongue behind. He concentrates on what a person says and is, on what one's actions and words reveal about that person. In vv 11 and 12, he uses examples from nature to illustrate why *these things ought not to happen in this way.* (See the comments on 1:2, 16, 19; 2:1, 5, 14; and 3:1 for a discussion of the significance of James' direct address of his audience as fellow believers.)

The Greek grammatical construction *ou chrē . . . tauta houtōs gegesthai* (*these things ought not to happen in this way*) is found only here in the NT. It is used by Hellenistic moralists to convey their "sense of outrage at 'what ought not to be'" (Johnson 1995, 262). Two conflicting actions should not come from the same person. This duplicity, like that of the double-souled person in 1:8, indicates something is wrong with the person.

■ **11** James compares the human mouth to the opening of an artesian **spring.** The formulation of his rhetorical question expects a negative answer: *A fountain cannot from the same opening pour forth both sweet and bitter water, can it?*

The Greek word for **water** is not explicit here. It is implied by the word **spring.** Springs were known for the quality of their water. Some had "fresh" water and others "brackish water" (NRSV), but none had both at once.

The verb translated **pour forth** (*bryō*) is found only here in biblical Greek (LXX or NT). In Josephus, other Hellenistic Jewish literature, and in the early church fathers, it refers to abundant water being forced out of an underground spring (BDAG, 184).

The Greek adjective *glykys* is the source of the English "glucose." It can describe the **sweet** taste of honey (Rev 10:9-10) or, as here, **fresh** tasting water. The word for **bitter** (*pikron*) describes water that is not drinkable. The parallel *halykon* (**salty;** from *hals,* **salt**) in v 12 indicates that here it refers to **salt water** or "brackish water" (NRSV).

■ **12** James again tries to grab his audience's attention by addressing them as **My brothers *and sisters*** (see 3:1, 10). The negative *mē* at the beginning of the sentence indicates that this rhetorical question expects a no answer. Of course, **a fig tree** cannot produce **olives** and a **grapevine** cannot **bear figs.** The analogy clinches his argument: *Neither can a salty spring produce fresh water.*

Figs, olives, and grapes are all endemic crops to the Mediterranean basin, well known to James' readers. James may allude to Jesus' teaching appealing to the grapes, trees, and their fruit in Matt 7:16-20. Good trees cannot bear bad fruit; nor bad trees, good fruit. Like trees, people are known by the visible results of their actions (see Johnson [1995, 263] for Greco-Roman parallels).

James' point is the same as in v 11. The fruit of a plant reveals its true identity. The water that flows from a spring indicates what kind of spring it is. Thus, what one says and does reveals the true nature of the person.

FROM THE TEXT

It is useless to try to disguise what is at the core of a person. No matter how hard we may try to guard our tongue, our true nature will eventually be revealed by what we say (see Jesus' comments in Matt 12:34-37). Everything in nature produces what it naturally is. A spring consistently produces the same kind of water. Fig trees always produce figs; and olive trees, olives. Hanging figs on a grapevine does not change its true identity.

For people to be godly, they must be changed at the core of their beings. Godly people say godly things and do righteous actions. Ungodly people say ungodly things and do unrighteous actions. As Christians, we are not to judge one another (see 4:11-12). But we can see from the words and actions of others what kind of people they are.

The logic here is the same as that reflected in James' discussion of faith and actions. Our profession of faith alone is not enough. Our actions reveal our true nature as persons of genuine faith, or not. Those who say they have faith, but whose actions betray their true faith-less core, demonstrate that their faith is not genuine.

D. Earthly and Heavenly Wisdom (3:13-18)

This fourth section of James' exposition treats a different but related topic, **wisdom** (vv 13, 15, 17). Its opening question, **who . . . among you** (*tis . . . en . . . hymin*), marks the beginning of three sections in the exposition (3:13; 5:13, 19).

Continuity with the closing analogy in the previous section is maintained in vv 17 and 18, which refer to **fruit**. At the same time, the references to **peace** in these verses anticipate, by way of contrast, the next section. In 4:1, James will address the problem of *wars and quarrels* in his communities (see Bauckham 1999, 65).

This brief section confirms for some scholars that James belongs to the wisdom genre and takes his inspiration from Proverbs. Others see Jesus' influence on James in his comparison and contrast of earthly and heavenly wisdom (see Matt 7:24-27; 25:1-8; Luke 6:46-49; 12:42-48). But these two influences are not mutually exclusive.

BEHIND THE TEXT

Wisdom has an important place in Jewish literature. So it is not surprising that James addresses the issue. Many scholars consider James the one example of Wisdom literature in the NT. He includes proverbs and discusses the nature of wisdom. In the Jewish and Christian traditions, wisdom always comes from God. The acrostic poem in Ps 111 affirms: "The fear of the LORD is the beginning of wisdom; all who follow his precepts have good understanding" (v 10). Proverbs echoes this same perspective: "The fear of the LORD is the beginning of wisdom, and knowledge of the Holy One is understanding" (9:10).

The contrast of earthly and heavenly wisdom became especially important in the first century. Jews and Christians were surrounded by a Hellenized culture that celebrated earthly wisdom. This may be best illustrated by the example of Philo of Alexandria, a first-century Jewish philosopher born and raised in Egypt.

Philo's Jewish philosophy was in the Greek tradition. His interpretation of the Mosaic law rewrote Jewish history with the aid of allegorical interpretation in the Greek tradition. His *Apology for the Jews* is known from fragments preserved in the writings of Eusebius, fourth-century Christian church historian (263-339).

As Philo recounts Joshua's conquest of the Promised Land, he obviously plays down its military aspects in favor of a conquest of another kind. Jewish wisdom demonstrated its superiority to pagan wisdom and prevailed. Thus, he concludes:

> Outsiders are left to choose between two possibilities, one that it [the conquest] was due to superior force, the other that the virtues of the in-

comers won the respect and submission of the native population. (*Philo* 1954a, Vol. IX, 407-11)

IN THE TEXT

■ **I3** James opens with a question: **Who is wise and understanding among you?** The adjective translated **wise** (*sophos*) is from the noun *sophia* (**wisdom**). The term incorporates the ideas of "sound judgment and good sense" and "expertise in any art" as well as deep knowledge that comes from "learned research" and insight into how things really are (Zodhiates 1992, 1300-1301).

The Greek adjective translated **understanding** (*epistēmōn*, **knowledgeable**) means "to know thoroughly," to have "expertise." This is the ancient "equivalent to . . . 'scientist'" (Zodhiates 1992, 639). Although **wise** and **knowledgeable** have a similar range of meaning, the latter places a greater emphasis on knowledge as such. Here it refers to those who think they have it all figured out. They are the educated intellectuals in the community.

Earlier in the Epistle, James addressed those who professed to have faith. His challenge to both them and those who claim they are **wise and understanding** is to show it by what they do. He uses the third person imperative to insist that persons of supposedly superior wisdom and intellect should *demonstrate* this *by means of a morally good lifestyle.* The verb translated *demonstrate* (*deixatō*, **show**) means "**to prove or make clear by evidence or reasoning**" (BDAG, 215). It reiterates the claim in 2:18 that just actions demonstrate true faith. Although the moral aspect is uppermost, **good** (*kalōs*, see 2:7; 4:17) also connotes excellence and beauty (Johnson 1995, 270).

James characterizes the visible evidence of true understanding as *gentleness* or **humility** tempered by **wisdom**. *Gentleness* (*praytēti*) carries the connotations of "*courtesy, considerateness, meekness*" (BDAG, 861). *Gentleness* is not a mark of weakness; it comes from strength of character.

Aristotle considered *praytēs* "the middle standing between two extremes, getting angry without reason (*orgilotēs*) and not getting angry at all (*aorgēsia*)" (Zodhiates 1992, 1210). Therefore, *gentleness* means "getting angry at the right time, in the right measure, and for the right reason" (Zodhiates 1992, 1210). The description of someone as a "gentle giant" might come close to what the word intends. This person, with the strength and ability to obliterate his or her opponent, chooses not to do so.

James may also have those in his audience influenced by Gnosticism (see the first sidebar on 2:18-20) in his sights. The word for **understanding** is not related to *gnōsis* (*knowledge*). So, some scholars see no connection to Gnosticism (Moo 2000, 168-71). Nevertheless, in later Gnosticism, actions of the body were separated from intellectual knowledge and had no bearing on one's salvation. Some gnostics flaunted their immoral lifestyles. James insists that those who are truly wise will live a ***morally good lifestyle.***

■ **14** James continues to challenge the vices of the supposedly ***wise and knowledgeable*** (v 13). The first he lists is ***bitter zeal*** (*zēlon pikron*, **bitter envy**). Overconfidence in the correctness of one's convictions can easily erode into "blind fanaticism." The zealot "sees himself as jealous for the truth, but God and others see the bitterness, rigidity, and personal pride which are far from the truth" (Davids 1982, 151).

The second vice is **selfish ambition** or ***self-interested rivalry*** (*eritheian*). Aristotle defines it as "'a self-seeking pursuit of political office by unfair means'" (Davids 1982, 151). In the NT, however, the vice is not limited to office-seekers. It refers to anyone who becomes jealous or angry enough over some issue that he or she withdraws (psychologically or physically) from the community.

James says that those claiming to be wise and understanding must not **boast** (*katakauchasthe*), if they have bitter jealousy and ***self-interested rivalry.*** Boasting can be used positively or negatively, depending on what one boasts in. In Jas 2:13, mercy's triumph (*katakauchatai*) over judgment is viewed positively (see 2 Cor 11:1-33).

Here, however, boasting is apparently inappropriate. Are they boasting in their "worldly wisdom" (Nystrom 1997, 206) or in their intellectual superiority? Are they trying to persuade people to follow them with fanatical zeal and partisanship? "Those who have jealousy and selfish ambition in their hearts (*kardias*, the seat of the will) have nothing to boast about" (Brosend 2004, 100). James addresses empty and dangerous boasting again in 4:13-17.

The command not to **deny** or ***lie against*** the truth refers to living in contradiction to Christian teaching ("the word of truth" in 1:18; see Acts 5:3). As believers, this truth is "planted" in them, so they should "humbly accept" (1:21) or "welcome" it "with meekness" (NRSV). This is **truth** not so much as a concept as a manner of life. To abandon the Christian lifestyle is to "wander from the truth" (5:19; Johnson 1995, 271-72).

■ **15** James negatively assesses the supposed **"wisdom"** of those who have bitter zeal and self-interested rivalry in their hearts. ***This wisdom is not coming down from above, but is* earthly, *sensual, and demonic.***

The participle ***coming down*** develops the theme introduced in 1:17. There "every good and perfect gift" is said to be "from above, coming down" (see 3:17). So "considered together with 1:5, it is clear that James regards genuine wisdom as a divine gift, a perception deeply rooted in the world of Torah" (Johnson 1995, 272; see Prov 2:6; Job 28:20-28).

But James considers the so-called **wisdom** of the supposedly "wise and understanding" (Jas 3:13) as definitely **not** from God. Instead, he depreciates it with three adjectives. The first, **earthly,** is a compound of two Greek words: *epi,* **upon,** and *gē,* **earth.** This "wisdom" is not heavenly, divine, or eternal.

The second adjective, **sensual** (*psychikē*), is related to the root *psychē* (**soul**). It is never used in a positive sense in the NT. Jude 19 tells us that the *psychikoi* (**sensual**) "do not have the Spirit." This is likely James' point here. Earthly wisdom is not a fruit of the Spirit.

The third adjective James uses to describe bitter and self-interested (v 14) "wisdom" is **demonic** (*daimoniōdēs*). Only here in the NT, it was perhaps coined by James (Brosend 2004, 100). This is the adjectival form of the noun for "demon" (BDAG, 210). This vaunted but false "wisdom" is **of the devil** ("devilish," NRSV). Recall that Jas 2:19 refers to monotheistic **demons** who **believe in one God** but **tremble with fear** because they persist in their rebellion against him (see 3:6; 4:7). These are strong words of condemnation. They set up the contrast with James' description of heavenly wisdom in v 17.

■ **16** James reiterates the two vices of v 14, omitting the adjective modifying envy. His meaning is unchanged. He explains, *For where zeal and self-interested rivalry are, there is instability and every corrupt practice.*

The first result of these vices is **instability** (*akatastasia,* **disorder**). A cognate, "unstable" (*akastastatos*), in 1:8 characterizes the **double-souled** person; in 3:8, the tongue as "a restless evil." It refers to "anarchy" (Ropes 1973, 248) or social **chaos** (see Luke 21:9; 2 Cor 6:5).

In 2 Cor 12:20 Paul lists *akatastasia* as a vice, alongside zeal (*zēlos*) and selfish rivalries (*eritheiai*). This is similar to James' use in v 16. He shares Paul's assessment in 1 Cor 14:33: "God is not a God of disorder [*akatastasia*] but of peace [*eirēnēs*]." There is no place for behavior that is disruptive and harmful to the community.

The second result of intercommunity rivalries is **every corrupt** practice. Practice (*pragma*) may mean **act** or **deed** (BDAG, 858-59). It is roughly synonymous with *ergon,* the actions that reveal one's faith (in 2:14-26). *Ergon* has a wider application to occupations and moral actions.

The adjective **corrupt** (*phaulon,* **foul**) describes the practices of the misguided zealots as "morally substandard" (BDAG, 1050; see Johnson 1995, 273). Titus 2:8 calls for **good actions** (*kalōn ergōn,* Titus 2:7), which will prevent outsiders from accusing Christians of anything "bad" (*phaulon*). Even outsiders recognize such practices as **evil.**

■ **17** James turns from vices to be avoided to virtues to be cultivated. These are all expressions of **the wisdom that comes from heaven.** James' discussion of vices and virtues stresses the positive. He balances two vices, "envy and selfish ambition" (v 16), with eight virtues. Each is an adjective describing godly wisdom. These virtues are not human moral achievements. They are the work of the Spirit in the lives of receptive believers.

3:15-17

James lists the first two virtues as **first** and **then.** He assigns no sequence or rank of importance to the remaining six. The number one characteristic of *wisdom from above* (contrast v 15) is that it is pure (*hagnos*). Those who receive it enjoy "freedom from defilements or impurities" (Zodhiates 1992, 73). They live "*holy*" lives (BDAG, 12; see 1 Pet 3:2; Phil 4:8). They exemplify true religion, as James defines it in 1:27: "Religion that is pure and undefiled [*kathara kai amiantos*] before God, the Father, is this: . . . to keep oneself unstained [*aspilon*] by the world" (NRSV; see the commentary on 1:26-27).

The adjective *hagnos* is from the same cognate family as *hagios*. Both terms mean "holy." *Hagnos* often has a more cultic sense than *hagios*. But his concern here is clearly not with ritual, but moral holiness, as throughout his Epistle. He describes holiness in terms of the sociological categories of purity and character (see Benefiel 2004, in Appendix A).

After setting the priority of purity, James follows with four alliterated virtues. Each begins with the letter epsilon. The first is *peaceful* (*eirēnikē*, **peace-loving, irenic**). That this is a major concern for James is evident in his twofold mention of **peace** (*eirēnē*) in v 18. Peace is obviously antithetical to the noisy confusion and instability of the zealots James reproves in vv 14-16.

Peace (*shalom* in Hebrew) is significant in the Jewish tradition. It is still used as a customary greeting. It means "wholeness, soundness, hence health, well-being, prosperity" and "more particularly, peace as opposed to war" (Zodhiates 1992, 519). God is the God of peace (Rom 15:33; 1 Thess 5:23), the one who gives peace.

The main blessing of the messianic kingdom of Jewish hope was peace (Lev 26:6; Num 25:12; Isa 54:10; Ezek 34:25; 37:26; Mal 2:5-6). Jesus offers his disciples his peace (in John 14:27; 20:19, 21). Paul considers peace with God a primary result of being justified through faith (Rom 5:1).

James stresses "peace" as characteristic of those who are "*peaceable*" (BDAG, 288). They do what they can to bring about peace. This adjective is used only here and in Heb 12:11 in the NT. Hebrews refers to it as the kind of fruit produced in the lives of divinely disciplined Christians.

The second alliterated quality is *gentle* (*epieikēs*, **considerate**; from *eikos* [*fair* or *equitable*] intensified by the preposition *epi*). Those marked by this quality are "*yielding, gentle, kind, courteous, tolerant*" (BDAG, 371). Paul encourages the Philippians, "Let your gentleness [*epieikes*] be evident to all" (Phil 4:5). Christian leaders especially need this capacity of being *easy to live with* (1 Tim 3:3; Titus 3:2).

The third quality in this alliterated set is *compliant* (*eupeithēs*, **submissive**; from from *eu* [*well*] and *peithō* [*persuade*]; Zodhiates 1992, 680). Its antonym (*apeithēs*) means "disobedient" in Acts 26:19 (see Rom 1:30). It is used as the opposite of *akatastasia* in Jas 1:8 ("unstable") and 3:16 ("disorder").

The quality of being *eupeithēs* appears in Philo's *Virtues* 15 and in Epictetus 2.10.8 describes those who are trusting and easily persuaded. In English this has the negative connotation of being naive and easily taken advantage of. But in Philo and Epictetus it is not negative. A better contemporary translation would be "team player." James describes one who goes along with the team plan and does not create conflict every time the plan changes.

Johnson notes that the first three virtues combined "amount to a definition of 'meekness' enjoined by 3:13" (1995, 274).

The final alliterated virtue is **mercy** (*eleous*). It is paired with **good fruit** (*karpōn agathōn*). These two nouns are part of an adjectival phrase, which begins with **full of** (*mestē*). **Mercy** is a classic virtue in the NT, primarily in imitation of God's example. Words in this cognate family appear in all the Gospels except John, most of Paul's letters, Hebrews, James (2:13; 3:17), 1 Peter, 2 John, and Jude. The parable of the unmerciful servant is the likely context of **mercy** in v 17. Christians are to be full of mercy because God has been merciful to them. Mercy is a response enabled by God's merciful activity in their lives.

James pairs **mercy** and **good fruit** as the visible products of the virtues he associates with the *wisdom from above.* The word **fruit** (*karpōn*) figuratively describes the observable results in a person's life (see, e.g., Matt 7:16, 20; Luke 6:43-44; John 15:5, 8).

Fruit in Paul's letters is often used in much the same way as James uses actions, visible results. Paul refers to "the fruit of the Spirit" (Gal 5:22; Eph 5:9), the *fruit* of Paul's labor (Rom 1:13; Phil 1:22), and the *fruit* of the readers (Rom 6:21; Phil 1:11).

The combination of James' virtue list to this point emphasizes qualities required for the ethics of cooperation, rather than competition (Johnson 1995, 274). These virtues are followed by two more alliterations, each beginning with the letter alpha. They are direct antonyms of the earlier vices. Greek uses the alpha prefix, much like English uses "un-," to mean "not."

The first of this pair is *without partiality* (*adiakritos*). This might be seen as a summary of the foray on favoritism in 2:1-13. In 2:4 James uses a verbal form of the vice (*diekrithēte*, *you show favoritism*). He chastises the community for catering to rich people and humiliating the poor. Johnson sees a conceptual link with "James' other uses of *diakrinō* in 1:6 and 2:4, both of which are connected to the concept of 'double-mindedness.'" He suggests that this word "means to be 'simple' rather than double in consciousness" (Johnson 1995, 274-75).

The second alliterated word in this section is *without hypocrisy* (*anypokritos*, **sincere;** see 5:12). Paul uses it in Rom 12:9 to command that love be genuine. In 2 Cor 6:6, this word indicates that Paul and his coworkers showed that they were servants of God by authentic love. In 1 Tim 1:5 and 2 Tim 1:5, Paul refers to faith that is without hypocrisy.

Hypocrites pretend to be someone or something they are not, as actors. The word in v 17 originally referred to inexperienced actors (Zodhiates 1992, 197). But in the NT, *anypokritos* has the positive connotation of being "**sincere**" or "**genuine**," that is, "**without pretense**" (BDAG, 91).

■ **18** This verse seem to allude to Jesus' beatitude (Matt 5:9) pronouncing peacemakers blessed. James writes literally, ***And the fruit of righteousness in peace is sown for those who make peace.*** He uses the same word for ***fruit*** (*karpos*) as in v 17. Here the ***fruit*** is **righteousness** that emerges from the seeds of **peace**. God raises **a harvest** (*karpos*) **of righteousness** and peace for those whose objective is to make peace. God blesses peacemakers with a legacy of righteousness and peace.

Moo defends the NIV translation: **Peacemakers who sow in peace raise a harvest of righteousness** (2000, 177). He thinks the verse speaks to what peacemakers produce. This reading takes the dative to indicate agency (*by*) rather than advantage (*for*, as in the NASB: "by those who make peace"; see Johnson 1995, 275).

But the verb *speiretai* is a passive, which James normally uses as a divine passive. If so, God raises the harvest of righteousness or justice on behalf of those who try to make peace. Brosend suggests that the dative carries the meaning of both advantage and agency. So he translates: "by those who are peaceable—*for* those who are peaceable . . . righteousness is sown and harvested only in peace" (2004, 101).

This is James' first favorable use of the noun **peace** (*eirēnē*). In 2:16 it appears in the hypocritical blessing of the destitute: ***Depart in peace.*** But here James summarizes this section on the virtues of heavenly wisdom, while paving the way to ch 4—his explanation of why there are wars and fights in his communities.

FROM THE TEXT

James says that the gentleness of intellectuals (see v 13) shows they are really wise and demonstrates their faith. If these verses are aimed at all those in his communities (Moo 2000, 168), they must all consider themselves intellectually superior. His Jewish-Christian audience may well have considered themselves superior to Gentile Christians in their understanding of the OT, the wisdom tradition, and the ethical standards of Judaism. Paul attempts to undermine this Jewish sense of superiority in Rom 2:17-24.

James' emphasis remains on the practice of one's faith, not on his audience. James is concerned about faith demonstrating the kind of wisdom described in v 19. The question of the character of the audience he addresses is not as important as it is for them to stay focused on the practical outworkings of faith (Brosend 2004, 104).

These admonitions apply to anyone who at any time might be tempted to feel superior to others. True gentleness, in the sense James discusses, can only come from those who have the strength and ability to outtalk or outsmart their opponents. But instead of relying on their rhetorical prowess, they wisely choose to restrain their power, using it to build up the community, not tear it down. Wesley comments that wisdom without hypocrisy is frank and open. Those who speak honestly love everyone and embrace all that is good. But they reject any ungodliness (Wesley 2003, 820).

Some people are too smart for their own good. They think they can live however they please. Perhaps, they imagine they are too cunning to get caught. There is a sense in which all power corrupts, whether it is physical, political, or intellectual. So James commands those who are intellectually powerful to prove how wise they are by treating their intellectual inferiors with gentleness and by a morally pleasing lifestyle.

The intellectually superior may be tempted to believe they know best in all situations. If they do not have godly submission in their hearts, they can easily be seduced to cause division in the community. "They claim that their rivalry is inspired. 'It is inspired, all right,' retorts James. 'It is inspired of the devil himself!'" (Davids 1982, 89-90). The "wise" must steer clear of the vices of bitter zeal and self-interested rivalry.

The virtues they should cultivate instead are purity, peace-making, gentleness, trustfulness, mercy, impartiality, and sincerity. These resemble the fruit of the Spirit Paul lists in Gal 5:22-23. James would probably agree that these virtues are possible only through the working of the Holy Spirit in one's life.

Purity is highly valued in the Jewish tradition. It is an expression of holiness. In fact, purity is one of the ways the holiness tradition has described the life of holiness (Benefiel 2004, see Appendix A). It is a life free from sin that imitates Christ. Wesley points out that true peace is tied to purity. This is because without purity, it is hard to have the peaceful characteristics of being quiet and inoffensive (Wesley 2003, 818).

Some of the virtues James mentions were also highly prized by pagans. But others were countercultural in James' day and are still seldom considered virtues in modern cultures. In the challenge-oriented society of the first century, conflict was natural and often used when a person sought to assert his or her own importance. Even today, peacemakers are often regarded as people who won't stand up for themselves or others.

Gentleness and trustfulness are still regarded as virtues for children, but not for those who want to get ahead in the world! Nevertheless, these are not weak words in James' vocabulary. They are virtues the strong need to restrain their ability to overpower and oppress the weak. It takes remarkable strength for the powerful to be gentle instead of dominating. It takes humility to trust our brothers or sisters in Christ. Many people are not reared to trust others. James wants us to expand our trusting circle to include those of the Christian community.

That is where the virtues of mercy, impartiality, and sincerity come into play. Community leadership that is merciful, impartial, and sincere will earn the respect of the entire community. This will allow for the building of trust within that community. Unfortunately, too many have grown up in "Christian" communities in which they witnessed so-called Christians who were unmerciful and judgmental.

Others have witnessed preference given to those who were more attractive, talented, or from more prestigious families than they. And worst of all, many have witnessed blatant hypocrisy in church leaders. We cannot blame young people who turn away from a church that justifies hypocrisy as part of what it means to be Christians.

James' words need to be heard clearly again in the twenty-first century. Leaders need to examine their motives continually. They may need to explain some of their difficult decisions so that the community can see their actions as merciful, impartial, and without hypocrisy. To the extent that each Christian is called to ministry, in some sense, all Christians are leaders who influence and shape the whole community.

E. The Double-Minded Must Humble Themselves (4:1-10)

This section opens with a question: *From where do wars and fights among you come?* Like the previous section, the opening question includes the prepositional phrase *among you.* Verse 10 ends the passage with a

> contrastive parallelism . . . which, beginning with the quotation in v 6, proceeds by admonitions employing parallelism (rare in James), and leads to the climax in verse 10 where reference to God's action forms an *inclusio* with the quotation in verse 6. (Bauckham 1999, 65)

The *inclusio* (literary bookends) device is obvious in the opening quotation in v 6b: **But he gives grace to the humble,** and the closing command in v 10: **Humble yourselves before the Lord, and he will lift you up.**

The first subdivision consists of vv 1-3, which emphasize unfulfilled desires as the reason for intercommunity fights. James suggests that the reason their desires are not fulfilled is because they ask selfishly.

Verses 4-5 confront members of the community who are praying outside of God's will as *adulteresses.* James charges that they want the impossible—to be friends with the world and with God.

The remedy for this situation is for the arrogant to humble themselves before God. Verses 6-10 describe this humility in several parallelisms: be submissive to God and **resist the devil** (v 7); draw **near to God,** cleanse your hands, **purify your hearts** (v 8); endure hardships, mourn and cry, change laughter to grief; and, joy to despair (v 9). The section closes with the command to humble oneself before God (v 10).

I. Desires Cause Fights (4:1-3)

BEHIND THE TEXT

Stoicism was the most influential Greek philosophy in the first century. Its founder, Zeno (334-262 B.C.), believed that ethics was central to philosophy. Stoics encouraged people to live in their society and to find tranquillity in their daily lives. They believed no one can change what happens to people, but people can control how they respond to life's events.

Stoic philosophers encouraged people to train themselves to respond to life more effectively. The purpose was to achieve inner harmony and to avoid the extremes of pleasure and pain. James' Jewish-Christian communities were undoubtedly familiar with this popular philosophy. Its influence is obvious in the writings of the first-century Jewish philosopher Philo of Alexandria. Stoic philosophical ideas were incorporated into second-century Christianity (Corrington 1990, 134).

Stoics believed the secret of contentment was summed up in the virtue of *enkrateia*, temperance (Corrington 1990, 136). At the same time, controlling desires was the key to living a virtuous life. Much like James, Musonius Rufus, a first-century Roman Stoic philosopher, taught that people develop healthy responses to life not simply by understanding virtue, but by practicing it (Vaage 1990, 129-30). Musonius (89, 16-17) contrasts pleasures (*hēdonē*) and virtue (*aretē*) as opposites (BDAG, 434). Resisting pleasures is at the heart of learning to be virtuous.

IN THE TEXT

■ I The question posed in this verse appears to follow directly on the concern for peacemaking in 3:18: *From where do the wars and fights in your community come?* James answers with a rhetorical question, which implies that fights come from their own selfish desires *doing battle in parts of your bodies.* This verse uses three different synonyms for wars, fights, or battles.

The first conflict word is **wars** (*polemoi*, **fights**). In the NT the term tends to have an apocalyptic flavor. It is used by Jesus in his prediction of the end times (Matt 24:6; Mark 13:7; Luke 21:9). It appears once in the Pauline Epistles (1 Cor 14:8) and once in Hebrews (11:34). Revelation uses it eight times. James is the only book in which it refers to this-worldly conflict.

The second conflict word is **fights** (*machai*, "**quarrels, strife, disputes**"; BDAG, 622). The word is derived from "sword" (*machaira*). Outside of James, only Paul uses this word in the NT (2 Cor 7:5; 2 Tim 2:23, Titus 3:9). In the LXX it means "quarrelling" (Gen 13:6; see Prov 15:18) between family and acquaintances.

James claims these **wars and fights** result from the selfish pursuit of **sensual pleasures** (*hēdonōn*). This word is stronger than **desires**. In most cases it has negative connotations even in Greek literature. Here and in v 3, James identifies it as the cause of contention in the community. In the NT, it refers only to physical pleasures (Luke 8:14; Titus 3:3; 2 Pet 2:13).

These **sensual pleasures** not only cause problems within the community but also **battle** (*strateuomenōn*) within the person. This third conflict word is derived from "soldier" (*strateuma*). Base **sensual pleasures** wage war against the higher moral principles within.

The phrase **within you,** "in your members" (NASB), is difficult to translate. The pronoun "your" is plural, indicating that James addresses a group of people. But he uses the word **members** (*melesin*), a term referring to the actual **limbs of the body.** But it can also be used metaphorically for members of a community (Rom 12:5; 1 Cor 12:27; Eph 4:25; 5:30). Visible intercommunity conflict reflects the invisible inner conflict within individuals caused by their desires for **sensual pleasures.**

■ **2** James begins with the usual verb for **desire** (*epithymeite*, **You want**). He continues to describe the kinds of conflict sensual pleasures cause within from v 1. The NIV supplies the word **God** to complete the thought, although it does not appear in Greek.

Those who desire sensual pleasures are not being fulfilled. Not only do desires for such things lead to **murder and jealousy** (**You kill and covet**), but they cannot be satisfied. James has already referred to the prohibition of murder in 2:11. Frustrated desires cause inner conflict. James says the reason for the **fighting and warring** within their communities and their unrealized desires, is that they are not asking for what will actually benefit them.

Since early in the church's history, interpreters have debated whether **murder** (*phoneuete*) was in the original text here. It seems difficult to imagine that James' readers had stooped to such a heinous act. One scholar, Oecumenius (ca. 990), spiritualized the murder as done in their hearts (see Matt 5:21-22). Erasmas (ca. 1466-1536) speculated that the text was originally *phthoneuete* (**you envy**). No ancient manuscripts support this reading. But it is plausible, since the theme of 3:13—4:10 is envy (Johnson 1995, 277).

Most modern scholars consider this solution unsatisfactory. Conjectural changes, without manuscript support, should be used only as a last resort. "'Killing' (*phonos*) is a common element in the *topos* [topic] on envy . . . and, for the Hellenistic reader, would have been expected in this context" (Johnson 1994, 277).

James uses two words related to getting or obtaining. The first is *echete*, the common word for having or holding something. The second word is the stronger compound word *epitychein* (from the intensifying preposition *epi* and the verb *tychein*, "to obtain"; Zodhiates 1992, 643).

James claims that desiring something and doing whatever they could—even murdering another—to get it does not help them attain their goal. In v 3, he explains what he means by **not asking for** their **own benefit.**

■ 3 Their prayers are misguided. They are **asking with evil intent.** They intend to use what they ask for **on sensual pleasures.** These Jewish Christians are asking God to give them things that they think will bring them pleasure. But they should be asking for what will develop character and virtue in their lives. God refuses to answer such self-destructive requests. Like his Stoic contemporaries, James understands pleasure as the enemy of virtue.

James uses a different word for getting in this verse than the two in v 2 (see 1:5-8). *Lambanete* (**You do not receive**) is a passive form of obtaining. The emphasis is on answers to prayers—receiving from God, rather than acquiring by aggression. Even if his hearers are not actually fighting to get what they want, they do not receive anything from God, because they plan to waste God's blessings on **sensual pleasures.**

The verb *dapanaō* means "**spend freely**" (BDAG, 212). In Luke 15:14 it describes the prodigal son's squandering his inheritance. "The persistent rage of the unsatisfied spendthrift will consume his entire being" (Wall 1997, 198) through his "extravagance" (Johnson 1995, 278).

James' readers are **asking badly,** with **wrong motives.** *Kakōs* is the common word for **bad** or **evil** in the NT. It carries the meaning of **worthless** from the perspective of eternity. God will not respond to prayers for worthless, temporal pleasures. Such a prayer, comments Johnson, "is a form of idolatry" (1995, 278).

FROM THE TEXT

James and his audience were steeped in a worldview that pleasures are the enemy of character. This is extremely countercultural to modern Western society. Commercials, TV programs, and movies continually bombard us with the belief that everything should "feel good." Our culture encourages us to do what is best for ourselves and not to worry about others. No wonder pastors find it difficult to preach on the positive value of suffering in the Christian life. Modern Christians do not understand that trials and difficulties build character (1:2-4).

A common saying today is "adversity doesn't build character, it reveals character." This reflects a belief that character is something one either has or doesn't have. There is no need to build or train one's character. James and ancient moralists would disagree.

James points out that we will never achieve the goal of making ourselves happy by the pursuit of pleasure. James rejects the notion that "the gift-giving God [can be] manipulated as a kind of vending machine precisely for purposes of self-gratification" (Johnson 1995, 278). God wants to give his children the desires of their hearts. But their hearts must be right with God or they will desire things that will destroy them. God loves us too much to grant such foolish prayers.

True contentment comes when we ask for things that will benefit us and others eternally. A community full of people looking for happiness in sensual pleasures will be rife with conflict, quarrels, and jealousy.

Selfishness is at the heart of conflicts in the church. When church members realize that they are to serve one another, everyone can reach the goal of contentment. They may receive what has eternal significance. Paul's admonition in Phil 2 applies here: "Do nothing out of selfish ambition or vain conceit, but in humility . . . look not only to your own interests, but also to the interests of others. Your attitude should be the same as that of Christ Jesus" (vv 3-5).

2. Friendship with Both the World and God Is Impossible (4:4-5)

BEHIND THE TEXT

James alludes frequently here to Jewish prophetic, wisdom, and intertestamental literature. Hosea's marriage to a prostitute is a metaphor for Israel's relationship to God (Hos 3:1). Because his wife was continually unfaithful to him, he had to buy her out of slavery. In the OT, those who left God to follow idols were called adulteresses (Isa 57:3, 7; Jer 3:20; Ezek 16:32; 23:47).

In the NT, the word describes those who "neglect God and their duty toward Him and yield themselves to their own lusts and passions" (Zodhiates 1992, 993; see Matt 12:39; 16:4; Mark 8:38; Rom 7:3; and 2 Pet 2:14).

Although James' familiar statement in 4:4 is not found verbatim in any known Jewish sources, it reflects first-century Jewish apocalyptic convictions. Friendship with the world and friendship with God are diametrically opposed in apocalyptic writings of intertestamental Judaism.

Friendship with God and Hostility Toward the World: Intertestamental Sources

- **Book of Enoch 48:7:** *For he hath preserved the lot of the righteous, because they have hated and despised this world of unrighteousness, and have hated all its works and ways in the name of the Lord of Spirits: for in his name they are saved.* (216-17)
- **Book of Enoch 108:8:** *Who love God and loved neither gold nor silver nor any of the good things which are in the world.* (281, also called *Fragment of the Book of Noah*)
- **Book of Jubilees 30:21-23:** *All this account I have written for thee, and have commanded thee to say to the children of Israel, that they should not commit sin nor transgress the ordinances nor break the covenant which has been ordained for them, (but) that they should fulfill it and be recorded as friends. But if they transgress and work uncleanness in every way, they will be recorded on the heavenly tablets as adversaries, and they will be destroyed out of the book of life, and they will be recorded in the book of those who will be destroyed and with those who will be rooted out of the earth.* (59; APOT, Vol. II, 1973)

IN THE TEXT

■4 James begins v 4 by maligning his readers as **Adulteresses** (*moichalides*). In the OT this term is used figuratively to identify Israel as the unfaithful wife of the Lord (Yahweh). Some later copyists of the ancient manuscripts took the word literally and wondered why only women were addressed, so they added "adulterers" to "adulteresses."

But the original term, **adulteresses** (Ezek 23:45), indicates that James and his community were steeped in Jewish literature and saw themselves as Jews. "Remember the Scripture . . . declares that God is a jealous lover and suffers no rival for the loyalty of the human spirit" (Ropes 1973, 261). The address indicates covenant disloyalty and the foolishness of such desires (v 3).

The rhetorical question in the next clause, **don't you know** (*ouk oidate*), is used only here in James. But it is used often by Paul (e.g., Rom 6:16; 1 Cor 3:16). This feature of diatribe style calls attention to a truth that should be self-evident to the whole community (see Mark 4:13).

James hopes his audience will understand that **friendship with the world is *hostility* toward God.** The word for **friendship** (*philia*) means the love of a friend for a friend. It connotes the warm human love between equals with similar values. The problem with **friendship with the world** is that it involves aligning oneself with the values of **the world. World** (*kosmou*) here refers not to planet earth but to the forces of evil aligned against God (see 1:27; 2:5; 3:6). *Hostility* (*echthra*, **hatred**) is a cognate of *echthros*, "enemy" ("**hating, hostile**"; BDAG, 419).

JAMES

4:4

James continues with the logical conclusion: *therefore, whoever chooses to be a friend of the world becomes a personal enemy of God. Therefore* (*oun*) appears here for the first time (see 4:7, 17). With it he calls attention to implications his hearers may not have considered.

James uses the indefinite *whoever* to indicate that one's relationship with God depends on personal choices related to the values of the world. The Greek word translated **chooses** (*boulēthē*) may be translated "*wish, want, desire*" and "*intend, plan, will*" (BDAG, 182; see 1:18; 3:4). We do not accidentally adopt the values of the world, we purposefully choose them.

James may have adopted the phrase **friendship with the world is *hostility toward God*** from Jesus in Matt 6:24: "No one can serve two masters. Either he will hate the one and love [*agapēsei*] the other, or he will be devoted to the one and despise the other. You cannot serve both God and Money." But James uses a different word for *love/friendship* (*philos*) here.

A similar topic is treated in 2 Tim 3:4: "lovers of pleasure [*philēdonoi*] rather than lovers of God [*philotheoi*]." This description of godlessness in the end times uses the same friendship term. But it certainly is not as strong a statement as James'. Johnson considers 1 John 2:15 the closest parallel: "Do not love [*agapate*] the world or anything in the world. If anyone loves [*agapa*] the world, the love [*agapē*] of the Father is not in him."

The passage is close enough to suggest the existence of a shared Christian tradition to which both John and James could appeal. The fact that John uses the language of "love" rather than "friendship," however, only heightens the perception of "friendship" language as distinctively James' own. (Johnson 1995, 279)

This should not be taken to suggest that Christians cannot make friends with people who are not Christians. But Christians cannot align themselves with the values and goals of the forces of evil fighting against God and his church. The one who chooses to do this becomes *a personal enemy of God.*

The verb translated *becomes* (*kathistatai*) has the meaning of being made or appointed something (see BDAG, 492). Those who align with evil place themselves in the position of being directly opposed to God. There is no middle ground for James. Choose the way of the world or the way of God!

This is a viewpoint common to Jewish tradition. It is also found in the first or second century A.D. Christian discipleship manual called the *Didache* (*teaching*). It begins: *There are two ways, one of life and one of death, but there is a great difference between the two ways.*

The word translated *personal enemy* describes one who hates and opposes another (see Rom 8:7). Here as the opposite of friend, the author emphasizes the personal nature of the choices people make. One who chooses to befriend evil chooses hostility toward God.

JAMES

4:4

140

■ **5** This verse is difficult to translate. It can be understood in several different ways. It does not directly quote any OT verse, thus context offers little help.

The introduction to the quotation is fairly straightforward. **Or do you think Scripture says *for no purpose* . . . ?** The verb translated **do you think** emphasizes one's opinion rather than a known fact. James uses the same word in 1:26 of a person who *"considers* himself religious."* **Without reason** or *for no purpose* translates the adverb *kenōs* (*"in an empty manner, idly, in vain"*; BDAG, 540). It describes how James' imaginary dialogue partner supposes Scripture speaks. James' concern here is not what Scripture says, but why it says it.

In most NT instances, the phrase **Scripture says** precedes a direct OT quotation. But in this case, the origin of the quote is unknown. Some scholars think it might be from a now lost Jewish apocryphal work. If this was familiar to James and his readers, it would give them a context for understanding the quotation we do not have.

The quotation itself is difficult. The only noun in the quotation, *to pneuma* (**the spirit**), can be either a subject or an object. If it is the subject, the quote says: **the spirit he caused to live in us *desires greatly with envy.***

In Greek the phrase **with envy** (*pros phthonon*) actually begins the indirect quote. This emphasizes how the human spirit desires or longs to possess things—enviously. The verb the prepositional phrase modifies, *epipothei*, is a compound of the intensifying preposition *epi* and the verb *potheō* (*"desire, wish* [for], *be anxious, strive after"*; BDAG, 839). This would indicate that the human spirit strongly strives after what it longs to possess.

But if the noun **spirit** is the object, God would be the implicit subject. As the Creator and Life-Giver, he is the one who caused the human **spirit** to live in us. And God is the subject of v 6. The Scripture-like quote would then be translated: ***God enviously longs for the spirit whom he caused to live in us.*** God intensely desires fellowship with his human creatures.

Many modern commentators take God as the subject. The problem is that envy is never elsewhere ascribed to God in the NT (Davids 1982, 164; Ropes 1973, 264). But the OT indicates that God longs for his creation (Job 14:15). And the recognition that God is jealous of his people's sole allegiance is frequent (see, e.g., Exod 20:5; 34:14; Deut 4:24). In these passages the LXX uses the synonym *zēlōtēs* (***jealous** or **zealous***) rather than *phthonon* (**envy**) as in Jas 4:4. These two words appear often in similar contexts. But James uses *zēlos* ("jealous," 3:14, 16) in a negative sense.

A careful grammatical and cultural analysis and the use of *phthonon* strongly suggests the reading that takes ***spirit*** as the subject: ***The spirit he caused to live in us envies intensely*** (see Behind the Text on 4:11-12 for an in-depth discussion of "envy"). If the human spirit envies, it needs the greater grace God offers (Johnson 1995, 281-82).

FROM THE TEXT

James points out to his readers who are fighting among themselves that they are not friends of God. They reflect the values and modes of relating to one another that characterize the evil world. True to his Jewish tradition, James reminds them that there are only two ways. He calls one way "friendship with the world," which will lead to destruction. The other way, which he implicitly encourages them to take, is friendship with God.

Sinful humanity desires friendship with the world, making them enemies of God. But this should not be true of Christians. Yet, there is no middle way. By default, humans are naturally enemies of God. James' readers have chosen to return to their old way of life. The next section gives the solution to this unfortunate situation.

3. Be Humbled Before God (4:6-10)

BEHIND THE TEXT

This section contains allusions to OT prophetic and wisdom literature as well as to Jesus' teaching. Verse 6 includes an exact quote from the LXX of Prov 3:34. James can assume that his communities are familiar with various types of Jewish literature. His preference for the LXX suggests that they read their "Bible" in Greek.

In the OT prophets, one hears:

- "Return to me . . . and I will return to you" (Zech 1:3 and Mal 3:7).
- "Your hands are full of blood; wash and make yourselves clean" (Isa 1:15b-16a).
- "O Jerusalem, wash the evil from your heart and be saved. How long will you harbor wicked thoughts?" (Jer 4:14).

Wisdom literature counsels:

- "But for me, it is good to be near God. I have made the Sovereign LORD my refuge; I will tell of all your deeds" (Ps 73:28).
- "Who may ascend the hill of the LORD? Who may stand in his holy place? He who has clean hands and a pure heart, who does not lift up his soul to an idol or swear by what is false" (Ps 24:3-4).
- "I hate double-minded men, but I love your law" (Ps 119:113).
- "The lowly he sets on high, and those who mourn are lifted to safety" (Job 5:11).

142

Jesus says in the Beatitudes, "Woe to you who are well fed now, for you will go hungry. Woe to you who laugh now, for you will mourn and weep" (Luke 6:25).

The concept of the Satan figure in Jewish tradition developed over time. In the early writings, Satan is a member of God's court whom God sends out to test his people (Job 1:6-12). After the Babylonian exile, probably under the influence of Persian dualism, the devil came to be understood as the personification of Evil (vs. God, the personification of Good). Contrary to the absolute Persian dualism in which Good and Evil are equal and opposite forces, Judaism retained the idea that God is greater than the devil and will punish him and those who follow him. But in the dark days of Exile, Israel had no difficulty accepting the idea that the devil had (temporarily, at least) wrenched control of the earth from God.

The NT and the LXX use *daimonion* primarily to refer to demons. The LXX uses *diabolos* to translate the Hebrew *ha satan* ("Accuser"). In the NT *diabolos* ("devil") is used primarily in the singular to refer to the prince of demons. In the plural, **devils** is translated "malicious talkers" (1 Tim 3:11) and "slanderous" or "slanderers" (2 Tim 3:3; Titus 2:3). This is the meaning of *diabolos* in classical Greek.

The term "Satan" (*satanas*) is used in the four Gospels, Acts, some of the Pauline letters, and Revelation, but not in the General Epistles. These primarily Jewish-Christian works follow the pattern of the LXX, translating the Hebrew *ha satan* as *diabolos*.

IN THE TEXT

■ **6** The question of v 5 continues with its answer expressed in contrast (*de*) to the envious desires of the human spirit. God is introduced as the new subject: **But he gives greater grace.** God wants desperately to have fellowship with his creation, so he took the initiative to change the human heart. Because the human spirit is so subject to envy, God **gives us more grace.** The continuous present tense of the verb means that God's grace is not a one-time indulgence. God is not finished with his generous giving.

Therefore, Scripture says: "God resists the arrogant, but gives grace to the humble." This is an almost exact quote from the LXX translation of Prov 3:34. The one exception is the use of Lord (*kyrios*) instead of God (*ho theos*).

This quotation aptly captures James' antithesis of earthly wisdom and the wisdom from above (3:13-18). The **arrogant** (*hyperēphanois*; by etymology: **high thinkers**) are **proud** and haughty people; BDAG, 1033; see, e.g., 1 Pet 5:5 [also quoting Prov 3:34]; Luke 1:51 [*God has scattered the arrogant*]; Rom 1:30; 2 Tim 3:2). The NT has nothing positive to say about the proud past, present, or future.

143

God opposes the proud but gives grace to the humble. Found only here in James, the word **grace** (*charin*) appears twice in v 6. **Grace** is a rich theological word. Here it means the "*favor*, . . . *gracious care/help, goodwill*" (BDAG, 1079) God offers the undeserving. This is not in response to a favor done by the person receiving grace. The term occurs throughout the NT. Paul and Luke/Acts use it extensively. It appears in Hebrews, 2 Peter, Jude, in the Johannine literature, and twice in Revelation (1:4; 2:21).

On the opposite end of the spectrum of the **arrogant** are the **humble** (*tapeinois*). James uses some form of the Greek root for **humble** four times (1:9, 10; 4:6, 10). In Matt 11:29, Jesus describes himself as "gentle [*praus*] and humble [*tapeinos*] in heart." He promises (in Matt 18:4 and 23:12) that those who humble themselves will be raised to a higher status by God (see Luke 14:11; 18:14; 2 Cor 10:1; 12:21; Phil 2:3; 3:21). First Peter 5:5-7 echoes the usage and context of James.

Two synonyms in Greek can be translated **humble** (*tapeinos*) in English. Jesus uses these words together in his self-description (in Matt 11:29) as "gentle [*prays*] and humble [*tapeinos*] in heart." *Praus* may be translated "gentle" or "*humble, considerate, meek*" (BDAG, 861). *Tapeinos* may be translated "**unpretentious, humble**" (BDAG, 989).

James' preference for *tapeinos* (**humble**) may be due to the need for his readers to become submissive to God. He defines the conditions under which adulteresses can repent and return to fellowship with God in the following verses.

■ **7** James begins with two commands: **Submit yourselves, then, to God. Resist the devil.** . . . To **submit** (*hypotagēte*) is a passive form of the verb "*subject*" or "*subordinate*." Thus, it means "*become subject*," "*subject oneself*," or "*obey*" (BDAG, 1042). In the NT it often refers to voluntary submission, as here. To be submissive is to trust and obey the one submitted to.

The verb translated **resist** (*antistēte*) means to "**be in opposition to, set oneself against, oppose** . . . **to be resistant to power, resist**" (BDAG, 80). This verb is also found in 1 Pet 5:9 in a similar context of resisting the devil (see Eph 4:27; 6:11; 1 Tim 3:6-7).

James does not call for mild resistance. Resistance means taking sides, speaking out against the adversary, and strategizing to foil his sinister plots. This resistance is not in human strength alone. When Christians stand up against the devil, they are promised: **he will flee from you.**

The verb translated **flee** (*pheuxetai*) is defined as "**to seek safety in flight**" (BDAG, 1052). The devil will not just walk away; he escapes as fast as he can.

Previously James traced sin back to desires of the human heart (1:13-15), but:

Now he reveals (as in 3:3, 15) that behind the evil impulse lies the devil: suprapersonal forces of evil are behind personal evil. Here James agrees not only with Paul . . . , but also with the gospel tradition. (Davids 1982, 166)

■ **8** In this verse James emphasizes the opposite to resisting the devil. He says, **Come near** (*engisate*) or **to God and he will come near** [*engiei*] **to you.** James' language recalls the imagery of Sinai. There Moses and the priests were invited to "approach" God (Exod 24:2; 19:22), but the people could not (Exod 19:21). In Deut 4:7 it was regarded as exceptional that "Israel's God was one who 'approached' people" (Johnson 1995, 284).

Echoes of the prophets are also heard: "Return to me . . . and I will return to you" (Zech 1:3; Mal 3:7). James uses *engizō* ("**draw near, come near, approach**"; BDAG, 270). The LXX uses a different verb, *epistrephō* ("turn, turn around, go back"), but the meanings are similar. The Hebrew verb (*šûb*, "return, turn, turn again, come again") used in the OT is close to the meaning of the Greek verb used in the LXX. The verb *engizō* brings out the desire to establish a close relationship with God. It is not just to be protected from the evil one, but to know God intimately.

James' context is slightly different from that of the prophets. Although he calls them **adulteresses** in v 4, he also calls them **brothers and sisters** in v 11. As he adapts the language of the prophets to his audience, he emphasizes the need to **move toward** God, rather than returning to God.

The second part of this verse again echoes Israel's Prophets and Psalms. James commands his readers: **Wash your hands, you sinners, and purify your hearts, you double-minded.** Isaiah counsels: "Your hands are full of blood; wash and make yourselves clean" (Isa 1:15*b*-16*a*; see Jer 4:14). The psalmist says that those who would be close to God must have "clean hands and a pure heart" (Ps 24:4). The heart in biblical psychology designates the seat of affection and decision (Gen 6:5; Deut 8:2). Thus, the pure heart describes one in right relationship with God (Matt 5:8; 1 Tim 1:5; Johnson 1995, 285).

The **sinners** (*hamartōloi*) are "those who act contrary to the law of God; they disobey God in their actions" (Davids 1982, 167). The **double-mined** (*dipsychoi*: **double-souled**; see the commentary on 1:8) differ. They are "those who try to be committed to both good and evil, God and the world" (Davids 1982, 167). The **sinners** are to cleanse their hands while the **double-souled** are to purify their hearts morally.

But this might be taken as an example of Hebrew synonymous parallelism. If so, the two subjects—**sinners** and **double-minded**—are merely alternate ways of referring to the same offenders. Likewise, the two metaphorical actions—washing hands and purifying hearts—refer to the same underlying reality. Thus, James addresses a single group with just one challenge: You, who are trying to be friends with both God and the world, need to recognize that you are sinners, who need to be morally transformed.

Cleansing (*katharizō*) and purifying (*hagnizō*) are similar and are often used together in parallel. Psalm 24:4 (LXX) uses *katharos* ("clean") instead of *hagnos* (**"pure, holy"**; BDAG, 13) in referring to a "pure heart." James uses the two significant verbs, "to cleanse" and "to purify" or "make holy." The command to purify your heart means that we are to dedicate ourselves to God or give ourselves up as an offering to God (BDAG, 13).

In the LXX of Ps 119:113, the psalmist says he hates **lawless men** (*paranomous*, **contrary to the law**). But the Hebrew refers to "double-minded men" (*seʿepim*; **divided, half-hearted**). James paraphrases the Hebrew in Greek, rather than quoting the LXX. If so, this indicates that he is familiar with both the Greek and Hebrew terms and uses the one that expresses best what he wants to say.

James first addressed double-souled persons in 1:8 as those who doubt God. These people have two competing wills or differing purposes in life. They are restless and unsettled because they have not figured out whom they will serve or what they want out of life.

Significantly, this address to the double-souled immediately follows James' request that they cleanse their hands and purify their hearts. A basic element of being holy is a settled allegiance to God. God expects nothing less than undivided commitment. Other interests may exist, but there is no question as to whose will is primary.

■ **9** James continues his series of imperatives: *Be miserable, mourn, and cry!* These three aorist verbs indicate that those who realize their sinful, double-minded condition, should begin to **Grieve, mourn and wail**.

Talaipōrēsate (Be miserable) occurs only here in the NT. It "indicates neither voluntary asceticism . . . nor an eschatological judgment, . . . but the inner sorrow and wretchedness one experiences when one realizes that he is in a sad condition" (Davids 1982, 167). This inner condition of misery is expressed in the outward actions of grieving—mourning and crying. The two words, **mourn and wail,** are synonyms often used together as visible expressions of deep grief.

There is a similarity here to the prophet Joel's emphasis on the nearness of the last judgment:

> Therefore, like Joel, he [James] calls on God's people to exhibit a heartfelt sorrow for sin that is the mark of true repentance—what Paul called a "godly sorrow . . . that leads to salvation and leaves no regret." (2 Cor 7:10; Moo 2000, 195)

This first sentence is followed by another command with essentially the same sentiment: *Exchange your laughter for grief and your joy for despair.*

James' readers must take sin seriously. Their **laughter** in their precarious position indicates that they are fools who ignore the judgment of God. If they could see themselves from God's perspective, they would realize their need for true repentance (see Prov 10:23; Eccl 7:6; and Sir 27:13).

> A carefree, "devil-may-care" attitude is typical of those who are "friends with the world." They live the hedonist philosophy "eat, drink and be merry, for tomorrow we die," a worldview that ignores the terrifying reality of God's judgment. (Moo 2000, 195)

The words translated as **grief** (*penthos*) and **despair** (*katēpheian*) are synonyms, which could both be translated as "sorrow."

James may be alluding to Jesus' teaching in the Lucan Beatitudes: "Woe to you who are well fed now, for you will go hungry. Woe to you who laugh now, for you will mourn and weep" (6:25). But his emphasis here differs in that he is describing how the **double-souled** persons should approach God. They must lament by acknowledging what they are and what they have done with great sorrow.

The laughter that characterized their lives before they recognized their true situation before God must be turned into sorrow for their sinfulness. James describes deep repentance. Divine forgiveness comes at great cost. Those who approach God to ask for forgiveness need to realize the appalling nature of their sin.

James' view of the Christian life is a serious one. He calls Christians to accountability. They have slid into "a casual attitude toward sin, perhaps presuming too much on God's forgiving and merciful nature" (Moo 2000, 195). But James also acknowledges that God gives good gifts and perfect presents (1:17).

■ **10** In vv 7-10, James has expanded on the Scripture quotation in v 6. He finishes this section with a final command, followed by a promise: **Humble yourselves before the Lord, and he will *honor you*.** This summary statement alludes to Jesus and Job. "The lowly he sets on high" (Job 5:11*a*). In Matt 23:12, Jesus says, "Whoever exalts himself will be humbled, and whoever humbles himself will be exalted" (Matt 18:4; Luke 14:11; 18:14). This saying of Jesus uses the same two verbs James uses here: *tapeinoō* ("Humble") and *hypsoō* ("lift . . . up," **exalt,** or **honor**).

In summing up this section, James refers back to his statement in 4:6 (see 1:9) that God is giving **grace to the humble** (*tapeinois*). He echoes Prov 3:34: "He mocks proud mockers but gives grace to the humble." If we humble ourselves (*tapeinōthēte*), God will give us grace and he will **lift** us **up** from our lowly position. Humility is important and necessary for true repentance.

Ancient Understanding of Envy and Jealousy

Jealousy (Jas 3:14, 16; 4:2) is an important theme throughout 3:13—4:10. The Greek words for *be jealous* (*zēloō*) and *jealousy* (*zēlos*) have a broad range of meaning. Positively, they can mean zeal. But in James, their meaning is always negative, as in jealousy or envy. In 4:5, the specific word for "envy" (*phthonos*) occurs.

Aristotle (fourth century B.C.) distinguishes assertive jealousy (*zēlos*) from envy (*phthonos*). He says, "The one, owing to competitiveness [*zēlos*], fits himself to obtain such goods, while the object of the other, owing to envy [*phthonos*], is to prevent his neighbor from possessing them" (*Rhet.* 2.11.1-4; cited in Malina 2001a, 127).

The Wisdom of Solomon (third century B.C.—first century A.D.) claims that death entered the world because of the devil's envy (*phthonos*, 2:24; http://www.earlyjewishwritings.com/wisdom.html).

In *The Testament of the Twelve Patriarchs* (A.D. 70-200), Simeon tells his children: "I was envious [*ezēlōsa*] of Joseph because our father loved him; and I set my mind against him to destroy him, because the prince of deceit sent forth the spirit of envy [*zelou*] and blinded my mind" (2.6-7). Deliverance from envy comes from God. Simeon warns his children that envy will destroy them (*T. Sim.* 2.8—3.6, http://www.earlyjewishwritings.com/testtwelve.html)

Philo of Alexandria, first-century Jewish philosopher, considered envy "the most worthless of all evils" (Philo 1950, III.1.3). His comments on the last five commandments indicate that "the root of transgressions against neighbor was envy" (cited in Malina 2001a, 129).

Patrocleas, in Plutarch's "Table Talk" (A.D. 46-127), wrote: "Envy, which naturally roots itself more deeply in the mind than any other passion, contaminates the body too with evil" (681 F-82, cited in Malina 2001a, 124).

In antiquity, envy was "a feeling of begrudging that emerges in face of the good fortune of others relative to some restricted good that is equally of interest to us" (Malina 2001a, 109). First-century culture thought everything was in limited supply, including "land, wealth, prestige, blood, health, semen, friendship and love, manliness, honor, respect and status, power and influence, security and safety" (Malina 2001a, 113). Thus, the evil of envy was discussed often. People tried to rid their lives of envy and to protect themselves from the envy of others. People hesitated to boast, since it invited the envy of others.

First-century people protected themselves from envy by hiding the evidence of any increase in wealth or status, by rejecting compliments, by sharing their wealth, and by buying amulets against the "evil eye." Envy in the heart, it was thought, came out through the eyes and caused loss and pain to anyone those eyes looked on (Malina 2001a, 120-26). Mediterranean cultures still use staring eye amulets to ward off the "evil eye." In modern Turkey the "blue eye" is a form of this evil eye amulet. Families hang a blue eye near the front door of their homes and in their cars. It is even painted on the nose of Turkish jets.

Modern societies tend to analyze envy psychologically as an emotion. People in most Western market economies do not usually have a concept that everything is limited. So envy is not as common an emotion as jealousy. But in the first century, envy was recognized by such behaviors as "ostracism, gossip and slander, feuding, litigation, and homicide" (Malina 2001a, 118).

This section of James warns against slander, litigation, and judging others. "Litigation in antiquity was not about justice, about getting at the truth of a case. . . . Rather litigation . . . is about shaming one's opponent, thus reducing him (or her) to public pity" (Malina 2001a, 119).

FROM THE TEXT

In v 6, James emphasizes that God is the one who initiates the relationship between himself and humans. He created us for fellowship with him and longs for that fellowship. In fact, he longs so much that he provides grace so we can respond to him. But he gives this grace only to those who recognize their lowly position, to those willing to be submissive to God.

In v 7, James encourages his readers to submit themselves to God. This requires humbling, cleansing, and purifying. He uses the purity language of holiness (see Benefiel 2004, in Appendix A).

James begins this section by indicating that God gives grace to the humble. Therefore, he commands his readers to be submissive to God. And he ends it with a command to humble oneself before the Lord (v 10).

John Wesley points out that we draw near to God through prayer: "Then draw nigh to God in prayer, and he will draw nigh unto you, will hear you; which that nothing may hinder, cleanse your hands—Cease from doing evil" (2003, 820). Wesley sees double-mindedness as a description of those who try to serve "God and Money" (Matt 6:24).

Brosend summarizes these verses: "At the center is a compelling call to claim friendship with God over (and against) the 'world,' to grieve one's sins, and to adopt a manner of life in keeping with one's faith" (2004, 113). One can hear a clear call to complete commitment to God and to a lifestyle that is pleasing to him.

Related to submission and humbling are cleansing and purifying. These are often seen in the holiness tradition as actions God does. Our response to his cleansing and purifying is consecration or submission. But in this section, James uses these terms in the Jewish or OT sense. The readers are commanded to cleanse their hands and purify their hearts. This is the OT way of saying that those who are seeking to be close to God need to stop doing what they know displeases God and begin to do what God wants.

Christians who realize that they have been taking sin lightly must be truly sorry and mourn their foolishness. God is a God of love. But he is also a God of judgment, which must be taken seriously.

James gives these commands to the double-souled—to those who want both the things of the world and the things of God. The Hebrew word echoed here means half-hearted. If Christians are serious about living close to God, James says they need to become seriously sorry for their half-hearted Christian lives and totally submit themselves to God.

Ropes characterized this humbling of themselves as an act of "single-hearted faith." We can be sure that "such a soul has a sure reward from God" (Ropes 1973, 272). When Christians do this, two things happen: the devil will flee and the Lord will honor them. What more incentive is there to live a fully consecrated life than freedom from sin and God's honor!

F. Do Not Judge Your Neighbor (4:11-12)

This sixth section of James' exposition changes the topic significantly. It begins with the personal address to **brothers and sisters.** The commands are not to slander or judge one another. God alone is qualified to judge. It is not the place of Christians to judge other Christians.

IN THE TEXT

■ **11** This verse begins: **Brothers *and sisters,* do not slander one another.** Again, **brothers** is collective, as James addresses his entire audience.

James' use of **brothers** is a striking switch from addressing sinners and double-minded persons in 4:8. Perhaps he illustrates the need for care in using the tongue as he advised his readers. "Rabbi Asi remarked: 'He who slanders another thereby slanders God'" (Martin 1988, 163).

James orders his hearers not to **slander** or speak against (*katalaleite*) one another. He warns his readers not to envy one another or promote competitive jealousy that will destroy their community. Slander was understood as the result of envy in one's heart.

James draws a comparison between slandering or judging one another and slandering or judging the Law. First, *the one who slanders a brother or sister* is assuming the role of their judge. Second, the one who *judges a brother or sister both slanders the law and judges the law.* To complete the thought, third, the one who *judges the law* is *not a doer of the law, but a judge.*

What is meant by *law* here? Nystrom thinks it refers to the "royal law" in 2:8 (1997, 249). Reicke suggests it "denotes the word, or the gospel" (1964, 47). James is probably referring to the Jewish Torah, perhaps more precisely the Ten Commandments as interpreted by Jesus. For James the Law is always a positive standard by which he measures his community. To speak against the Law is blasphemy, since one would be speaking against God.

Righteous people in James' view are doers *of the law,* not *a judge* over it. They submit themselves to the Law. The judge here is not one who is bound by the Law as our modern judges are, "but more as the royal judge, the fountain of right, *i.e.* such a judge as God is" (Ropes 1973, 274).

People consider themselves above the Law when they criticize it. Critics of the Law are no longer submissive to God and his royal law (2:8). Judging the Law "does more than break the law, it treats the law as if it did not matter, as if it were not in force. In short, it . . . finds it not worthy of adherence" (Nystrom 1997, 249).

■ **12** James begins v 12 with the same grammatical construction he used in 2:19, **God is one.** This is the traditional formula of monotheism in Judaism. James says, **The Lawgiver and Judge are one.** Placed first in Greek, *one* emphasizes that God alone can judge, because he gave the Law (Exod 24:12). God is also **the one who is able to save and destroy** (see Matt 10:28). God is both **Lawgiver and Judge** because he is the one who has the power both to save and to destroy humanity.

After James has established the awesome authority of God, he asks a rhetorical question, **But you, who are you, judging your neighbor?** "So who, then, are you to judge your neighbor?" (NRSV), asks James with obvious irony. He uses the singular *you* here, indicating he may have a specific example in mind—a particular slanderous judge in the community. Only God has the authority to judge. To usurp his place is to blaspheme God.

FROM THE TEXT

This section corresponds closely to the previous one. The issue again is submission to God. James identifies the outward actions of slander and judgmentalism as indicative of a lack of submission to God. Our relationship to God has community consequences. We cannot be submissive to God and treat our brother, sister, or neighbor as if we imagine we are God.

James' comments are not meant to discourage honest confrontation within the body of Christ. When done in an effort to build up another, it is justified. These cautions are intended "to make clear a strong warning that the line demarking proper from sinful discourse is easily and often unknowingly crossed" (Nystrom 1997, 250). James has already included himself among those who "stumble in many ways" (3:2). Far too often we are guilty of the same (or worse) faults we judge our brothers and sisters for.

James may have been sensitive to the reputation of the churches in their various Diaspora communities. This might be comparable to Paul's concern for Christians "to lead a quiet life, to mind [their] own business and to work

151

with [their] hands, . . . so that [their] daily life may win the respect of outsiders" (1 Thess 4:11-12). Paul rejects as shameful the practice of Christians taking other Christians to court, airing their dirty laundry "in front of unbelievers!" (1 Cor 6:6; see vv 1-6).

God is the one who gives the law of love. The Christian's response to the clear Word of God is submission, not critique. When Christians judge their brothers and sisters from their limited perspectives, they are disrespecting God. Jesus, in Matt 7:1, warns the people not to judge, lest they be judged. It is God's job to judge, not the Christian's. Furthermore, human judgments have no ultimate consequences since only God can save and destroy humanity. So, what is the good of Christians even attempting to judge others?

G. Do Not Boast About Tomorrow (4:13-17)

This seventh section of the exposition begins with *Come now.* It is also used at the beginning of the eighth section (5:1). Here it addresses the topic of making plans without considering the Lord's will. James wants to make sure his readers realize how small and powerless they really are in comparison to God.

He closes this section with a proverb on the sin of omission. The shift to the third person in v 17 "contrasts with the second-person address of verses 13-16" (Bauckham 1999, 65). This proverb at first glance seems unrelated to the rest of the section. But it essentially urges the readers: Now that you know what to do, do it!

BEHIND THE TEXT

To understand this section, modern readers need to understand two behind-the-scenes issues. One is that people with first-century Mediterranean culture tried to protect themselves from the envy of others (see sidebar "Ancient Understanding of Envy and Jealousy" above). People were warned not to boast, which would invite the envy of others. Boasting was not avoided simply because it made the boaster look proud, as in modern Western society. It was also to be avoided because it could invite harm to the boastful person, his family, or his community.

The second issue is that the first-century society was what scholars call a "peasant" society. Not everyone was poor. But that everyone, whether king or beggar, had a "peasant" mentality.

Peasant society was based on a rural culture, where land ownership and agriculture were the basis of wealth. Most landowners had two homes, their country home and their city house. The country home was their main base and the city house was a place where meetings, commerce, and socializing with other elites took place.

The two main institutions in a rural society are kinship and politics. The role, status, economic level, and religion of everyone in the society depend on their family background. The status of a person in the political system is determined by the kinship system as well. Political roles are available only to the proper people from the "best" families. The interests and values of the "best" families shape the whole society (see Malina 2001a, 81-88).

Cities were primarily market centers, not entirely unlike modern shopping centers. Ancient markets needed to import supplies so that those in the surrounding rural society could survive. Revelation 18:12-13 lists some of what first-century cities imported:

> gold, silver, precious stones and pearls; fine linen, purple, silk and scarlet cloth; every sort of citron wood, and articles of every kind made of ivory, costly wood, bronze, iron and marble, cargoes of cinnamon and spice, of incense, myrrh and frankincense, of wine and olive oil, of fine flour and wheat; cattle and sheep; horses and carriages; and bodies and souls of men.

We also know that Paul and some of his coworkers were craftworkers who made tents, coats, and other items from cilicium (a strong, water-repellant haircloth made from the black goats of Cilicia). Markets provided an outlet for farmers and craftsmen to sell or barter their excess goods in what was primarily a noncash society.

Wayne Meeks concludes from the NT data that the typical Christian was a free artisan or small trader (2003, 73). There is evidence of high-status Christians as well as slaves, but the middle status was well-represented. Because the Jews were a conquered people, it is likely that James' community belonged primarily to the middle status of artisan (like Paul) or small trader.

Cities were divided into different sectors based on what products were being sold or services being offered, much like modern department stores. The artisans and traders, however, dealt directly with their customers. So when Paul entered a city he could ask where the tentmakers were. Acts and Paul's writings indicate that he would make acquaintances in the tentmakers area, join with some family, and start working with them (Acts 18:2-3).

Hospitality was a highly valued virtue and was important in making possible the economic lives of artisans and traders. Thus, traders or artisans could go to a city where they heard that workers in their profession were needed. There they would stay with other people of their ethnic, religious, or kinship groups for a period of time. They would work with the family or pseudo-family group to pay for their lodging and other needs.

■ **13** This verse begins with a direct address to the merchants and traders in the community. The opening command, **Now listen** (lit., **Come now**), was an informal way of addressing one's associates (BDAG, 9). It is found only here and in 5:1 (addressing the rich) in the NT. This phrase appears in similar conversational writings (Xenophon, 431–355 B.C., and Epictetus, A.D. 55-135; Davids 1982, 171).

James identifies his addressees as **you who say, "Today or tomorrow we will go *into such and such a* city, *work there for* a year, carry on business and make *a profit*."** These people are part of the communities to whom James writes. If scholars are correct, such merchants represent a large part of the community (see Behind the Text above). The contrast between this address and James' usual, "my brothers and sisters," is noteworthy. This address is "brusque and admonitory" (Moo 2000, 201-2).

Some commentators think James is addressing the rich here. But the cultural context, as NT cultural scholars understand it, doesn't support that. Some of the merchants or traders might be rich. But inclusion in this group doesn't guarantee that they are rich. The tone of the address suggests that "the attitude of these Christians [is] unworthy of who they really are" (Moo 2000, 202).

The reference to **today or tomorrow** indicates the immediate future and is important to the point James makes in v 14. It is a part of the trader's job to seek out profit-making possibilities. A decision to go to a certain city, take wares, and trade them for a profit was only common sense to the merchants. They probably knew people in this city, knew there was a market for their goods, and made careful and concrete plans. This is really not the issue for James (see vv 14 and 15).

Trade (*emporeuomai* [root of the English "emporium"], **carry on business**) is found only in this verse and in 2 Pet 2:3. There it refers to false "teachers" who "in their greed . . . will exploit" their hearers "with stories they have made up."

Make a profit (*kerdainō*, **make money**) is used more often in the NT. However, outside the parable of the talents (Matt 25:14-30), the meaning elsewhere is primarily metaphorical—that is, gaining something or someone—rather than the specifically business profit.

■ **14** The grammatical difficulty of this verse in Greek resulted in alternate readings in the ancient manuscripts (see Johnson 1995, 295-96). These readings, however, do not "alter" the intended meaning.

The word **know** (*epistasthe*) is not the common word for know (*ginōskō*). *Epistamai* is a compound verb from the preposition *epi* ("over") and the verb *histēmi* ("stand"). It emphasizes having "**a firm mental grasp**" or a thorough understanding of all the data (BDAG, 380).

The next phrase, *to tēs aurion*, is translated literally *the thing of tomorrow*. No one may know **what will happen tomorrow** in detail. Some scribes attempted to improve the grammar by making the singular neuter article plural—*the things of tomorrow*. This corresponds more closely with Prov 27:1 (in the LXX), to which James probably alludes.

What is your life? (*poia hē zōē hymōn*). *Poia* is an interrogative pronoun from *poios*. It is used to ask a qualitative question, "What kind of or what sort of . . . ?" (Wallace 1996, 346). This fits the context of the verb **you . . . know** in this verse. It can introduce a direct or indirect question. Here, it is probably an appositional indirect question: **You do not even know what will happen tomorrow,** *that is, what kind of life you will have.*

The tenuousness of life is captured in the next clause. It explains why one can't plan on tomorrow. *For you are a vapor that appears for a little while and then disappears.* The word translated *vapor* (*atimis*) is a passing **mist,** steam seen briefly, only to vanish quickly (BDAG, 149). It is a metaphor for nothingness. In the grand scheme of things, people's lives are transient, uneventful, and inconsequential. Their lives resemble the steam that comes off a pot of boiling water.

One important manuscript (Sinaiticus) omits the metaphor *For you are a vapor.* But the meaning remains the same. The transitory nature of life is a common theme in Jewish and Christian literature (see Prov 21:6; Job 7:7, 9, 16; Ps 39:5-6; and Luke 12:15). "Ecclesiastes is a commentary on the meaning of life, and its thesis is that human existence is like a mist" (Wall 1997, 220).

James has already alluded to the transitory nature of the lives of the rich in 1:10-11. In Jewish apocalyptic literature (*4 Ezra* 7:61; *2 Bar.* 82:3; *1 En.* 97:8-10) "the wicked are compared to a mist or smoke that will disappear" (Johnson 1995, 296).

■ **15** James now indicates the proper attitude these merchants and traders should have. **Instead you ought to say, "If the Lord wills, indeed** [*kai,* "then" or "and"] **we will live and do this or that." Instead** (*anti*) indicates a contrast between what they have been doing and what they should be doing.

James starts with the basics. Whether we live or die is in God's hands. So what we do while we are alive should be what God wants. The phrase *If the Lord wills* is often referred to as the *conditio Jacobaea*—**James' condition.**

James uses the term **Lord** (*kyrios*) here as in the LXX—a reference to God. It does not appear to refer to Jesus. The change from "If God wills" (used in the pagan world; Ropes 1973, 280) to "*If the Lord wills*" may indicate a Jewish-Christian flavor (Moo 2000, 205).

In the NT the idea is "found with remarkable frequency" as "'the will of God' (Rom 12:2; 1 Cor 1:1; Heb 10:36)." Jesus spoke of "the 'will of the father' (Matt 7:21; 12:50; 18:14; 21:31) or 'the will of the one who sent me' (John 4:34; 5:30) or 'the will of God' (Mark 3:35)" (Johnson 1995, 297).

Two worldviews at odds are represented in vv 13-17. The first primarily ignores God—it is "marked by boastful self-reliance (4:13-17) and selfish indulgence (5:1-6)" (Moo 2000, 200). James urges his Christian audience to respond biblically and reaffirm that God providentially provides all we need (Moo 2000, 201).

■ **16** With *nyn de* (**As it is;** lit., ***But now***), James picks up the merchant's worldview introduced in v 13. He reminds his readers that **boasting** can create problems. He says, **you boast *in your arrogance.*** **Boasting** can be used in both a positive and negative sense. When used in a positive sense the Greek verb *kauchaomai* is generally translated "rejoice" or "glory in." People boasting of what they perceive gives them honor. When Christians boast in the Lord, whether God or Jesus Christ (Rom 2:17; 5:11; 1 Cor 1:31; 2 Cor 10:17; Phil 3:3), they identify the source of their honor and status in God rather than in their own accomplishments.

James accuses these merchants and traders of boasting in their ***arrogance*** (*alazoneiais*): they **boast and brag** as fools. This precise term is used only twice in the NT, here and in 1 John 2:16. The noun *alazōn*, "***boaster***" or "***braggart***" (BDAG, 41; see Rom 1:30; 2 Tim 3:2), is "a stock character, expressing empty arrogance" in the Greek philosophical tradition (Johnson 1995, 297).

The word ***arrogance*** in this verse means to show off what one pretends to be or have. The arrogant are overly proud hypocrites. They are charlatans who claim to have cures or products that can do amazing things.

Arrogance has negative connotations in the context of merchants and traders. James claims that because they do not include God in their business plans, they are like charlatans. God gives the strength and wisdom to make good business plans, so he must be the author of these plans. Otherwise, merchants will make plans they cannot fulfill.

James concludes this verse with **All such boasting is evil.** He defines the type of **boasting** he is talking about and proclaims it *evil.* The word for **evil** (*ponēra*) is in all but seven of the NT books. James also uses it in 2:4.

Boasting, whether in good things or bad, invites envy. ***Boasting in arrogance*** is foolish and dangerous. It invites envy for no reason. It invites sorrow and pain as a result of another's envy; it is wicked, malicious, and misleading to others. This **evil** consists of both physical suffering and evil in a moral or spiritual sense (BDAG, 851-52).

■ **17** This verse takes the form of a maxim or proverb. It is introduced by ***Therefore*** (*oun*), which introduces a conclusion to 3:13-16. It shifts from a second person (**you**) to a third person (**he**) subject; and, from the specific to the general. The maxim serves as a transition to the new topic in 5:1-6. As a proverb it defines the sin of omission. ***Therefore, to the one who knows to do good and does not do it; to that person it is sin.***

James encourages the merchants and traders to heed what he says. Now that they know how they should plan their lives, they must do it. The failure to "preface one's endeavors with prayer and place one's projects within the will of God" may be the sin of omission referred to in this passage (Johnson 1995, 298).

The word translated **good** (*kalon*) is the common word for good. Paul uses it extensively in 1 Timothy to describe the qualifications for Christian leaders and to fight the good fight (e.g., 1:18; 3:7; 6:12). The Gospels use it in talking about good fruit (Luke 6:43), good works (Matt 5:16), and the good shepherd (John 10:11). James uses the word in 2:7 ("noble name"); 3:13 ("good life," i.e., moral lifestyle); and, this verse. Surprisingly, he does not use it to describe "works," actions demonstrating true faith, in ch 2. The actions James mentions are in response to God's work in human lives. They are good because they are a result of God's work. Thus, there is no need to identify them as good or bad. This verse comes close to referring to **good** works, but James omits the noun "works" (*erga*, "actions").

The word *hamartia* is usually translated **sin** in the NT. Luke uses the word in his version of the Lord's Prayer (11:4: "forgive us our sins"). Paul uses it extensively in Rom 6—8. ***Sin*** in the NT means a departure from divine or human standards of uprightness, a state of being sinful, and a destructive evil power (BDAG, 50-51).

So *hamartia* (***sin***) can refer to specific sins as well as any deviation from God's truth or law. James insists that those who neglect to do good are guilty, when they know to do it. The sin of omission is not to be taken lightly as a mistake or fault. People are just as guilty for not doing good as for doing evil.

FROM THE TEXT

Three main theological issues appear in this section. First, God is the source of the Christian's daily physical strength. One's life, mental abilities, talents, and gifts are all from God. When Christians plan their lives without acknowledging God's involvement or asking for his direction, they are un-grateful and disrespectful of the God who is the source of their lives. Their arrogance, in thinking that they are the ones that make things happen, will eventually bring sorrow and pain into their lives.

James' response to the "business plan" of these merchants is similar to Jesus' response to the rich fool (in Luke 12:20). The rich fool planned to tear down his barns and build bigger ones: "'You fool! This very night your life will be demanded from you. Then who will get what you have prepared for yourself?'" James is not this direct, but he does emphasize the transitory nature of life itself.

The people James addresses are functional atheists. They are compartmentalizing their lives. In their "business world," they do what they feel is best; but in their "spiritual world" they try to follow God's will. James is trying to break down the sacred and secular distinctions in these Christians (Brosend 2004, 127). This observation may be anachronistic as the first-century Jews, Christians and pagans, saw everything through a sacred lens. But it is also true that James observed that these merchants were making assumptions about their lives without taking the Lord into serious consideration.

Functional atheism is certainly common in the twenty-first century among Christians. Today, Christians need to break down the artificial sacred-secular distinctions. They must realize that God is present and needs to be a part of their plans from the beginning. They should not make their plans and then ask God to bless them.

Second, James recognizes the transitory nature of human life. God has always existed, and in the light of eternity, the few years of our lifetimes are like a blink of an eye. This reinforces James' point that Christians need to ask for God's direction in their lives. He is all-wise and understands what is most important in life.

Third, the nature of the sin of omission is the last of the three theological issues stressed in this passage. It is not enough just to avoid doing the wrong things. Christians have to do the right God expects of them. This fits James' earlier discussion on faith in action. Actions are a response to God's presence in the Christian's life. They are positive actions that build up the community and make a difference in the world. When Christians do not do what God has prompted them to do, they are as guilty as when they do something they know is wrong.

H. Warning to the Corrupt Rich (5:1-6)

The eighth section of the exposition begins as the previous one, with **Come now** (*age nyn*). But here, those addressed are **rich people.** Commentators debate whether or not they were members of the Christian community.

James strongly denounces the rich and their oppression of the rest of society. It resembles passages in the OT prophets' descriptions of the corrupt rich. The section concludes with a possible allusion to the crucifixion of Jesus characterized as a murder orchestrated by the rich.

BEHIND THE TEXT

James, perhaps, echoes warnings to the corrupt rich, a frequent theme in the OT prophets (see Amos 2:6-8; 4:1-3; 5:7, 10-12; 8:5, 6; Mic 2:1-2, 8-9; 3:1-3, 11; 6:10-12). Micah 6:8 summarized the message of the eighth century B.C. prophets: "And what does the LORD require of you? To act justly and to love mercy and to walk humbly with your God." Isaiah 1:15-16 accused the rich of having "hands . . . full of blood" and needing to "wash and make [them]selves clean." Verse 17 advised: "learn to do right! Seek justice, encourage the oppressed. Defend the cause of the fatherless, plead the case of the widow." Isaiah 10:1-2 warns against depriving the poor.

During the so-called intertestamental period, "the rich" came to be identified with those who compromised with Israel's pagan overlords. And the righteous people, honored for not compromising with them, were called "the poor" (see 1 and 2 Macc on the Maccabean revolt). Jesus identified earthly riches as treasures moth and rust would destroy (Matt 6:19-20; Luke 12:33).

IN THE TEXT

■ I The opening invitation, **Now listen,** was an informal way of addressing one's associates (see on 4:13). *Come now* is not to be read "as a summons to see the foolishness" of the rich. It is a "cry to bewail the punishment coming upon them" (Davids 1982, 175). Thus, it is like the prophetic "Woe-oracles." In the Prophets (see Isa 1:8), such language warned the audience "to prepare for strong words" announcing the doom of those addressed (Brosend 2004, 131).

That James directly addressed *the rich* would seem to indicate that they were among the intended recipients of the letter.

In antiquity riches consisted in "clothing, gold and silver, and land" (Brosend 2004, 132; but see Moo 2000, 212-13).

Evidence suggesting that the rich were members of the community James addressed includes the following:

1. The rhetorical device *Come now* is used in both 4:13 and 5:1. This makes the merchants and the rich synonymously parallel. If merchants were in the community (not debated), then it seems likely that some were rich as well.

2. The advice to the rich in the community is found after James addresses them as *brothers and sisters* (see 5:7-8, 10-11).

3. The reference in 5:11 to the endurance of Job, a rich man who stayed true to God even after losing everything, suggests that rich believers were conceivable (Jas 5:2 also alludes to Job 13:28).

4. The word *miseries* echoes Isa 59:7, the context of which suggests that Israelites who have lied and perverted justice may confess and

be redeemed, even those who were conniving and had shed innocent blood.

5. The illustrative example in 2:2-3 implies that both rich and poor entered the Christian synagogue James addressed.

But some evidence argues against the possibility that there were rich people in the community:

1. James has only words of warning for the rich, no words of advice comparable to that he offered the merchants. (This is persuasive only if 5:7-12 addresses a different group).

2. All the prophecies alluded to, which use the word *howling* (Isa 13:6; 15:3; and 16:7), are against the enemies of Israel. Thus, the rich could be enemies of the community. James 2:6 indicates that the rich were oppressing James' community.

The author urges the rich to **Weep and wail** because of their dismal future. James parallels two words expressing sorrow, **weep and wail.** The first, **weep** (*klausate*), typically describes external expressions of sorrow. It is closely associated with repentance. It appears in the Gospels describing actions by Jesus, Mary Magdalene, and Peter. Also it is used in the beatitude in Luke 6:21. James uses the word once here and once in 4:9, where he urges his double-souled readers to repent.

The second word, *howl* (*ololyzontes*), which occurs only here in the NT, is an onomatopoeia word (BDAG 2000, 704). That is, it attempts to represent the sound of one who is crying aloud. By the first century its common meaning was to cry out or shriek, whether in joy or pain. It appears in pagan Greek literature as well as in the LXX (Isa 13:6; 15:3; and 16:7).

James seems to use the word under the influence of Isaiah. There it occurs in oracles against Babylon and Moab. These enemies of Israel would howl because of the destruction the day of the Lord was about to wreak upon their lands. The word *miseries* confirms this.

What the rich are to **weep** and *howl* over are *miseries.* If James alludes to Isaiah, these *miseries* are coming as judgment from God. Romans 3:16 quotes Isa 59:7, which uses the singular noun, **misery.** James uses the verbal form of this word in 4:9 (**Grieve** or *Be miserable!*). Both contexts indicate that those addressed are part of the religious community. The word "wretched" in Rom 7:24 and Rev 3:17 is a cognate of this noun (*talaipōros*).

These rich people are about to experience misery upon misery. The verb **coming** in the present tense may indicate that the *miseries* are already on their way and keep plaguing them.

■2 James begins to describe the current condition of the rich: *Your riches have become corrupted and your clothes have become moth-eaten.* He alludes to Matt 6:19-20 in the Sermon on the Mount. There Jesus advises his

160

disciples not to "store up for [them]selves treasures on earth, where moth and rust destroy." They are instead to store up "treasures in heaven." Since one's heart will be where one's treasure is, his followers are to accumulate treasure that will last forever.

Job 13:28 compares the physical wasting away of a sick person to *a moth-eaten garment* (LXX). Isaiah prophesies that those who condemn him *will all become old like a garment; and a moth will eat you all up* (LXX).

The term for *riches* (*ploutos,* **wealth**) is common in the NT. It is used negatively as a burden and false hope in the Synoptic Gospels (e.g., Matt 13:22). Paul uses the word metaphorically in a positive sense, referring to the "riches of Christ" (Eph 3:8). He uses it negatively in 1 Tim 6:17. There he tells Timothy to "command those who are rich . . . not to be arrogant nor to put their hope in wealth, which is so uncertain." Revelation echoes a similar evaluation of riches in 18:17. Hebrews 11:26 uses the term paradoxically, identifying as great riches "disgrace for the sake of Christ." For James, *riches* are temporary and earthly.

The verb **rotted,** which describes what has happened to their riches, is in the perfect tense. This implies that their *riches have already become corrupted* and the effects of that corruption continue to be felt. The perfect tense may anticipate the demise of the rich, with an emphasis on their wealth as temporal (Davids 1982, 175). Thus, the rich were not yet suffering the loss of their possessions and imagined security (Davids 1989, 114).

The word **rotted (*corrupted,* *decayed*)** appears only here in the NT (BDAG, 921). Although metaphorical usage is possible, there is an organic feel to the word. Since the first-century culture was agriculturally based, it is possible that their **wealth** consisted in agricultural products, which would be subject to literal decay. Since clothing was made of natural fibers, these were subject to decomposition.

The word for **clothes** (*himatia*) is the common NT word for "*clothing*" or "*apparel*" (BDAG, 475). It is used for any piece of clothing, but also for the outer cloak, robe, or coat. In Matt 26:65, the high priest tears his clothing (*himatia*). The plural form indicates that they wore more than one piece of clothing. This would be consistent with their economic status.

The adjective James uses to describe what happens to the clothing, *sētobrōta* (*moth-eaten*), appears only here in the NT. The same word in Job (13:28 LXX) describes Job's aging as comparable to what happens when moths eat a woolen garment. The holey clothes of these rich people were not a result of overuse; they were destroyed from being hoarded.

■ **3** James continues on the theme of hoarded riches wasted rather than used for good purposes. He warns the rich: **Your gold and silver are corroded** [*ka-*

tiōtai, only here in the NT]. **Their corrosion [*ios, poison;* see Rom 3:13] will testify against you and eat your flesh like fire.**

The Greeks used the same word for rust and poison. The listener or reader determined its meaning contextually. Since rust corrodes metal (but not normally gold or silver!); and some poisons corrode the inside of a person, their actions are similar. Here James employs the similarity to indicate that the rust of hoarded **gold and silver** will become a poison and eat their **flesh like fire.**

Matthew 6:19-20 uses the metaphor of "*eating*" (*brōsis*) twice for corrosion or "rust." Jesus emphasizes the hoarding of "treasures in heaven," where they will not corrode. Jesus knows that where our treasure is, is where our hearts will be (v 21).

Rust (*ios*) is found in Ezek 24:6, 11-12 (LXX) in the cooking pot parable, which God instructed Ezekiel to tell the *provoking house.* In the parable, the rust ("impurity") was so thick on their pot (= lives) that God was unable to remove it, even by intense fire. In Ezekiel and in Jas 5:3, rust indicts that its owner will be subject to imminent judgment by God. Here rust refers to end-times judgment: "In the apocalyptic image rust is almost a living avenging force" (Kittel 1965, 335). God's judgment falls on the corrupt rich because they would let their gold and silver rust rather than use it to aid the poor.

James tells the rich that the corrosion of their rusty hoarded gold and silver will witness **against** them in God's court of justice (see 2:6). The testimony is not to them, but is against them—a *witness* for the prosecution (Davids 1982, 176).

Fire (*pyr*) often appears in apocalyptic and judgment contexts throughout the Bible. Fire was used to purify metals. It became a metaphor for purifying the hearts and minds of people by means of trials and tribulation. As part of the description of hell in the Gospels, **fire** is a metaphor for judgment. Frequently in Revelation and in all four Gospels it refers figuratively to judgment (Matt 18:8-9; 25:41; Mark 9:43-49; Luke 3:9-17; 17:28-35; John 15:5-8; see also Heb 10:27; 12:18, 29).

James uses **fire** metaphorically three times. The first two in Jas 3:5-6 refer to the destructive power of the human tongue. Here in 5:3, the effect of the rust is to consume the **flesh** of the miserly rich **like fire.**

The word translated **flesh** (*sarkas*) is in the plural and refers specifically to the meaty part of the body. In the first-century context the body was thought to consist of flesh (*sarx*) and bones (see the commentary on 2:26).

The apocalyptic and judgmental contexts of fire indicate that the rich will be severely judged for hoarding their **wealth** (not in Greek; added by the NIV), rather than using it to meet the needs of others. **You have hoarded** [*ethēsaurisate, treasured up;* see Matt 6:19-20] . . . **in the last days.** When used positively, it means "***store up***" or even "***save***" (BDAG, 456). In James, it definitely has a negative connotation. This rich man is not frugal, but miserly.

In the last days could refer to the rich saving up for a secure retirement (see Luke 12:19-21). But it is best taken here as another apocalyptic reference. For Jewish Christians in the first century, the time beginning with the coming of the Messiah was considered the last days.

■ **4** ***Behold*** (*idou*) both indicates a new topic in James' indictment of the corrupt rich and heightens the drama of the charge (Johnson 1995, 301). The rich not only hoarded their wealth but also failed to pay their employees.

The parallelism is typical of Jewish Wisdom literature:

• The wages you failed to pay the workmen who mowed your fields are crying out against you.	• The cries of the harvesters have reached the ears of the Lord Almighty.

In the first part, the withheld **pay** of the workers is personified as ***screaming.*** The injustice is inescapably obvious (see Luke 10:7; 1 Tim 5:18). In Hab 2:9-11, "the stones of the wall . . . cry out" against the one "who builds his realm by unjust gain." In Luke 19:40, Jesus told the Pharisees that if his disciples did not praise him then "the stones will cry out" (see Gen 4:10). "In important times and unjust situations even inanimate objects call to God" (Brosend 2004, 134).

The OT literature on this topic (e.g., Lev 19:13) and the present context make it clear that James refers to the unjust withholding of wages as both unjust and deliberate fraud (Johnson 1995, 302). Most Greek manuscripts have the verb *apostereō*, which means to "***rob, steal, despoil, defraud***" (BDAG, 121). Two of the better manuscripts read *ho aphysteremēnos*, "which has been withheld" (NASB). But *aphystereō* occurs nowhere else in the NT (only in the LXX of Neh 9:20 and Sir 14:14; Moo 2000, 216).

In Mal 3:5 God threatens judgment on "those who defraud laborers of their wages." In the second part of the parallel construction, **the cries of the harvesters have reached the ears of the Lord Almighty.** The screams and loud cries have been heard by God (see Exod 2:23-24; 3:7). These are not just metaphorical. In the first century day laborers lived at the subsistence level. If they were not paid that day, they and their families did not eat.

The term for God, **Lord Almighty** (*kyriou sabaōth* = **Yahweh, Lord of the Armies, Lord of Hosts;** BDAG, 909), emphasizes God's omnipotence. In the NT, the description *sabaōth* (***Armies***) occurs only here and in Rom 9:29, quoting Isa 1:9 (LXX). Isaiah connects God's holiness to his omnipotence in his inaugural vision of the Lord on his heavenly throne. He reports hearing the seraphs' song: "Holy, holy, holy is the LORD Almighty; the whole earth is full of his glory" (Isa 6:3). If James alludes to Isaiah's divine name, he associates justice and power in his understanding of God. The corrupt rich have reason to fear, repent, and return to the good graces of this powerful and holy God. The themes of social justice, holiness, and power dominate this verse.

The perfect tense of the verb in the phrase **have entered into the ears of the Lord of the Armies** may emphasize that the cries of the farm workers in the past are still ringing in God's ears (see Isa 5:9). "God has already heard of these things. Once more, James is clearly evoking the experience of Israel in Egypt" (Johnson 1995, 302).

James uses aorist adjectival participles, *tōn amsantōn* (**those who mowed**) and *tōn therisantōn* (**those who harvested**), to indicate that the farmhands' work is completed. According to the gracious provisions of Israel's law, they should receive their pay immediately. There is no question about whether they have fulfilled the agreement. The term **your estates** (*tas chōras hymōn*) indicates that the work of these laborers did not involve only a small plot of land, but extensive acreage (Ropes 1973, 288).

■ **5** James' indictment of the unjust rich is reminiscent of the OT prophets. They similarly accused the rich of living in luxury and self-indulgence, while the poor were suffering. For them the end of the world as they knew it was near (see Amos 2:6-7; 4:1; 5:11-12; 6:4-6; 8:4-7; Ezek 16:49; Jer 5:26-28).

Two different words describe the self-indulgent lifestyle of the corrupt rich in another parallel construction. The verb **lived luxuriously** (*etryphsate*) appears only here in the NT. The noun form (*tryphē*) occurs in Luke 7:25, where Jesus contrasts John the Baptist's rustic way of life with the lifestyles of those who lived **in luxury** in palaces. In 2 Pet 2:13, a related verb (*entryphōntes*) describes the "reveling" ways of the false teachers.

In the NT, lives of conspicuous consumption and **self-indulgence** are never viewed positively as a Christian lifestyle. This is especially true when it is associated with *epi tēs gēs* (**upon the earth**). This may have "a straightforward literal sense: they have lived well 'off the land'" (Johnson 1995, 303). But **on earth** stands in contrast to the afterlife (Ropes 1973, 290). The corrupt rich live in luxury **on earth** in contrast to the future torment in Hades that awaits them (see Luke 16:19-31). A luxurious way of life and preoccupation with oneself alone compromise a person's integrity of spirit, body, and mind.

The second verb is a synonym, **lived riotously** (*espatalsate*). It also means "to indulge oneself beyond the bounds of propriety" (BDAG, 936) by eating and drinking to excess. It means to live in order to satisfy all the senses (see 1 Tim 5:6). The irony of self-indulgence is that it proceeds **the day of slaughter** (see Acts 8:32, quoting Isa 53:7; Rom 8:36, quoting Ps 44:22).

This specific setting, **the day of slaughter,** appears in Jer 12:3 and in the Jewish pseudepigraphal book of *1 Enoch* (16:1). Jeremiah 12:3 is part of the prophet's prayer warning the prosperous ungodly people that God would "Set them apart for the day of slaughter." They will be well deserving of the coming judgment.

Although **day of slaughter** lacks the definite article in Greek, most commentators take it to refer to the Day of Judgment, or at least the day of judgment for the corrupt rich (Ropes 1973, 290-91).

> Now "feeding the hearts" becomes, by implication, equivalent to "stuffing" or force-feeding an animal to fatten it for the slaughter. The rich oppressors' self-indulgence is perceived ironically as preparation for self-destruction "in the last days." (Johnson 1995, 304)

There is a double-heedlessness in this image of fattening. Instead of heeding James' call for repentance (4:9), "the rich have chosen the opposite, a self-indulging luxury that renders them like fatted calves ready for slaughter" (Brosend 2004, 135).

Some translations translate the expression as "a day of slaughter" (NASB, NRSV). This could refer to the rich gorging themselves while the poor are dying for lack of enough to survive. Their desperate situation is due wholly to being unjustly denied their rights by the rich. The **slaughter** applies to the condition of the poor (see Ps 44:22; Isa 34:2, 6; Jer 25:34; Ezek 21:15; *Sib. Or.* 5.377-80; *1 En.* 94:9; 98:10; 99:6).

The application of *slaughter* to the poor fits this context well, because James lists the atrocities of the rich in vv 4 and 6.

John Wesley perhaps stands alone in interpreting *a day of slaughter* as referring to "a day of sacrifice—Which were solemn feast-days among the Jews" (2003, 822). That is, the rich ignore God's commands to do justly and care for the poor while worshipping at a religious festival!

■ **6** James continues to accuse the rich. The first verb, **you have condemned** (*katadikasate*: you have found/pronounced guilty [BDAG, 516]; see Matt 12:7, 37; Luke 6:37) evokes the violent courtroom image of Jas 2:26.

That the second verb, **murdered** (*phoneusate*), is frequent in the NT (e.g., Matt 5:21; 19:18; 23:31, 35; Mark 10:19; Luke 18:20; Rom 13:9) and is a testimony to the violent times during which Christianity was born. The term appears elsewhere in Jas 2:11 (twice) and 4:2. The LXX of Exod 20:15 uses it in one of the Ten Commandments: "You shall not murder." It means wrongful killing of a person. Whereas condemning may be done lawfully when the evidence requires, murder is never lawful.

The victims of both actions are **innocent men** (lit., *the righteous one, ton dikaion*). Accordingly, neither action is justifiable. The victim is identified in the singular. Scholars debate whether it refers directly to those the rich were taking advantage of, to Jesus, or to James.

The latter view presumes that the letter was written after his death by one of his disciples. The grammar seems to favor Jesus as the victim. The

5:5-6

definite article persuaded early commentators like Oecumenius, Bede, Cassiodorus, and Wesley suggest this (2003, 822). If Jesus is intended, James makes the rich responsible for the condemnation and execution of Jesus, in addition to their other sins (see Matt 23:29-32; 27:1).

The adjective *righteous* (*dikaios*) is used extensively in the Synoptic Gospels, John, Acts (3:12-16; 7:52; 22:14), and other NT writers (1 Pet 3:18; 1 John 2:1, alluding to Isa 53:10-12; Heb 10:38, citing Hab 2:4) as a messianic title—*the righteous one.* Romans 1:17 and Gal 3:11 cite Hab 2:4. Until recently Protestant scholars assumed Paul used *the just* to refer to justified believers. But some "new perspective" scholars take even these passages as references to Christ, *the righteous one*—the vindicated Messiah who vindicates believers.

Modern commentators generally think James' reference to *the righteous one* points to poor righteous believers who are being unjustly treated by the rich. They see "nothing in the context" that "has prepared us for the introduction of Jesus at this point" (Moo 2000, 218). There is even less reason to identify him with James (Johnson 1995, 304).

James' use of the word **condemned** may refer to a kind of judicial verdict bought by the rich (see 2:6). This would "reflect OT and intertestamental teaching directed to situations in which rich people use their wealth and influence to deprive the righteous poor of their rights and their living" (Moo 2000, 129; Ropes 1973, 291). Sirach connects murder and depriving someone of his means of making a living: "To take away a neighbor's living is to commit murder; to deprive an employee of wages is to shed blood" (Sir 34:22 NRSV).

Their sin of murder is only made worse in that *the righteous one* did not *resist* them. Not only was he **innocent,** but he was also defenseless, or unwilling to fight back. *The righteous one does not resist* (*antitassetai*) his murderers. This verb appears four more times in the NT (Jas 4:6; Acts 18:6; Rom 13:2; 1 Pet 5:5). Some suggest that the clause should be read as a question: "Does [God] not oppose you?" (Johnson 1995, 291; see Davids 1982, 180).

FROM THE TEXT

The accusations are typical of OT prophetic voices. The rich are corrupt and oppress the poor. But in many parts of the world today "the oppression has intensified. Salaries are very low and often withheld. Racial and sexual discrimination is common. Who can deny that the *ptōchos*, the poor, are many in Latin America?" (Tamez 1990, 78). James teaches that God expects the rich and powerful to deal justly with those who are poorer and weaker.

First, the rich are not to hoard their wealth, but to give to those in need. What good are corroding and moth-eaten treasures? John Wesley had three rules of Christian prudence: "Gain all you can . . . save all you can . . . give all you can" (1955, 326). By "save" Wesley recommended frugality, not building one's investment portfolio. What are those who have accumulated far more "stuff" than they can ever use to do? One practical response to this passage might be to go through our closets and give away usable clothes we have not worn for a year. We don't need them; and there are others who do.

Second, employers should pay their workers a fair, living wage. The object is not to see how little one can get others to work for, but to provide them with a fair wage so they can feed and clothe their families. When employers take advantage of their employees, God is not pleased and will do something about it.

Third, those who "own" anything should practice good stewardship. In fact, God is the source of everything we "own." We are only managers of what God gives us to use responsibly. If we have been gifted with the ability to make money, he expects us to use that money to glorify him. And his command is to love our neighbors as ourselves. Why would we lavish luxuries on ourselves and our families, just because we can? Why misuse our God-given gifts?

Fourth, the powerful are to use their power to help others, not to keep their status or retaliate against those they perceive as potential challengers. The powerful of James' day attacked the innocent Jesus, and ultimately murdered him. The powerful still abuse their power to assassinate the character of innocent people whom they consider threats to the status quo.

The rich need to expect loss and to trust God nonetheless. James will allude to Job, an exemplary rich man who lost everything but still trusted God (v 11). It is difficult for the rich to trust in God when they have their riches to depend on.

Wesley understood this verse as addressing the emotional need of the oppressed poor for justice. "The apostle does not speak this so much for the sake of the rich themselves, as of the poor children of God, who were then groaning under their cruel oppression." That the "miseries of the rich will come 'Quickly and unexpectedly'" indicates that God will not let the oppression go on without eventual justice: "the final vengeance which will then be executed on the impenitent." Wesley sees the rich in this passage as unbelievers who oppress poor believers (2003, 822).

"The purpose of the verses is partly to dissuade the Christians from setting a high value on wealth, partly to give them a certain grim comfort in the hardships of poverty" (Ropes 1973, 282). Both the rich and the poor can learn from James' strong warning to the rich.

Great literature speaks to several different audiences, and James is an excellent example of this. After he had been visited by the last spirit, Scrooge says in Dickens' *Christmas Carol*: "Men's courses will foreshadow certain ends, to which, if persevered in, they must lead. But if the courses be departed from, the ends will change. Say it is thus with what you show me!" (http://www.dickenschristmascarol.com). It is not too late for us to change.

I. Patience in Suffering (5:7-11)

James' request addressed to his **brothers and sisters** begins the ninth section of his exposition. The topic changes abruptly from a warning to the corrupt rich (5:1-6) to call for Christians to be patient because the **appearing** (*parousias*) of the Lord is near. They must not grumble against each other, because they, too, will stand before the judge who is about to come.

Verses 7-11 conclude with the example of the OT patriarch Job. He ties both sections (5:1-6 and 7-11) together, because he was a rich man remembered for his patience. These verses also function "as something of a hinge between 4:11—5:6 and the final exhortations in 5:12-20" (Johnson 1995, 311).

BEHIND THE TEXT

Jewish Christians closely associate the last days with the appearance of the Messiah. In this passage, James compares preparation for the second coming with farming. There is the preparation of the soil, the planting, the waiting for the rains to come, and finally the harvest. While they await the coming of Christ, there is work to do. To stand around and grumble wastes the precious time of preparation for Christ's return.

Job was the parade example of patience in the first century. He was a "blameless and upright" (Job 1:1) wealthy man, who endured the trials Satan put him through with God's permission. God was sure Job trusted him, but Satan insinuated that Job's trust existed only because of his wealth and comfortable life.

In his trials, three of Job's friends come to comfort him. They all assume his suffering is divine punishment for his hidden sins. Job maintains his innocence. Even his wife urges him, "Curse God and die!" (Job 2:9) because of his trials. But Job refuses. He calls on God to explain himself but does not waver in his trust in God. In the end God vindicates Job and restores his wealth, health, and family (Job 1:1—2:13; 42:7-17).

IN THE TEXT

■ **7** James begins with the inferential conjunction *oun* (**then**). In light of the certain punishment of the rich (5:1-6), **therefore** he exhorts his readers: **Be patient . . . until the Lord's coming** (*parousias*).

The NT describes patience as a characteristic of God (Matt 18:26; Luke 18:7; 2 Pet 3:9) and humans (Matt 18:29; 1 Cor 13:4; 1 Thess 5:14; Heb 6:15). Paul lists "patience" (*makrothymia*) as a fruit of the Spirit (Gal 5:22).

The imperative verb *makrothymēsate*, **Be patient,** means "**remain tranquil while waiting**" or "**bear up under provocation without complaint**" (BDAG, 612).

James encourages believers to remain even-tempered through the trials and hardships they face. The verb implies more than mere endurance, but active forbearance—"'patience and long-suffering'" (Johnson 1995, 313). Rather than give up when things get hard, they are to remain steadfast in their faith and active for God. As they do, they prepare for the coming of the Lord. Patience is usually used in the context of the attitude "of a superior to an inferior." Since God shows *makrothymia*, the community must likewise show patience.

James 5:7-8 contains two of the seventeen NT references to the *parousia*—**the Lord's** <u>coming</u> (emphasis added) (Matt 24:3, 27, 37, 39; 1 Cor 15:23; 1 Thess 2:19; 3:13; 4:15; 5:23; 2 Thess 2:1, 7-8; Jas 5:7, 8; 2 Pet 1:16; 3:4, 12; 1 John 2:28).

Parousia is not just a specialized word for the second coming of Christ as it is often used in English. It is also used for the coming of Stephanas (1 Cor 16:17), Titus (2 Cor 7:6-7), Paul (2 Cor 10:10; Phil 1:26; 2:12), the lawless one (2 Thess 2:9), and God (2 Pet 3:12). Its primary meaning is "***presence***" (BDAG, 780).

The term *parousia* was never applied to God in the LXX. It is used in secular literature to refer to the arrival of a king. The phrase *parousia tou kyriou*—**the Lord's coming**—appears for the first time in so-called intertestamental Jewish literature with reference to God. In the NT, it most frequently refers to the second coming of Jesus Christ (see Johnson 1995, 313-14).

James illustrates how Christians are to demonstrate patience and what they are to do while awaiting the coming of Christ by appealing to the example of farmers. They plant their crops and wait expectantly for rain and the eventual harvest.

The farmer waits (*ekdechetai*). The verb also means "***expect***" (BDAG, 300). The term **valuable crop** (*timion karpon*, ***precious fruit***) he awaits refers specifically to the end product of farming—***the harvest.***

The adjective *timion* is usually used to describe jewels or precious metals like gold and silver. This is the only passage in the Bible in which it characterizes fruit. James may contrast the hoarded and corroded wealth of the rich with this truly ***precious fruit.*** James does not specify the type of metaphorical fruit Christians patiently await. But the word *karpos* in 3:17 and 18 is associated with the peaceful life resulting from "the wisdom that comes from heaven."

The farmer endures the waiting and work it takes to plow and fertilize the soil, plant the seeds, wait for the rains to come, and allow the crop to mature. James does not use the generic word ***rain*** (*hyetos*) in the phrase **autumn and spring rains.**

The adjective *proimon* means simply **early** (BDAG, 870). The noun *opsimon* means "**late rain**" (BDAG, 746). The language and imagery "reflect the climatic conditions specific to Palestine, where fall rains in October are followed by those in mid-November" (Johnson 1995, 315). Some later manuscripts add the word *hyetos* to clarify James' meaning for urban readers living in a different climate.

■ **8** Just as farmers wait expectantly and patiently, James encourages his readers to do the same. **You too, be patient, strengthen your hearts, because the Lord's coming** [*parousia*] **has drawn near.** The verb translated **strengthen** (*stērixate*) means "**set up, establish, support**" in the sense of "**confirm**" (BDAG, 945). This verb, only here in James, is used thirteen times in the NT, usually in this figurative sense. Paul identifies God as the one who strengthens or establishes believers.

Here, James figuratively urges his audience to have strong and stable **hearts** (*kardias*). He refers not to the emotions of his audience, but to their "will and its decisions" (BDAG, 509). To **strengthen your hearts** is to reinforce your resolve, to stand firm and steady, regardless of how long or difficult the wait. James' audience should reconfirm their decision to follow Christ to the end.

The reason for the two commands in v 8 is because **the coming of the Lord has drawn near** (see v 7). The perfect tense of the verb **has drawn near** (*ēngiken*) emphasizes that the action has already happened and that the effects of the action linger. This could be taken as an example of "realized eschatology." But the already of the kingdom of God is balanced by the not yet (Johnson 1995, 316; see Luke 21:8; Rom 13:12; 1 Pet 4:7). With the dawning of the last days, the second coming is near, but it has not yet occurred. "The Judge is standing at the door!" (v 9).

James "does not want his readers to remain simply passive in their waiting . . . ; they are to focus themselves" (Johnson 1995, 315). The call for them to "purify your hearts" in 4:8 is similar. These invitations "stand in contrast to the 'deception/indulgence of the heart' in 1:26 and the 'stuffing of the heart' in 5:5" (Johnson 1995, 315).

■ **9** James' next appeal, **Don't grumble** [*stenazete*] **against each other, brothers and sisters, so that** [*hina*] **you will not be judged.** The verb *stenazete* means to "**complain**," "**sigh**," or "**groan**" because circumstances are not to one's liking (BDAG, 942). According to Mark 7:34, Jesus groaned (*estenaxen*) when a deaf man was brought to him for healing. Hebrews 13:17 encourages its audience to obey their leaders so they can do their work with joy and not with groaning (*stenazontes*).

Paul's letters refer to groaning within oneself (Rom 8:23, 26; 2 Cor 5:2). James 5:9 is the only passage in which complaining is confrontational—**against** (*kat'*) another believer. Johnson sees this as "a thematic (not verbal) allusion to Leviticus 19" (1995, 316). In Lev 19:18, this command immediately precedes the great command to love one's neighbor: "'Do not seek revenge or bear a grudge against one of your people, but love your neighbor as yourself. I am the Lord." This appears to be a main theme of James.

Those who complain about their fellow believers are in danger of judgment. James seems to allude to Jesus' command in Matt 7:1: "Do not judge, or you too will be judged." The verb **you will be judged** (*krithēte*) has a wide range of meaning in the NT (see BDAG, 567-69). The next clause suggests that James referred to eternal judgment by God: **The Judge is standing at the door!**

James introduces this warning with a demonstrative particle (*idou*, **Look, Behold**), which the NIV leaves untranslated. This calls his audience's attention to the importance of the warning that follows.

The verb translated **is standing** (*estēken*) is in the perfect tense as was **has drawn near** in v 8. This places **the Judge** as parallel with **the Lord**. The judge has arrived at **the doors**, where he awaits entrance (BDAG, 42; compare Mark 13:28-29; Matt 24:32-33).

In v 8 the immanence of **the Lord's coming** is to encourage the readers to patient endurance. The reminder that **the Judge is standing at the door** is to motivate them to be on their best behavior. The judge is "Hearing every word, marking every thought" (Wesley 2004, 822).

■ **10** James again addresses everyone in the congregations to which he writes using the masculine plural **Brothers,** which includes both women and men. He issues yet another imperative directive: ***Take the prophets who spoke in the name of the Lord as an example of suffering hardship and of patience.*** The NIV translation, **an example of patience in the face of suffering** is also possible (Johnson 1995, 311; Ropes 1973, 298).

James calls on their collective memory of the OT. The prophets called to preach to Israel and Judah were ridiculed and persecuted for announcing God's word to those who didn't want to hear it (see Johnson 1995, 317-18, for references).

The word translated ***example*** (*hypodeigma*) "can mean either 'sample/illustration' or, more specifically, a 'pattern/model' presented for imitation" (Johnson 1995, 317). Mention of the example of the prophets' endurance indicates that James implicitly urges his audience to imitate them. It is not that they should become masochists, seeking suffering for its own sake. But they are not to give up their perseverance to avoid it either.

The noun translated ***suffering hardship*** (*kakopathias*) is a compound noun from ***bad*** (*kakos*) and suffering (*pathos*). It appears only here in the NT. The verbal cognate, however, is found in v 10 (see 2 Tim 2:3, 9; 4:5). The meaning of the word ranges from a general word for "*suffering, misfortune, mis-*

5:9-10

ery" to *"strenuous effort"* or *"perseverance"* (BDAG, 500). James appears to refer to the dangers and opposition that come from remaining faithful to Christ and fulfilling one's calling (see v 7 on *makrothymias*).

■ 11 Again James gets his audience's attention by beginning with *idou,* **Look** (paraphrased **As you know** in the NIV). He reminds them of something they all believe in common: **we consider blessed those who have persevered.** With the first person plural, **we consider blessed** (*makarizomen*), he identifies himself with his readers.

James identifies the source of this saying: ***You heard of the endurance of Job and saw what the Lord finally brought about.*** Job is the classical example of a godly person who endured undeserved suffering. James can take it for granted that his audience has **heard** about the endurance of Job. He uses the most common Greek word for hearing. In various NT contexts, it conveys the force of attentive listening, obeying, learning, understanding, or comprehending (Zodhiates 1992, 113-14).

James associates **heard** and **have seen.** Their hearing implies their understanding of Job's endurance in popular thought. "The portrayal of Job in the canonical book is scarcely that of the 'patient Job' . . . Perhaps James is referring to apocryphal traditions transmitted in assemblies such as the synagogue" (Johnson 1995, 319). This estimate of Job appears first in the *Testament of Job,* probably written about the same time as James' letter.

Perseverance or ***endurance*** (*hypomonēn*) is a synonym of "patience" (v 10). James uses ***endurance*** twice in this verse, once as a noun and once as a verb. He earlier employed it in 1:3-4 as a noun and in 1:12 as a verb. Patience is usually used in relationship to people; ***endurance*** is putting up with circumstances or inanimate things. ***Endurance*** (*hypomonē*) is "**the capacity to hold out or bear up in the face of difficulty, . . . *fortitude, steadfastness, perseverance*"** (BDAG, 1039).

Usually the things endured are considered evil or as occasions for suffering for one's faith. ***Endurance*** indicates a quietness of mind when putting up with difficult circumstances, whether real or perceived. It also indicates a consistency of character and temperament even when frustrated by adverse circumstances.

Endurance

Endurance or the verb "to endure" is found in Matthew and Mark with an eschatological sense: those that endure to the end. Paul uses it twenty times in his letters. In 1 Cor 13:7 it is a characteristic of love. In 2 Tim 2:12, he quotes an early creed or hymn, also eschatological: ***If we endure, we will also reign with Christ.*** In 1 Tim 6:11, **endurance** is one of the qualities Paul advises Timothy to pursue; in 2 Tim 3:10, it is a quality Paul claims to have.

Hebrews uses the word five times. In 12:1-2, the anonymous author urges readers to endure, following the model of Jesus, who because of the joy set before him, endured the cross. Hope makes **endurance** possible (see 2 Pet 1:6; Rev 1:9; 2:2, 3, 19; and 3:10; 13:10; 14:12).

Saw (*eidete*) is from *horaō* rather than from *blepō*, the common word for physical seeing. *Horaō* means **"to perceive by the eye, catch sight of, notice"** (BDAG, 719). James uses the verb twice, first in 2:24 where he concludes that "you see that a man is justified by works and not by faith alone" (NASB). Second, he employs it here where the readers know the ending of Job's story and *saw* what the Lord finally brought about in Job's life.

The root word (*horaō*) appears in all the Gospels. It is never used in the physical sense, except when something was unclear or far away (e.g., Mark 8:24). The Johannine literature uses it extensively, primarily in seeing some manifestation of God. The use of this word in the Gospel of John, the most reflective Gospel, makes sense. In Paul's letters, Acts, Hebrews, and 1 Peter the emphasis is on perceiving, whether in a physical or metaphorical sense.

The last part of this compound sentence is cryptic in Greek; literally, *you saw (perceived) the end of the Lord. The end* (*telos*) can mean a termination in respect to time (see Luke 1:33). In James' use, it denotes result or final goal (see BDAG, 998). Thus, the translation **you . . . have seen what the Lord finally brought about.** Though used only here in James, *telos* appears often in the NT, mostly in an eschatological sense. Paul uses the word as does James: *the **end** of the law is Christ* (Rom 10:4, emphasis added).

Augustine and others have interpreted *Lord* as referring to Jesus. If so, *the end of the Lord* refers to what was accomplished through the cross and the resurrection. Most scholars today, however, see it as a general reference to God. Their reasons include the reference to the Lord's compassion and mercy, often used in the OT to describe God, and its previous use in v 10 where it obviously means God (see Johnson 1995, 320-21; Ropes 1973, 299; Davids 1982, 188).

Here, because the readers knew the end of the story, they understand *that the Lord is sympathetic and compassionate.* Since the ability to endure depends largely on hope, they need to understand that God *is very sympathetic and compassionate.*

The word translated *sympathetic* (*polysplanchnos*) is a compound word, made up of *polys* ("many" or "much") and *splanchnon* ("bowels"). In Greek, like "heart" in English, "bowels" is a metaphor for the center of the emotions. Thus, it means *"sympathetic, compassionate, merciful"* (BDAG, 850). This adjective and its noun (*polysplanchnia*), found only found here in the NT, are used in other early Christian writings as an attribute of God (Clement of Alexandria, Acts of Thomas, Hermas' Vision and Mandate; Davids 1982, 188).

The adjective *oiktirmōn,* **compassionate,** is used only to describe God or a divine attribute humans are to emulate. It is also translated *"**merciful**"* (BDAG, 700). It is not considered as strong a word as *eleos,* **mercy. Compassionate** occurs only here and twice in Luke 6:36: "Be merciful just as your Father is merciful." The verb form (*oiktirō*) appears twice in Rom 9:15 (citing Exod 33:19). The noun (*oiktirmos*) is used five times for both human and divine **compassion** (Rom 12:1; 2 Cor 1:3; Phil 2:1; Col 3:12; Heb 10:28).

FROM THE TEXT

This eschatological passage encourages James' readers to have patience in the face of trials and suffering. This is because the Lord is returning soon. The period before Christ's return was a time to cultivate the hearts of people and to bring in the fruit—those who are ready to receive Christ. It is not a time to waste on self-indulgence, but for working and waiting for the second coming. It is also a time to strengthen our hope, to nurture our souls, and to make ourselves ready to meet God.

Nystrom points out that "nothing can be done to speed the *parousia* on its way. . . . Difficulties within the community must be dealt with, and the correct understanding and practice of the faith and works dynamic must be taught and maintained" (1997, 286). James believes the coming of Christ is near, but he does not neglect the moral education of the people of God. If the alleged "faith" of Christians is not evidenced by actions, it does not really exist.

There is too much good to do before Christ returns. Thus, there is no time for judging/complaining against other Christians. God's people need to get busy with the ministry God has for them to do. Those who judge and complain have taken their eyes off of the Lord and the ministries he has assigned them as his followers. Such idle Christians, who complain and judge, will themselves be judged for not completing the tasks God assigned them and for disrupting the unity and harmony of the community.

In addition to patience, Christians need to cultivate endurance. Endurance is possible for those who have hope. James' community was familiar with the story of Job. They understood that after his trials, there was restoration and hope. The God whom James serves is a God who is sympathetic and compassionate.

Those who serve God single-heartedly experience the love of God beyond their imagining. Knowledge of God's love makes endurance possible; and endurance makes the Christian life on earth possible. Endurance builds Christian character and makes victorious living possible, despite temptations and trials. It is essential for spiritual formation. Only those Christians who endure will reign with Christ.

J. The Simple "Yes" and "No" (5:12)

This brief tenth section of the exhortation stands alone. Some take it as "a genuine transition to the end of the letter" (Johnson 1995, 326). It repeats the direct address, **brothers and sisters.** The entire verse, after the introductory address, "is the aphorism, given special emphasis by the opening 'above all'" (Bauckham 1999, 65). James felt no need to elaborate on his command not to swear other than to encourage direct and honest speech.

BEHIND THE TEXT

This section echoes Jesus' teachings found in Matt 5:34-37. Whereas the ancient teachings of Judaism were to keep any oaths made to the Lord, Jesus tells his followers not to swear at all. They must "simply let [their] 'Yes' be 'Yes,' and [their] 'No,' 'No'" (Matt 5:37). In 5:12, James summarizes the teaching of Jesus on this subject.

IN THE TEXT

■ 12 James changes topics abruptly, from a call to patient perseverance (in 5:10-11) to instructions to speak so simply and honestly that oaths are unnecessary (see 3:1-12; 5:9). He insists: **And first of all, my brothers and sisters, do not swear by heaven, or by the earth, or any other oath.** James reemphasizes what he said in 4:13-16. We do not control our lives; God does. To swear that something will happen is arrogant and evil.

The connecting phrase **And first of all** or **Above all** is literally, **But before all things** (*pro pantōn de*). It prepares "the reader for the importance of what is to follow" (Brosend 2004, 149). It is of fundamental importance to realize that we live at the mercy of God. God's will must be the will of the Christian.

James' command, **do not swear by heaven or earth, or any other oath,** is best understood in the context of Jesus' words in Matt 5:34-37. This is "the closest parallel to a saying of Jesus in the entire letter" (Brosend 2004, 150). Jewish tradition accepted oaths. They forbade only breaking oaths, especially those made to God (Lev 19:12). Jesus, however, prohibits all oaths. For humans to swear under oath presumes that they can change God's decrees.

James assumes his readers understand the arrogance of those who **swear by heaven or earth.** In 4:14 he reminded them that they don't know what will happen tomorrow. Their lives are no more lasting than the steam coming off boiling water! They understand life much better if they say, "If it is the Lord's will, we will live and do this or that" (4:15). Most commentators do not believe James prohibited swearing in solemn occasions or in a court of law. His concern was with frivolous oaths.

James comes to the same conclusion as Jesus. **Let your "Yes" be yes, and your "No," no, or you will be condemned.** Only the final clause differs from what Jesus said: "anything beyond this comes from the evil one" (Matt 5:37*b*). The meaning is much the same. Arrogance comes from the evil one and reflects a lack of submission and humility before God.

This is "a call to simplicity and truthfulness" (Johnson 1995, 341). It functions as "the conclusion of James's warnings and admonitions on negative speech, not the beginning of a section on the positive uses of speech" (Brosend 2004, 152). Perhaps it serves a transitional role, connecting the two.

FROM THE TEXT

This passage emphasizes the need to be straightforward with each other and with God. There should be no need for Christians to swear that we are telling the truth, lest others assume we lie otherwise. We should be *known* for truth-telling. Of course, we need compassion, tact, and diplomacy in communication. But if a "yes" is communicated when "no" is the answer, confusion and pain result.

James encourages Christians to know their thoughts and express them honestly and straightforwardly. Relationships benefit from honesty. Most relational problems come from dishonesty and deception.

K. Prayer Offered in Faith (5:13-18)

The eleventh division of the exposition begins with a series of three questions related to possible conditions of Christians within the community: suffering, cheerful, or sick. James follows these questions with commands on how to deal with each situation. He then expands on the subject of prayer for the sick, in which he links physical healing and the forgiveness of sins. The section ends with the example of Elijah's powerful prayer life.

BEHIND THE TEXT

James does not conclude his Epistle with the expected personal greetings and final advice typically found in ancient letters. But he does employ a health wish that was common at the close of letters (Davids 1982, 191). This health wish (vv 13-18) consists of a series of three questions and answers. The last question on illness has an expanded answer with an illustration from the life of the prophet Elijah. The stories of Elijah found in 1 Kings, Jewish apocryphal works, and the Talmud present him as a man of prayer.

Elijah of Jewish Legend

First Kings 17:20-22 tells the story of Elijah praying for the dead son of the widow at Zarephath and bringing the child back to life. First Kings 18 is the famous story of Elijah's contest with the prophets of Baal on Mount Carmel. When he calls on God, God answers with fire that consumes the altar and the sacrifice.

This same chapter implies that Elijah prayed for rain during an extended drought and that God sent a heavy rain in response.

The apocryphal book 2 Esdras and some Talmudic passages also emphasize the importance of prayer in Elijah's ministry. This inspirational literature was familiar to Jewish Christians in the early first century. "And Elijah [prayed] for those who received the rain, and for the one who was dead, that he might live" (2 Esd 7:109 NRSV).

This section might have been constructed with "If . . . then . . ." clauses. But it is a characteristic of James to use questions as conditional sentences. The Epistle contains twenty-two questions. These questions, along with the parallelism in v 17 (*proseuchēi prosēyxato*: **In prayer, he prayed**), indicate a Jewish source or author. The unusual grammatical construction also in v 17 (instead of a *hina* clause the use of the gentive—*tou me brexai*: **that it would not rain**) adds support to this judgment (Davids 1982, 198). "Such rapid-fire questions and directives are common in the diatribe" (Johnson 1995, 329) of Hellenistic rhetoric.

Oil (Isa 1:6; Mark 6:13; Luke 10:34) was widely used as medicine in antiquity. So were wine (Luke 10:34; 1 Tim 5:23), balm (Jer 8:22; 46:11; 51:8), and eye salve (Rev 3:18). When ancient readers heard the words of Jas 5:14, their understanding would be: Seek medical assistance, then pray for the healing of the sick person. God is ultimately the Healer, but sick Christians should not refuse medical intervention.

The modern understanding and treatment of disease is quite different from that of the first century. In James' time, healing was not the getting rid of disease, but the "bringing [of] understanding and meaning to a situation—making sense of the world, or better, (re)creating a world that comprehended the disease" (Brosend 2004, 160). The objective was to restore the person to the community, not just to bring them back to vitality and health. Thus, the forgiveness of sins was an important part of the restoration of the person to the community.

The music of the Jewish tradition in the first century consisted of the Psalms. In fact, the verb form of the Greek word for "psalm" (*psallein*, "to psalm") means to sing. In Eph 5:19 and Col 3:16, the author adds "hymns and spiritual songs," perhaps including songs familiar to Gentiles. But since the communities to which James writes are all Jewish, he uses "to psalm" in a call for joyful singing.

IN THE TEXT

■ **13** In this verse, James intends to comprehend the whole spectrum of emotions and needs present in the Jewish-Christian communities. Instead of constructing a series "if-then" clauses offering advice, he uses interactive questions and answers. His first question is: *Is anyone among you suffering?*

The word for *suffering* or **trouble** is a colorful word in Greek (see the commentary on 5:10). The context suggests suffering as an emotion, perhaps depression, brought on by difficult circumstances. James' command to those suffering emotional pain to **pray.** Christians should recognize that God is in control and pray in the face of suffering.

The second question covers the other end of the emotional spectrum. *Is anyone cheerful?* The word translated *cheerful* (*euthymei*) is probably the closest word in Greek to **happy.** A person who is **happy** is encouraged by his or her circumstances—"feeling good" (*eu-*) as opposed to "feeling bad" (*kako-*; Johnson 1995, 329).

James commands this happy person to sing. *Let this one sing a psalm.* The songs Jewish Christians sang were psalms. The Greek verb is *psallō,* *sing a psalm.* Frequent in the LXX, it originally indicated a song with string accompaniment. Eventually it indicated any song of praise (Davids 1982, 192).

■ **14** James continues to give advice through rhetorical questions: *Is anyone feeling sick among you?* James uses *asthenei* to indicate sickness. It literally means to be without bodily strength (BDAG, 142). Occurring only here in James, it is the most common word in the NT for physical ailments. It is also used figuratively of mental and spiritual weakness (Rom 4:19; 1 Cor 8:7, 11-12).

The word *nosos,* *disease,* refers a specific sickness. Feeling sick or weak (*asthenei*) is a symptom resulting from the disease. Matthew uses both terms in 8:17 to translate the prophecy of Isa 53:4. Jesus carried not only our weaknesses brought on by sickness but the disease itself. Both are linked to the human sin.

In the NT, sickness is linked both to evil spirits (Matt 17:18; Luke 13:11) and to sin (1 Cor 11:30; Mark 2:5). Verse 15 suggests that James sees sin in some way related to weakness or sickness.

James commands: *Let the sick person summon the elders of the church, and let them anoint this one with oil, and pray over him or her in the name of the Lord.* James specifically uses the term *church* (*ekklēsias*), not **synagogue** (as in 2:2). This church is a specific local Christian community, an association of believers (Acts 15:22; 1 Cor 4:17; Phil 4:15). James uses the Greek terms for *church* and **synagogue** once each.

The **elders** (*presbyterous*) in first-century Jewish tradition are those respected for their seniority and leadership in the assembly. They were responsible for the Jewish community. In the first century they were usually the oldest (thus **elders**) group of men. The term was also used specifically for members of the Jewish Sanhedrin, the highest governing body for Jewish civic and ritual laws. The "characterization 'elders of the assembly' suggests something more than the older members of the community; it points to official leaders" (Johnson 1995, 330).

These **elders** are called together and instructed to **pray** [*proseuxasthōsan*] **over** (*ep'*) the sick person. The preposition **over** may indicate that the person is too ill to move or function as "shorthand for laying hands on the person during the prayer" (Moo 2000, 238; see Matt 19:13).

Proseuxasthōsan (**pray**) comes from the common word for the act of praying in the NT (see the Lord's Prayer in Matt 6:9-13; Luke 11:1-4). It is used extensively in the Synoptic Gospels, Acts, and in the writings of Paul. James employs the term in 5:13-18 to designate praying for oneself (v 13), intercessory prayer (v 14), and for specific petitions (vv 17-18).

Here, an intercessory healing prayer follows the anointing **with oil**. Olive oil (*elaiōi*) was one of the most common medicines of the first century. After appropriate medicine was administered, the elders were to pray for the healing of the believer. God is the one who ultimately heals and makes the medicine effective, but medicine is important to the healing process.

Anointing with Oil

Anointing with oil in Jewish tradition was used to ask for God's special blessing on the person anointed. Kings were anointed by priests to confirm God's choice of them to lead their people. The use of oil also indicated wealth and joy. The practice of anointing with oil is mentioned in only one other passage in the NT. In Mark 6:13, it is used as a means of physical healing. This was in the context of the ministry of the twelve, whom Jesus sent out to preach, drive out demons, and anoint sick people with oil for their healing. The parable of the good Samaritan mentions the use of oil [*elaion*] and wine in the Samaritan's immediate care of the injured man's wounds (Luke 10:34).

The intercessory healing prayer was to be prayed **in the name of the Lord** (probably God). This could indicate that, in addition to sin being connected with sickness, James may have considered some sickness the result of evil spirits. Exorcisms were carried out **in the name of the Lord** (Jesus; according to Acts 19:13).

Christians, however, were also to baptize (Acts 8:16), preach (Acts 9:27, 29), be imprisoned and die (Acts 21:13), be washed, sanctified, and justified (1 Cor 6:11), give thanks (Eph 5:20), stay away from heretics (2 Thess 3:6), and everything else (Col 3:17) **in the name of the Lord.** So perhaps even the anointing was in his name. This phrase invokes the authority by which all is done. So it is not surprising that they are to anoint with oil and pray for healing **in the name of the Lord.**

■ **15** James describes the **prayer** of the elders (v 14) as **offered in faith.** He employs *euchē*, an abbreviated form of the normal word for **prayer** (*proseuchē*) found only in James. In Acts 18:18 and 21:23 *euchē* refers to the "vow" Paul is asked to make. This may indicate that ***the prayer of faith*** for healing was a ritual prayer, much like marriage pronouncements today.

Several Greek verbs can be translated ***heal***. James chooses the least specific and most general word, *sōizō* (***save***) (e.g., John 3:16-17). A related word, *diasōzō*, may also describe physical healing (Matt 14:36; Luke 7:3). But its usual meaning is "**rescue or deliver from a hazard or danger**" (BDAG, 237; e.g., Acts 27:43; 28:4; 1 Pet 3:20). This is the closest synonym to James' term. Other NT verbs translated ***heal*** include *therapeuō* (e.g., Matt 4:24; see John 5:10; Acts 4:14; 5:16; 8:7; 17:25; Rev 13:3, 12) and *iaomai* ("***restore***"; BDAG, 465; see Jas 5:16).

James' employment of *sōizō*—salvation—as healing is consistent with his use of the word *asthenei* for ***feeling sick*** in v 13. Perhaps also affecting his choice is the presence of *kamnonta*, identifying ***the one who is weary with sickness***. This refers to the weakness that accompanies sickness. It could also refer to the associated depression. Regardless, **the prayer offered in faith will make the sick person well.**

James assigns no power to the human agents in the healing; **the Lord will raise him up.** The verb *egerei* connects with the Gospel accounts of Jesus' healings (e.g., Mark 2:9; Luke 5:23-24; John 11:29). The term also recalls "the resurrection, whether of Jesus or the sick person" (Johnson 1982, 333; see Jas 1:18; 5:20). The emphasis, however, is plainly that the Lord heals the sick person. God is the healer, not the elders, not the ritualized ***prayer.***

If he has sinned, he will be forgiven. The causal connection between sin and suffering is taken for granted in both the OT and NT and in Judaism. In John 9:1-3, Jesus seems to deny it. But in 1 Cor 11:29-30, Paul affirms it (Johnson 1995, 333; Davids 1982, 194-95). James appears to allow for the possibility here.

James was unconcerned with the cause of the person's suffering. His point is that God will not only heal the person but also forgive the person's sin (see the commentary on 1:15; 2:9; 4:17). The future passive verb translated ***it will be forgiven*** (*aphethēsetai*) is a divine passive. That is, God heals and forgives. Neither healing nor forgiveness just happen spontaneously.

The same verb for "forgive" appears here as in the Lord's Prayer (Matt 6:12, 14-15; Luke 11:4). It means "**release from legal or moral obligation or consequences**" (BDAG, 156). Forgiveness entails giving up on punishing the wrongs done. It is the opposite of holding a grudge. God abandons his right to hold sins against those he forgives.

■ **16** Because James relates sin to illness, he urges his readers to confess their sins to one another and pray for each other. He shifts his attention from the individual sick person to the entire community: **Therefore confess your sins** to each other and pray for each other so that you may be healed. This is no longer about a single sinner (v 15), but about the entire community. The three verbs in v 16 are all second person plurals—*you all.* James uses the connective **Therefore** (*oun*) to tie confession and prayer to v 15, in which he assures his audience that God will heal and forgive those prayed for.

James' readers are to be proactive. By being mutually accountable, confessing their **sins** and interceding in prayer for one another would spare them from the necessity for healing of sickness due to unconfessed sin. The present imperative verb urges them to *keep confessing* (*exomologeisthe*). This is not to be a onetime confession, but an ongoing practice of total transparency and mutual communal concern.

The root of the imperative verb *exomologeisthe* occurs ten times in the NT. And it refers to "the confession of sins" in half of these instances (Jas 5:16; Matt 3:6; Mark 1:5; Acts 19:18; 1 John 1:9). Otherwise it means "a profession of faith" (Phil 2:11), usually in praise to God (Matt 11:25; Rom 14:11).

James writes to Jewish Christians who need to recognize their need for ongoing confession of **sins** and intercessory prayer. Without these, they cannot remain healthy in spirit, mind, and body (see on the commentary on 4:17 for more on sin [*hamartia*]).

As with the abbreviated form of the noun *euchē* (**prayer**) in v 15, here James uses the shortened form of the verb **pray**—*euchesthe* rather than *proseuchesthai*—"wish" in Rom 9:3 but "pray" elsewhere (Acts 26:29; 27:29; 2 Cor 13:7, 9; 3 John 2). Longer forms are used of prayer in the sense of talking to God and/or specific prayers to God. The shorter form more often expresses a desire or wish. James refers to intercessory prayer, in which one prays or wishes for God to heal another.

The assurance **you may be healed** (*iathēte*) involves a passive subjunctive verb. It is a provisional promise. Those may find healing when they confess their sins and Christians pray. (See the comments on v 15 for the synonyms for cures from disease in v 15.)

James follows his dual command with an observation: *The petition of a righteous person is very strong.* Here he uses a completely different word, *deēsis*, for **prayer**. Often translated prayer in the NT, *deēsis* emphasizes prayer as a request or petition (BDAG, 213). Sometimes *proseuchē* and *deēsis* are paired together as synonyms (e.g., Eph 6:18; Phil 4:6; 1 Tim 5:5). Such passages highlight prayer as more than communing with God, but entails making specific requests of God.

In Greek, James' observation begins with *Poly ischyei*: intercessory prayer has *great power.* The Greek word order emphasizes the incredible strength of the prayers of righteous people. He ends the sentence with a participle indicating the manner in which it is strong: *as it is effective.* It is difficult to translate this literally (see Johnson 1995, 335; Gal 5:6).

A free translation would be: *The intercessory prayers of a righteous person are extremely effective with God.* God hears and answers such prayers. The effectiveness of the requests is not in the praying itself, as if prayer is powerful or magical. Their effectiveness arises from the goodness and unlimited ability of God (Davids 1982, 197).

■ **17** James gives a familiar example from history (see sidebar on Elijah above). *Elijah was a person* [*anthrōpos*] *of like feeling to us.* All four Gospels refer to **Elijah.** He played an important role in Jewish messianic expectation. Every Passover he was expected to return to announce the coming of the Messiah. In Rom 11:2 Paul mentions Elijah as one who "pleads with God against Israel" (NRSV). God answered him with the assurance that there were still 7,000 Israelites who had not betrayed Yahweh and worshiped Baal.

James uses the generic word *anthrōpos*—**human,** a **person** who belongs to the human race (BDAG, 81). In order to emphasize Elijah's humanity, James describes him as *a person of like feeling* [*homoiopathēs*] *to us,* one **just like us.** Elijah had the same feelings, fears, and faults as James' readers.

Homoiopathēs appears only here and in Acts 14:15. In the Acts account, the people of Lystra tried to worship Paul and Barnabas as the gods Hermes and Zeus. When Paul and Barnabas realized this, they explained that they were just ordinary people—"human like you." Just so, "Elijah was a human being like us" (NRSV).

James illustrates what can happen when ordinary people pray: Elijah **prayed earnestly that it would not rain, and it did not rain on the land for three years and a half years.** In Greek, James uses the cognate construction, *in prayer he prayed.* This was a common Semitic way of intensifying the verb. Elijah requested a drought; and his prayer was answered. If an ordinary human was able to influence nature by praying, how much more would God grant intercessory requests for forgiveness and healing!

James refers to the OT account of Elijah's prophecy in the time of King Ahab (1 Kgs 17). James has interpretively added the word for prayer and the time sequence from Jewish tradition (see Luke 4:25; Johnson 1995, 336).

■ **18** Elijah not only prayed for an extended drought but subsequently prayed for rain. First Kings 17—18 does not specifically say Elijah prayed; this comes from traditions preserved in Jewish noncanonical literature (2 Esd 7). **Again he prayed, and the heavens gave rain, and the earth produced its crops.** James' phrase, **the earth produced its crops,** expands the OT account, providing a link with 5:7.

James emphasizes that God is the one who gives (1:5, 17; 4:6). He answers the intercessory prayers of righteous people. Elijah was not praying for drought or rain for selfish reasons. He was locked in a life-and-death struggle with the evil Israelite king Ahab and the religion of Baal. If Elijah was not effective in demonstrating the power of the true God in contrast to the false god Baal, the whole nation of Israel could be lost.

FROM THE TEXT

James offers different advice for different people in different situations. This is no one-size-fits-all formula. The suffering are to pray, not panic or simply bemoan their pain. Help and relief come ultimately from God. So they were urged to go first to the Source of help.

The cheerful are to sing praise to God. God is the source of the Christian's hope, the giver of life and all good things. Christians need to acknowledge God and his work in their lives.

The sick are to seek medical help and to call for mature Christians to pray for their healing.

Confession and intercessory prayer are essential to healing. Modern medicine recognizes the intimate relationship between illness and hope or anxiety. God created human beings as whole beings, so one's relationship with others and with God affects one's physical body as well as one's mental state. Stress is a well-known cause or accelerator of the most common life-threatening diseases such as cancer and heart disease. James encourages his readers to make the relationships in their lives right, confessing to each other, so that they might be healed.

Today, many people overlook the stresses in their relationships with God and others. They stake their hopes for healing on medical science alone. Medication may relieve their symptoms or even cure their diseases. But with stress-related diseases, medicine may bring only temporary or partial relief. People must learn to deal with the situations that cause their stress.

The last principle James offers is that God grants the requests of his righteous people. When a Christian's desires are in line with God's, he is more than willing to answer prayer.

Moo addresses the questions raised by godly people who are not physically healed (2000, 243-45). He rejects the answers that (1) this kind of healing was only for the apostolic age, that (2) the healing will take place in God's timing (perhaps in the afterlife), or that (3) the faith of the sick person was insufficient to effect the healing.

Instead, the text indicates that the faith relates to the elders who pray for the sick person. Moo concludes, "A prayer for healing, then, must usually be qualified by a recognition that God's will in the matter is supreme. And it is clear in the NT that God does *not* always will to heal the believer" (2000, 244-45; see 2 Cor 12:7-9).

L. Turning the Wanderer Back (5:19-20)

This twelfth and final section of James' exposition begins with the repeated address: **My brothers and sisters** (*adelphoi*). It treats an issue different from prayers for the sick. Given James' close connection between sickness and sin, there is some continuity.

James seems unconcerned about reaching out to unbelievers. This verse is as close as he gets to evangelism. He encourages the community to reach out to those who have wandered from the truth. Perhaps this includes not only backsliders but also Jews who have not yet accepted Christ as Messiah.

This section and the Epistle closes with a proverb (aphorism) and a biblical allusion (Prov 10:12). This "was probably already familiar in the form of a saying employed in Christian paraenesis (1 Pet. 4:8; *1 Clem.* 49:5; *2 Clem.* 16:4)" (Bauckham 1999, 65-66).

What appears in these final verses is what is emphasized throughout the letter—speech, this time in terms of truth.

> Throughout his composition James . . . shows just what kinds of speech reveal the "friendship with the world" that is enmity with God (4:4): heedless and self-deceiving speech (1:13-14), flattering and discriminatory speech (2:3), blaspheming speech (2:7), cursing speech (3:9), slandering speech (4:11), arrogant speech (4:13), recriminatory speech (5:9). All such modes of speech seek to assert the self at the expense of the truth and at the expense of others. (Johnson 1995, 340)

Johnson makes a strong argument for viewing vv 19-20 as integral to 5:12-20. Far from a number of disjointed exhortations here at the end, this is a unified discourse on the positive modes of speech for building up the faith community through prayer.

BEHIND THE TEXT

This final section (vv 19-20) identifies James' purpose for writing: to return people to the truth. The theme of returning to the truth is a common one among the General Epistles with a Jewish-Christian flavor, especially James, Peter, and Jude. James regarded Jews who rejected Jesus as Messiah as having wandered from the truth.

Jesus began his preaching ministry with the call, "Repent, for the kingdom of heaven is near" (Matt 4:17). He was preaching to the Jews in Galilee. At the close of his ministry he addresses the Sadducees in Jerusalem saying, "You are in error because you do not know the Scriptures or the power of God" (Matt 22:29). Luke recounts Jesus as informing the Pharisees and teachers of the Law, "I have not come to call the righteous, but sinners to repentance" (Luke 5:32).

Jesus taught in the temple, in synagogues, in the open places, and even from a boat. With rare exceptions (see John 4; Matt 15:21-28), his audience was Jewish. Even when he healed the demon-possessed daughter of the Canaanite woman he told her, "I was sent only to the lost sheep of Israel" (Matt 15:24).

In light of this, it is important to realize that James is not just addressing the Jewish-Christian community in these two verses. His letter as addressed to "the twelve tribes" **in the Diaspora** may include all the Jews "scattered among the nations" (see Bauckham 1999, 14). If so, James may also be encouraging his readers to bring back to the truth their fellow Jews who did not yet understand Jesus as Messiah. James' letter is often seen as nurturing rather than evangelistic in nature (Davids 1982, 198; Johnson 1995, 338). Yet these last two verses, if taken within the context of the twelve tribes, may indicate his passion for evangelizing or perhaps better, restoring (Brosend 2004, 161-62) his fellow Jews.

IN THE TEXT

■ **19** The last two verses of James are one conditional sentence. Verse 19 is the "if" clause; v 20, the "then" clause (see NASB and NRSV). James addresses the whole church with the personal address, **My brothers and sisters.** The Greek masculine plural (*adelphoi*) indicates either a group of men or a group of men and women.

James begins the sentence, **if anyone among you should wander from the truth and someone should bring him back** . . . The verb *planēthē* (**wander**) comes from the root of the English word "planet." They were called "planets" because, unlike the "fixed stars," they appeared to wander about the night sky. The wandering of persons comes about because they are mistaken about something or have been deceived (BDAG, 822). It is not because they have deliberately chosen to turn away from the truth. For James, unbelieving Jews have not accepted Jesus as their Messiah, because they have been deceived by their leaders. They would follow Jesus, if only they could see the truth.

Several commentators do not take the verb "to wander" as an unintended turning from the truth. They see this wandering as implying "that the person is guilty of apostasy" (Martin 1988, 218). In the OT, wandering is a "transgression of the law, especially idolatry." In Jewish apocalyptic literature wandering "takes on the ethical dualist sense" (Davids 1982, 198).

Wandering is also considered a transgression in the NT. But it often includes the qualifying idea of a person being mislead or deceived, and so a victim of involuntary sin. In 1 Tim 1:13, Paul writes of his preconversion Jewish experience: "Even though I was once a blasphemer and a persecutor and a violent man, I was shown mercy because I acted in ignorance and unbelief."

Hebrews says of Israel's High Priest: "He is able to deal gently with those who are ignorant and are going astray [*planōmenois*], since he himself is subject to weakness" (5:2).

The context in James indicates that the author is concerned about those who sincerely want to do right, but have been led astray. The book of James was written to bring those wandering ones to an understanding of the truth (see 1:16). But James also reveals his perplexity concerning Christians whose actions do not match their profession of faith—"this should not be" (3:10). Surely, these were among the wandering sinners needing to be brought back to the way of wisdom.

The **truth** (*alētheias*) is "the whole code of religious knowledge and moral precept accessible to the members of the Christian church. To err from it means any departure from the right path in thought or conduct" (Ropes 1973, 313). Johnson sees the stress here to be on "the proper 'way' of behaving, as in 2 Peter 2:15" (1995, 337). Truth for James includes both aspects; right belief will result in right actions (see on 1:18 and 3:14).

The verb translated **bring . . . back** means to *turn* someone *around* (BDAG, 382; see, e.g., Isa 6:10; Acts 3:19; see Davids 1982, 199). This may call for one to walk alongside the wanderers and correct their direction to keep them on the right path (see Matt 18:12-18; Gal 6:1). But, in the NT to **bring . . . back** (*epistephēi*) is generally a matter of "turning back to the faith from which one has strayed" (see Mark 4:12; Luke 1:16; Moo 2000, 249).

■ **20** Verse 20 begins with a textual variant. The first word in the best texts reads, **Let one know** (*ginōsketō*), a third person singular imperative. Some ancient manuscripts have the second person plural imperative **Know!** (*ginōskete*). Scribes probably made this change to agree with those addressed in v 19, "My brothers and sisters" (NRSV) and/or to remove the ambiguity later in the sentence (Metzger 1971, 685-86). Later scribes introduced other changes to deal with the ambiguity.

The best text reads literally, **Let the one turning a sinner out of his wandering way know that he will save his soul from death and will hide a multitude of sins.** The ambiguity is whether the converter or the converted **will save his soul out of death.** This confusion led some manuscripts either to leave out **his** (*autou*) or move it after **death.** This makes it clear that the converter will save the soul of the converted from death. This seems to be the intended meaning of this passage. But the text is ambiguous. Later scribes merely wanted to make this clear (see Ezek 3:21; Matt 18:15).

It is possible to read the verse to mean that when Christians see a brother or sister wandering from the truth, these Christians have the responsibility of bringing that one back. In doing so, such responsible Christians save their own souls, because they have done what God has asked them to do.

Most commentators think that James means that the soul of the wandering sinner will be saved. Davids comments: "The need to assign the one promise to one party and the other to another appears illogical; James is quite able to express parallel ideas in parallel phrases (cf. 4:7-9!)" (1982, 200-201).

The second question is: Whose sins are covered? Is it the corrector (Dibelius 1975, 258; Ropes 1973, 315-16) or the one whose soul is saved? It is likely that both expressions refer to the wanderer (Martin 1988, 220; Davids 1982, 201). Perhaps James left these questions ambiguous because either meaning was appropriate.

A question remains as to the precise meaning of *will hide a multitude of sins.* To what does *hide* or **cover** (*kalypsei*) refer? Most interpret **cover** as a synonym for forgiveness (Pss 32:1; 85:2; Rom 4:7). Others, however, understand it in terms of the prevention or suppression of sinning (Prov 10:12; 1 Pet 4:8). Thus, it refers to future rather than past sins within the community (Johnson 1995, 339). At stake would be the continuing faithfulness of the church to the truth (5:19; 1:18). For this, mutual correction is indispensable.

Several later manuscripts add the affirmation *amēn* (**Amen**) to bring v 20 to a formal conclusion. One adds *because to him is glory into the ages (forever), amen.* The original text of James seems to end abruptly. It includes no closing benediction, prayer, or greetings, expected in letters of the time. So scribes added the affirmation to give it a fitting closing.

FROM THE TEXT

James concludes his letter with his central purpose in writing the letter. Although James goes into detail in describing the truth and how it works itself out in the lives of those who believe it, it comes down to one thing. The purpose of the Christian community is to keep everyone on the path toward God. This is what James has tried to do through his letter; and it is what Christians should do within their sphere of influence.

There are three important theological ideas in v 19: "(1) Christians have the opportunity and the responsibility to care for one another through the task of loving doctrinal and moral correction" (Nystrom 1997, 318). As has been seen from the beginning, James is not focused on evangelism in this letter. His concern is for the spiritual education and moral development of his readers' communities. This does not mean that James does not value evangelism. But in this letter, it is not his priority.

"(2) The penalty for sin is death; James will not equivocate on this" (Nystrom 1997, 318). James is not interested in sugar-coating the gospel. Whether one wanders into sin, or sins rebelliously, the penalty is death. So a Christian community should care for each one's spiritual condition with this solemn understanding that sin leads to everlasting death.

"(3) In this process, the agent of reconciliation 'covers' a multitude of sins" (Nystrom 1997, 318). This work of reconciliation is very significant because those who lose their way will die spiritually and their evil works will be revealed on the Day of Judgment.

Martin agrees that "death here is that of eternal consequence rather than only a physical demise" (Martin 1988, 219). The Christian community is charged by James with turning the wanderer in the direction of God's truth, resulting in life everlasting and the hiding of awful sins under the blood of Jesus.

As Nystrom says, "Sin is a problem both corporate and personal" (1997, 320). The spiritual condition of a fellow Christian is of concern to the whole community. James asks his readers to join him in this ministry of reconciliation—of bringing others to the knowledge and truth of God as revealed in Jesus Christ. This knowledge will result in and be validated by a lifestyle pleasing to God.

There are fifty-nine imperatives in the Epistle of James. In brief, James is a call to action. The letter is replete with exhortations and rebukes. So it is fitting that the concluding lines "turn to the community with an encouragement to intervene on behalf of fellow Christians who may have difficulty in the spiritual matters that James has been discussing" (Moo 2000, 249).

The Christian way is what we are all in together as a community. Therefore, to "wander from the truth" is a serious matter. The "truth" is something one does or obeys as well as knows (see 1:18).

> The truth from which one has wandered is not just intellectual or doctrinal (though that would be involved); it includes the practical righteousness indicated by the Hebrew word *ĕmet*, which the Greek OT usually translates with the word *alētheia*. It encompasses both thought (truth) and deed (fidelity). (McCartney 2009, 263).

Wandering from the truth may take place in surprising places, even in Christian congregations. Some may prefer that their pastors soothe and entertain them, rather than confront them with their unfaithfulness to the truth of the gospel. James has confronted his congregations with difficult truths throughout his Epistle. Now he urges them to go and do likewise. Looking after "orphans and widows in their distress" (1:27) is hard work. But that is what true "religion" demands. Truth calls for humility and peace-making, which are even more difficult (3:13-18).

Is leading wanderers back to the true but difficult gospel James proclaims too daunting a task for average churchgoers in the twenty-first century? Surely pastors, like James, must sometimes lead their people where they'd rather not go. They must expose them to timely issues they'd prefer not to think about. Dare they confront rich church members and risk losing their financial base? That is truly difficult for pastors who cannot ignore the well-being of their families.

James is quite clear on what must take place. Whether an entire congregation or only a few persons are wandering from **the truth,** the instruction is the same: We are to **bring** [them] **back.** Will we be doers and not just hearers of the word (2:14-26)? Will we help bring back the wandering sheep to the fold?

James' fifty-nine imperatives dominate the Epistle's one hundred and eight verses. His repeated exhortations throughout were intended to **bring** his readers **back** to the truth of the gospel: to such things as "Religion that God our Father accepts as pure and faultless" (1:27), to "the royal law" (2:8), to "the law that gives freedom" (2:12), to "faith and . . . actions . . . working together" (2:22), to disciplined and consistent speech (3:1-12), to "the wisdom that comes from heaven" (3:17), to the humble path of friendship with God (4:4), to lives of intercessory prayer for one another (5:13-16).

APPENDIX A

Languages of Holiness by Ron Benefiel, Ph.D. (Revised June 2004)

	Purity	Power	Love	Character
Images	altar	Great Commission	Great Commandment	kingdom of God
Scripture	Rom 12 I Thess 4	Acts 2 Acts 1:8	Prodigal Son; I John	Sermon on the Mount
God's activity	cleansing	empowering for service	reconciling; transforming	creating a new community
Response	consecration	receptivity	responsive cooperation	submission
Sin	eradicated	conquered	excluded	corporately confessed
Focus	personal/sexual morality	Spirit-filled life	right relationship	Christian practices
Mission	set apart/called out	personal evangelism	love for God and for people	prophetic witness
Experience	crisis (by faith)	Crisis (presence of the Spirit)	process/growth	formation in community
Psychology	self-sacrifice	abundant life	relational unity	corporate intimacy
Practices	testimony/personal devotions	witnessing prayer	acts of kindness/time with God and other believers	Eucharist/ hospitality/ acts of mercy
Hymns	"I Surrender All"	"The Comforter Has Come"	"Love Divine, All Loves Excelling"	"The Church's One Foundation"
Ecclesiology	gathered remnant	Spirit-filled church (individuals)	family of God (individuals)	already not-yet Kingdom
Soteriology	saved/ sanctified	saved and filled with the Spirit	reconciled to God; filled with love	person as part of the church
Prophets	P. Palmer	Finney	Wynkoop	Hauerwas
Dangers	legalism	subjectivism	antinomianism	externalism